D0391973

THE
WALK-ON-WATER
SYNDROME

Dealing with Professional Hazards in the Ministry

THE
WALK-ON-WATER
SYNDROME

EDWARD B. BRATCHER

Foreword by Dr. Wayne Oates

WORD BOOKS
PUBLISHER
WACO, TEXAS

A DIVISION OF
WORD, INCORPORATED

THE WALK-ON-WATER SYNDROME
Copyright © 1984 by Edward B. Bratcher

All rights reserved. No part of this book may be reproduced in any form whatsoever, except for brief quotations in reviews, without written permission from the publisher.

Unless otherwise noted, all Scripture quotations are from the Revised Standard Version of the Bible, copyrighted 1946, 1952, © 1971, 1973 by the Division of Christian Education of the National Council of the Churches of Christ in the U.S.A., and are used by permission.

Quotations marked TEV are from the *Good News Bible,* the Bible in Today's English Version. Copyright © American Bible Society, 1976.

Library of Congress Cataloging in Publication Data

Bratcher, Edward B., 1924–
  The walk-on-water syndrome.

Bibliography: p.
  1. Pastoral theology. 2. Clergy—Psychology.
I. Title.
BV4011.B653 1984   253'.2   84-19486
ISBN 0-8499-0430-7

Printed in the United States of America

Contents

CONCORDIA UNIVERSITY LIBRARY
PORTLAND, OR 97211

Foreword

Out of the depths of his own involvement, Dr. Edward Bratcher speaks to the personal and ministerial dilemmas of being a pastor. This is a report from the front line of the spiritual combat, to use Augustine's phrase, unique to being a minister in the parish-congregational-church setting.

Furthermore, Dr. Bratcher draws upon the extensive service he has rendered as a consultant and counselor to pastors and their families who are under duress from stress situations in their work. He empathically offers "mosaic" case situations of pastors. By mosaic situations, I mean that the case is not necessarily that of a given individual but a mosaic of factors drawn from the experiences of many people. As a result, the cases are Mr. or Ms. Everyperson's story. You as a reader will find your own situation, about which you may be quite isolated, described here. You will "connect up" with the author and feel genuinely understood.

Another deep well of wisdom from which Ed Bratcher draws is a two-year, full-time, subsidized research project he did about the personal and vocational needs of ministers. He consulted with individuals and groups of pastors across a broad spectrum of Protestant churches. His detailed study of the many research projects on the effectiveness and personal well-being of ministers is included in detail in this book. Therefore, reading this book will give you the gist of these studies and save you from reading many others. As a result, this book is a treasure house of hard facts about ministry.

This is the kind of book a new pastor should read ahead of time to find where the hazards as well as the hopes of pastoring a congregation can be found. Specific guidance to help turn hazards into challenges and to find the unreality in hopes is given.

I am honored to introduce my friend of many years, Ed Bratcher, to the reading audience. He is a person of steadfast devotion to Christ, persistent enthusiasm for being a pastor, and sterling personal integrity. He is a "Barnabas" to all pastors, "a son of encouragement."

WAYNE E. OATES, PH.D.
Professor of Psychiatry and Behavioral Sciences and
    Director of Program in Ethics and Pastoral
    Counseling, University of Louisville School of Medicine
Senior Professor of Psychology of Religion and Pastoral
    Care, The Southern Baptist Theological Seminary

Preface

This book is about the parish ministry and the need to strengthen it. The clergy needs help! The laity needs help! Both need help to find greater fulfillment in the parish ministry. What do I mean by fulfillment in ministry? I mean both competence and satisfaction in performing the duties required to maintain a *vital* parish ministry.

Clergy and laity are functioning far below their God-given potential because they are facing problems and obstacles that leave them discouraged and cause them great emotional and spiritual pain.

A survey of 4,665 Protestant ministers showed that 58 percent felt that the work of the church seemed futile or ineffectual.[1] Reverend Roy Oswald, a behavioral scientist and authority on clergy burnout, believes that one out of every four clergy is burned out and another 25 percent are under great stress and may be on their way to burnout.[2] Even though no comparable survey has been made of the laity, I believe that the feelings of frustration and burnout among the laity parallel those of the clergy.

This lack of fulfillment within the parish ministry is a problem that requires urgent attention, for the strength of the Christian movement is directly related to the strength of the parish ministry. It has been my goal, therefore, to find ways to strengthen the parish ministry.

In this book, which is a result of my attempts to achieve that goal, I focus attention on the personal and vocational needs of ministers. I do this for at least three reasons. First, I believe that if ministers can identify areas where they hurt, and if laymen can understand ministers better, then, with this greater insight, the laity and clergy can work together to find solutions to some of the problems facing ministers. Second, speaking from my personal experience as a minister, I present those problems which I know best. I do not in

9

any way want to imply that the problems of the laity are not as important as those of the clergy. Third, I assume that fulfillment for both clergy and laity is interrelated. Therefore, help for the clergy will in turn mean help for the laity.

The nature of the current crisis within the ministry influenced me to take a problem-centered approach in which I identify major clusters of problems that form obstacles blocking fulfillment in ministry for the clergy. Although I suggest some solutions, I place greater emphasis on the problems themselves. But my intention is not to be discouraging. Rather, I believe that neither clergy nor laity has faced openly and honestly the problems which plague the clergy, and that solutions await clear identification of the problems. Also, I believe that detailed solutions depend on the particular needs of each congregation as well as on the distinctive traits of the different forms of church government. Therefore, it is impossible to recommend solutions that would fit all ministers and congregations.

In addition to this clarification of my purpose let me explain my use of certain terminology which potentially could be misunderstood.

For example, the men and women who serve on a church staff are variously called Pastor, Minister of Music, Director of Religious Education, Youth Worker, Director of Social Ministries, Associate Pastor, etc. For the sake of clarity and ease in identification I use the words "minister" and "clergy" in an inclusive sense to describe both men and women who are serving in church-related vocations.

The words "minister/clergy" and "laymen/laity" are used to differentiate two different groups within the church. According to my biblical and theological perspective, this seems improper. In fact, the use of these terms and the division which they imply are part of the lack-of-fulfillment problem. All Christians are ministers. However, words have to be found to differentiate those who are vocationally involved in the parish ministry and those who are not. Therefore, I have chosen the words most commonly used. By "ministers" I mean all individuals vocationally involved on a paid basis in the parish ministry. By "laymen" I mean all those serving on a voluntary basis in the parish ministry and whose vocational pursuits are or have been outside the organized church.

The words "parish," "congregation," and "church" (small "c") are used interchangeably. I do not intend for there to be any denominational overtones in these words.

There are times when referring to ministers I used the masculine third person pronoun to include both men and women. I found it awkward to use his/her or she/he on every occasion. I recognize that the needs and pressures of ministers who are women are not exactly like those of ministers who are men. However, because there are common human needs, I believe that what I have written applies, in most cases, equally as well to women and men, even though the general nature of this book does not allow me to elaborate on the more specialized problems related to the ordination and placement of women ministers.

Finally, this book reflects my pilgrimage as a minister— one which began in 1948 and continues to this day. But it was during the years 1972 through 1974, when I served as Consultant on the Ministry at The Southern Baptist Theological Seminary and spent time researching, writing, and speaking on the personal and vocational needs of ministers, that I gained special insight into that pilgrimage. I contend that *ministers are not miracle-workers—they cannot walk on water; but they can learn to swim.*

Acknowledgments

It is impossible to name all who have made this book possible. But I would be remiss if I did not make an effort to acknowledge my indebtedness. I am grateful to: E. E. Steussy and Leonard Holloway who made possible through financial support and personal guidance my two-year position as Consultant on the Ministry at The Southern Baptist Theological Seminary; the staff and faculty of The Southern Baptist Theological Seminary for their acceptance and support of my work and study related to fulfillment in ministry; and the faculty and students of Midwestern Baptist Theological Seminary where, on two different occasions, much of this material was tested in the classroom.

Special thanks must also be expressed to: Suzanne, Dick, and Mike, my children who lived through the experiences in this book and contributed their insights; Wayne Oates who supported my efforts in countless ways including writing the preface; the members of Manassas Baptist Church who encouraged, and at times prodded, me in my writing, and who granted me time to teach and to write; Dan Verner who read the manuscript and offered suggestions in style and wording; Edith Woody who deciphered my hieroglyphics and typed and retyped the manuscript while carrying on her duties as secretary of Manassas Baptist Church; and Kathleen Mohr for her personal interest in helping clarify my ideas through meticulous editing.

Most important of all has been the love and faith which Marjie has extended to me as I have struggled to find fulfillment in ministry.

Chapter 1

A Search for Fulfillment

What is the greatest problem a minister faces? This is the question most often asked during the years I have been studying and reflecting on the personal and vocational needs of ministers. My answer to the question has varied. On some occasions I have said loneliness. On other occasions I have focused on such problems as the lack of a support system, role conflicts, and the expectation to walk on water.

The fact that I have given different answers at different times to that very question indicates to me that there are several "greatest" problems facing ministers today. Moreover, the answer depends, in part, on the individual and the parish he or she is serving.

But before examining specific obstacles to fulfillment in ministry, I want to relate the tragic experience of one young couple which provides an overview of the personal and vocational needs of ministers. (Their names have been changed but the story is neither a composite nor has it been overdrawn. And although some of their problems were created by Baptist polity, their struggle is not uniquely Baptist.) When Karl West graduated from seminary, he and his wife, Jane, were excited about his having completed this important step in preparation for the ministry. The only mar in their happiness was the fact that Karl had not yet received a call to a church. But even this problem did not cause them undue anxiety because they had already overcome many other hurdles to reach graduation.

Karl and Jane could look back with satisfaction and confidence over the years in the military, in college, and at the seminary.

Karl and Jane's experiences were similar to the experiences of other rejoicing graduates. Karl had grown up in a Christian home. His church attendance had been above average, and there had been times when he was an adolescent that he had wondered if God were calling him to preach. But Karl's induction into the military during the Korean War had caused him to put aside his questions about God's will for his vocation.

While stationed in a southern state, Karl was invited by a friend to attend a Southern Baptist church. His first reaction was to say no, because of his negative image of Southern Baptists. But having nothing better to do, he later agreed to go. The church was small, the people were very friendly, and the seminary student who served as pastor appeared to have a real interest in servicemen since he himself had been in the military during the Second World War. Several young members made Karl feel at home and even encouraged him to become active in the youth and music programs of the church. As a result, Karl began attending the church regularly.

A few months later, Karl again questioned whether God was calling him to the ministry. In part, this may have been the result of his active involvement in the church. But also, it was at this particular time that Karl and Jane were married. It was only natural, therefore, that the question of his vocation came to the forefront.

Karl and Jane talked a great deal about Karl's growing conviction that God was calling him to a church-related vocation. They even talked with the pastor of their church. And, after a great deal of discussion and prayer, they decided God was indeed calling Karl to the ministry. He and Jane told the church about their decision and made plans to go to college and seminary after Karl's discharge from the military.

He enrolled in a Baptist college. College days were difficult for Karl and Jane, as they are for many married students. Jane worked, took care of the apartment, cared for their newborn baby, and encouraged Karl in his studies.

While still attending college, a great opportunity came for Karl to serve a small country church. Even though they knew the demands of being a pastor would add to their stress, the

Wests decided Karl could not pass up the experience. An ordination council was called, and upon recommendation of the council, Karl was ordained. Later Karl would wonder if he had really been ready for ordination.

Seminary years rapidly followed college. During those years, Karl and Jane developed close friendships with other students, on whom they depended for help to face the financial crises associated with being a student, the disappointments and frustrations of church work, and the pressures of academic demands. Moreover, they believed that these friendships would provide support for whatever difficulties might be ahead. This, however, did not prove to be true because eventually their friends moved to many different parts of the country.

As their friends moved away, Karl and Jane began to experience loneliness and anxiety. And their stress was compounded when the anticipation of becoming a full-time pastor gave way to a gnawing sense of concern as the summer months wore on and no church called Karl. Because he had not grown up Southern Baptist and was from a state where there was no organized Southern Baptist work, Karl did not have a concerned church, pastor, or executive secretary to help locate a church for a home-state boy. The seminary's placement office was doing its best, but its influence at that time was not as great as it is today.

Finally, toward the end of the summer, Karl was in touch with a new congregation. Seven families made up the church membership. Their finances were very limited, but they promised to pay a salary of seventy-five dollars a month plus provide a modest home as a parsonage. Although the church was being sponsored by another church, it had no significant backing either of finances or leadership.

Confident of God's leading, willing to serve in a difficult situation, and probably somewhat desperate to find some place to go, Karl and Jane packed their few belongings and plunged into their work.

An interesting aside is that about five weeks after Karl moved to that church, he received a telephone call from the chairman of a pastor search committee indicating that his church, which had several hundred members and was at that time paying a salary of six hundred dollars a month plus parsonage, would like to consider him as their pastor. Karl replied that he believed God had led him to the smaller congregation and that it would not be possible to consider this offer.

The years went by. Karl served the church and, to help lighten the financial burden, also worked at various times as a painter, a carpenter's helper, and a schoolteacher. Sure, there were difficult times, but there were also many sources of satisfaction. Karl and Jane enthusiastically performed the many duties which were thrust upon them. Among other things, Karl was pastor, music leader, Sunday school teacher, and part-time janitor, while Jane was wife, mother, organist, and worker in the missionary society. But they were rewarded when the church grew both numerically and spiritually, and a new building was eventually constructed.

However, during these productive years for the church, personal debts grew for Karl and Jane. In fact, Jane became emotionally ill and had to be hospitalized, which further complicated their problems. Financial pressures increased and Karl felt he had to resign as pastor and accept a position in a nonchurch related vocation that paid a much larger salary.

A few months later, a church from a nearby state asked him to be pastor. This church provided a minimum salary, but Karl believed it would be large enough to cover his financial responsibilities. Excited about getting back into the ministry, he accepted the offer. His first few months there were satisfying and happy. However, the recurrence of Jane's emotional illness again brought financial problems and growing debts.

It was at this time that Karl learned the local high school needed a substitute teacher. He made arrangements, without first consulting with the deacons, to teach once a week on his day off. But his decision did not please the deacons. Some of them believed that, despite Karl's and Jane's heavy financial burdens, if they used their money wisely, they would not need the extra job. Moreover, no previous pastor of that church had ever served in any capacity other than as pastor. So the deacons asked Karl not to teach. He agreed.

In a few months, mounting financial pressure brought the decision to leave the pastorate once again and seek employment that would help them find their way out of their financial jungle. Karl made a brave attempt to enter business for himself.

He failed. The only answer was to declare bankruptcy. At this juncture, a friend from a town where Karl had served as pastor assured him that he would be able to secure a job in the personnel department of the plant where he worked. (It is ironic that this friend who was most willing to help was not a professing Christian, although he had occasionally attended the church that Karl had pastored.)

Karl secured the job and it appeared that the old pressures would be lessened, that a new life was ahead. But the newfound peace was broken about four years later when Jane suffered another period of serious depression. She felt quite guilty about her emotional problems and was convinced that it was really her fault that Karl was not in the ministry. Months of ups and downs passed. Family problems increased, and divorce was even discussed. But through it all Karl and Jane hoped that solutions could be found. Then Jane began using medication unadvisedly. Physical weakness and emotional exhaustion led to her accidental death at age forty when she choked while eating.

Karl is now remarried. He and his wife have found financial security, and the children appear to be making good adjustments. Karl continues to preach from time to time and is active in the church where he is a member.

As Karl reviewed with me what I had written about his and Jane's experiences, he expressed some of his feelings concerning his years as a pastor. He was angry over the inadequate salaries he was paid—he now makes more than twice as much as he ever made as a pastor. He feels that he could have coped better with many of his problems if his income had been greater. And he added the ironic note that he received only a few *weeks'* training to equip him for his job as a sales representative, whereas he spent several *years* preparing himself to be a pastor.

Karl also resented the constant pressure for him to live up to standards which he could not reach. One specific expectation was in regard to tithing. Karl openly admitted to the deacons that his financial condition was such that he could not tithe. However, he felt he was not understood, and since he was the pastor he must set an example. This burden to set an example and be "ten feet tall" was the basis for resentment directed toward the deacons, followed by self-hatred for his failure to be a good example. This vicious cycle took a tremendous toll on Karl's sense of self-worth. Today he remembers the pressure to tithe as a devastating experience which he believes was unjust and unnecessary.

Karl identified other emotions as he looked back on his years as a pastor. One was the feeling of being trapped. At each major juncture he and Jane spent a great deal of time in prayer. From prayer they found strength and a measure of peace. However, there was no place to turn, no one to help. The trapped feeling expressed itself in different ways. Karl felt caged by the "system." No one had the power or the resources to help him solve his problems. He felt that the harder he tried to help himself, the less response he received from the system. For example, his departure from the pastorate the first time was not seen by the denominational executive as an indication of serious personal needs but rather as an indication that he had "copped out." Moreover, in every situation there appeared to be no middle alternatives. At every juncture he felt he was in a no-win situation.

Another emotion Karl remembered was the feeling of futility. It seemed that the administrative demands of church business kept him frustrated because they required time which he believed should be devoted to being a pastor and a preacher.

Nevertheless, Karl said he was not bitter toward the church. He has even continued to preach on a part-time, supply basis. He said he has found a new freedom in the proclamation of difficult truths. He no longer feels the pressure of having to please a congregation—the pressure that often causes a pastor to dilute his understanding of the gospel to avoid being fired.

When Karl talks about his experiences he raises questions about himself and the church as a vocational system: Where could he have turned for help? How could he have avoided some of the mistakes he made? How could he and Jane have developed a better relationship? What about placement? What about friends to talk to? What about someone to help in times of financial crisis? Although Karl believes in the church, he has serious doubts about the present condition of the ministry as a vocational system.

Karl's doubts and experiences illustrate most of the issues which I believe are involved somehow, in each minister's personal quest to find fulfillment in ministry: an effective support system, placement, role conflict, adequate salary, the meaning of call and ordination, acceptance of our humanity, the meaning of success in ministry, and the role of the minister's family. Although in coping with these problems many ministers have been strengthened rather than scarred by them, I contend that far more have been scarred than we are willing to admit. Moreover, much of this hurting and scarring is unnecessary. There is a tragic waste of human resources and potential when we fail to help one another.

Karl's and Jane's experiences make clear the fact that many factors contributed to their problems. Some of the problems were personal, but a majority were the result of the church as an occupational system. I agree with a statement made by the authors of *Ex-Pastors:* "If our argument occasionally suggests that the church is chiefly at fault, it is because we see system pressures at work which many clergy do not, and what to them seems principally to be their own inadequacy, our analysis reveals as a deck stacked against them."[1]

*   *   *

In the next chapters the obstacles to fulfillment in ministry are identified and guidelines for overcoming these obstacles, although sometimes only partial, are presented. But what is truly needed is an understanding of the problems and a commitment to their resolution by all who are involved in the church as a vocational system so the parish ministry may become God's instrument in the ministry of reconciliation.

Chapter 2

Human Beings Like You

Paul and Barnabas understood their humanity. When the crowd in Lystra wanted to offer sacrifices to them, "they tore their clothes and ran into the middle of the crowd, shouting, 'Why are you doing this? We ourselves are only human beings like you!' " (Acts 14:14–15, TEV).

Too few laypersons and ministers have the understanding of Paul and Barnabas. Many laypersons expect ministers to be ten feet tall and able to walk on water. More often than not this expectation is also accepted by the minister, who then finds himself in a vicious cycle—not being able to live up to the expectation, yet constantly trying to.

Recently, this assumption—that ministers are superhuman—was the subject of one episode of a popular TV series. This particular episode is about a preacher who, while wrestling with a decision to quit the ministry or not, seeks professional counseling. Then one Sunday, following the service at which the counselor is his guest, the pastor announces his resignation.

In the final scene, we see the counselor talking to his wife. He is depressed over the fact that he has helped a minister make a decision to leave the ministry. But his wife, seeking to console him, points out that, after all, the pastor had made the decision himself and the counselor had only helped him clarify the issues. Still thinking about his role in the pastor's decision, the counselor shares his feelings about ministers. He claims that as a child he had thought his minister was seven feet tall. Actually, the minister had been only five feet three inches, and had stood on an orange crate. One Sunday the orange crate had broken, and the preacher had held onto the mike and kept talking without missing a word. An incredibly faultless person, capable of accomplishing the impossible, said the counselor, was what he thought a preacher really was and should be.

My point is this: The choice to use this issue—the superhuman nature of ministers—as the basis for a popular TV show indicates the prevalence of such an attitude. The writers assumed, and I believe correctly, that the average TV viewer would understand the setting and would also laugh at the ridiculous attitude which is normally held. (The program, therefore, offers some hope for overcoming the view that ministers are superhuman and for removing this obstacle to fulfillment in ministry.)

An understanding of the nature of the problem posed by the perception that ministers are practically infallible can be gained from a study made by Hugh A. Eadie. In his study of Presbyterian ministers in the Church of Scotland, Dr. Eadie found that most ministers enjoyed better physical health than other occupational groups. However, the picture was entirely different when it came to mental health. In the group under forty-five years of age, three out of four had emotional and psychological complaints.

Eadie describes what he refers to as a "parsonic personality" (i.e., the personality of a parson). This, he explains, is an individual who suffers from a guilt-neurosis syndrome and tries to be "omnipotent and omnicompetent on the one hand, and all-loving and all-lovable on the other." When a clergyman fails to achieve such inhuman perfection, Eadie notes, the results range from simple depression to compulsive sexual fantasies.[1]

SOURCES OF THE SUPERHUMAN VIEW

I asked a class of seminary students whether they found that being expected to be superhuman was a problem for them. After a few moments of silence one student spoke. He said,

"I want to tell you where I find myself. I have worked through my understanding of God's call for me as a pastor. Now I am struggling with the question of my humanity. I find that members of my congregation are pushing me to be superhuman. I find also that I want to be superhuman." Nothing more was said by the other members of the class. It was obvious that they all understood and agreed. Now they were looking to me as the professor for answers.

I believe the problem is the fault of both the laity and the clergy. William Hulme writes:

> It is hard for the layman to accept the sinfulness of his pastor. The saints seem superhuman. Intellectually he can accept the fact that his pastor is a sinner. "He's a human being just like us," he says. But to accept this emotionally is another matter.
>
> Most of us would like to think that there is someone around who is better than we are. The likely candidate for this position is the minister. As one church councilman put it, "I know my pastor takes a drink—in fact, I like him to have a drink with me. I know he's married—and therefore that he does—well, that he does certain things. This is all fine and dandy. But dawgone it! I still want him to be up *there!*" As he said this he gestured with his hand slightly above his own head. "I want my minister to be a cut above me."[2]

This attitude is not just something I have read about. I have encountered it frequently. One example that I remember took place when my wife and I were guests of a deacon and his wife. They invited us to go with them to a play which was being held in a town that was a two-hour drive from where we lived. Therefore, during the drive, we had plenty of time for a leisurely conversation. Because of my friendship with this deacon, I felt I could be honest and open with him. I told him about the period of depression I had been going through as a result of criticisms I had received for some of the stands I had taken in sermons. I could not understand why matters of disagreement had to lead to people's not attending church, stopping financial support, suggesting that the pastor should either keep silent or consider leaving. I spoke on how I had hoped my relationship with the congregation had been long and strong enough that disagreements could be faced openly and honestly and, where there were mistakes, that the members and I could respond with confession and forgiveness. I concluded by saying that I was depressed over what to do and how to face the future.

My friend listened attentively and politely. When I finished he said, "Ed, I don't understand how you can become depressed. You are a seminary graduate. You have a doctor's degree. You have studied the Bible. You are a Christian man. You help many people. And I don't see how anyone who has studied as much as you have and knows the Bible as well as you do can ever become depressed. As Christians we are supposed to have hope and be optimistic."

Like many others, my friend had fallen into the natural temptation of believing that men and women who are dealing with the "holy" are, thereby, holy themselves. This was the apostles' experience at Lystra. Paul and Barnabas were talking about God, and since through God's power a man had been healed, the people were convinced that Paul and Barnabas themselves were gods. The same thought processes exist today. If you are talking about God, have been called to a church-related vocation, and have been ordained, you are considered superhuman. The aura that pervades the laity's understanding of God's call to a church-related vocation has led to the heresy that ministers are more than human.

The problem would not be so difficult to overcome if it stopped there. But we make it doubly difficult because, when the laity place the clergy on a pedestal, the clergy give a helping hand, enjoy the intoxication of the higher elevation, and strive to stay on the pedestal. The cycle repeats itself.

The paradox is that although the Bible teaches that pride and the desire to be like God are the sources of man's tragic fall, it is precisely at this point that we as ministers most often succumb. The serpent which entices us to believe that we can be like God is often a member of the pastor search committee, saying, "You are just the person we are looking for. You have all the qualifications that we need to solve all of our problems." And like Adam and Eve, we eat this enticing fruit and die—die to our humanity and become *less* than human.

But claiming that the minister tries to walk on water simply because of pride is too harsh. There is usually another element in his personality. Most ministers are conscientious—concerned about values, about self-improvement. The student quoted above also said, "Jesus commanded us to be perfect as our heavenly Father is perfect." The student's yearning to be able to walk on water was genuine and sincere. I reminded him that we need to remember that we also have the biblical teaching that we are sinners and that we are saved by grace, not by our achievements. So the drive to become the best person possible, by the grace of God, must never be distorted to mean that we can be superhuman. Specifically, we must not permit being superhuman to become a goal we either believe we have reached, and therefore fall into the sin of self-righteousness, or a goal we believe that we can reach, and therefore fall into the pattern of hating ourselves when we do not reach it.

Another virtue which can lead to the sin of believing we are more than human is the virtue of sensitivity. By being sensitive to the needs of people and anxious to help people, we pressure ourselves into believing we can accomplish more than we are really able. Seeing the hungry multitudes, we come to believe that God has called us to multiply the loaves and fish and feed the five thousand. Too often we forget that we are to be faithful and offer our five loaves and two fish and let God do the feeding. As ministers, we need to ponder the cartoon that depicts the beauty of the skies at sunset and has the question written across the skies, "Are you trying to take the job of your boss?"

RESULTS OF TRYING TO WALK ON WATER

Trying to walk on water leads to several attitudes that can be destructive to the minister, both personally and professionally. And these attitudes are so prevalent that they need to be dealt with if there is to be any fulfillment in ministry for either the clergy or the laity.

Feelings of Inadequacy and Low Self-Esteem. Reuel Howe and Carlyle Marney worked with thousands of ministers, and as a result of their work, they expressed similar views in slightly different ways. Reuel Howe wrote, "He [the minister] usually feels like a bastard. He gets no assistance in self-acceptance. Ministers receive very little pastoral care. Many of them are sick about themselves—their self-esteem is very low, and it needn't be. One of the jobs we work at here is to restore to people a sense of self-esteem and a knowledge of their resources. It's just appalling."[3] In a letter to Dr. Karl Menninger, Carlyle Marney said, "I'm excited by the prospect of your doing a book for ministers. You say they should not fear being reproachful (Jeremiah, et al.)—but Doctor—90 percent of the clergy we see do not have sufficient sense of 'I' worth, integrity, ego maturity—to say Boo! to a Church mouse, much less a culture."[4]

The reasons for experiencing low self-esteem are numerous but can be expressed in one statement—the pastor is expected to "walk on water" and he cannot, and he becomes angry with himself because he cannot. Dr. Roger K. White, a psychiatrist who has counseled many ministers, stated that the minister is under constant pressure to accomplish far more than he is capable of doing.[5] Some of the expectations that the average congregation has of its pastor are:

(1) He must be a perfect moral example.

(2) He must provide moral and emotional support at all times regardless of his own condition.

(3) He must be an able administrator both in the church and in the community.

(4) He must be an able public speaker on any and every topic.

(5) He must perform as an actor—keep people on the edge of their seats at all times, be able to act in all settings (i.e., funerals, weddings, picnics, baptisms, etc.).

(6) He must serve as a philosopher—a teacher of values—even though the people agree beforehand that they will not listen.

(7) He must perform as a counselor, a role which is particularly emotionally exhausting.

If any man could accomplish all of these tasks, he would also be able to walk on water.

Looking at the problem from another standpoint, one sees

that almost nothing a pastor does can ever be considered "finished." A sermon could always have had more preparation; a counseling session could always have been more effective; the task of visitation is never done, etc. Faced with tasks that are never finished, the pastor yearns for at least one that has been completed. In fact, a fellow pastor said he enjoyed hunting because when he killed a squirrel or deer, he could see a job that had been finished, and that accomplishment made him feel good.

For an individual to have good mental health he must feel that he has succeeded at some task. Therefore, when the pastor tries to walk on water and fails, symbolically speaking, he gets out the cat-o'-nine-tails and flays himself to motivate himself to greater efforts and achievement. And because he never succeeds in walking on water, he continually feels that he is a failure and he develops behavior patterns which lead to poor mental health.

Part of this pattern is, again, the vicious cycle of self-punishment after each failure. Unfortunately, this cycle is further compounded by the tendency of the minister to be a perfectionist. The minister does not set his *goals* at perfection; rather, he demands perfection of himself. When a person sets his goals at perfection, he does so out of a healthy sense of self-worth. When he demands perfection of himself, he is seeking to establish his self-worth. Since he naturally falls short of his goal, he is continually punishing himself for being a failure.

The end result is self-hatred, often masked by an attitude of superiority and infallibility. Although I am not a psychologist, I suspect the reason many preachers cannot admit to anyone else that they make mistakes or cannot accept criticism from their laymen is not because they believe they somehow have divine powers and cannot make a mistake, but rather the opposite. They have such a feeling of inadequacy they have to take the stance of infallibility to be able to live with themselves. It goes without further elaboration that this self-hatred/infallibility complex leads to all kinds of conflicts with the members of the congregation and results in the pastor's becoming isolated from those who would genuinely like to share his problems and burdens. One deacon put it to me this way: "I have tried to be a friend to my pastors but have found quite often that there isn't room for both of us on that pedestal." I suspect that what this deacon has seen is not really a pedestal as much as it is camouflaged self-hatred.

Unresolved Anger. We learn quite early that anger is not an acceptable emotion. Our society suggests that we handle anger by repressing it. As children, our environment taught us not to show anger against someone who is bigger and stronger than we are; therefore, we learned to suppress it.

As Christians, we have labeled anger as sin. We have not differentiated between the emotion of anger and destructive action based on anger. As a result, our mistaken Christian view reinforces the view of our society—we should repress our anger.

The pastor is also reminded that as a paragon of virtue he must not lose his temper. Once, when I was apologizing to a deacon for losing my temper, he looked at me and said, "Ed, preachers aren't permitted to lose their tempers."

Not only does the pastor face the problem of not knowing how to deal with his anger, but he also finds himself in a position that produces a great deal of anger. Dr. Robert S. Glen, professor of psychiatry at the University of Texas' Southwestern Medical School in Dallas, has observed that stress produces anger, and inasmuch as the pastor is constantly under a stress situation, he builds up tremendous amounts of anger.[6]

An example of the stress situation that leads to anger is being "on call" seven days a week, twenty-four hours a day. The telephone rings. The familiar voice of a church member says, "I hate to call you at home and on your day off, but Mr. Jones has had a heart attack and is in intensive care. I thought you would want to know." What can a minister say? He is glad that someone has taken the initiative to call him, so he can't get angry at the person who called. He can't get angry at Mr. Jones for having a heart attack. But the minister is angry, and rightfully so. The stress of being called on his only day off makes him angry. But there is no one to whom he can vent his anger. So he keeps it bottled up and silently prays for help.

Again, when a pastor is unable to walk on water he may become angry at God, as witnessed in Jeremiah 15:18 and 20:7. Jeremiah directs his anger against God, calling him a

"deceitful brook" and a "deceiver." How could he do that—
and get away with it? Dr. Robert Glen has commented, "God
is big enough to absorb our anger." We can tell God off in
the moments of our anger without upsetting him and having
him destroy us with a bolt of lightning.

Often the tremendous store of unresolved anger comes pouring out in bitter sermons and periods of depression. No pastor
has to be reminded of the angry sermons he has preached or
of the diatribes he called prophetic preaching, while down in
his guts he knew those sermons were nothing more than a
lashing out at those who had hurt him. These bitter sermons
lead to self-hatred and then to greater anger for being forced
to walk on water and a vicious cycle is started. Unresolved
anger is the source of a cycle that can be described in a para-
phrase of the words of James 3:6: "Unresolved anger is a world
of wrong, occupying its place in our bodies and spreading
evil through our whole being! It sets on fire the entire course
of our existence with the fire that comes to it from hell itself."

Fear of Intimacy and Its Consequence, Loneliness. One pastor has described the minister as "the loneliest man in the
world." There is far more truth than ministerial exaggeration
in that statement. Often the source of the loneliness is the
fear of intimacy. The minister is afraid that if he permits anyone
to get too close to him that person will find out he really
can't walk on water.

Even after many years of talking about openness, I still
find it very difficult to practice. I tend to want to be the answer
man, the "savior" of those in trouble. Therefore, I quickly
fall into the pattern of always trying to help and seldom permitting anyone to help me.

This pattern is the result, in part, of the typical pastorate.
In the first few months of any pastorate a minister receives
a great deal of adulation. This adulation is sweet, like honey.
He relishes it, but it soon becomes bitter because he feels that
it is not truly deserved. Unfortunately, adulation has an addic-
tive quality to it. One soon realizes that it is destructive, but
finds that it is difficult to live without. To continue to receive
the adulation, the minister must keep his parishioners at arm's
length.

At first glance the relationship between most ministers and

their parishioners does not appear to be one of holding off the other at arm's length. There appears to be a genuine camaraderie between the minister and the parishioners. Laughter, jokes, and verbal banter are a part of the relationship. However, a closer examination may reveal that these are really devices to keep the relationship on a very superficial basis.

Ministers also fear intimacy with peers. Studies have shown that ministers look upon their peers not as colleagues but as competitors.[7] And one of the primary reasons for this competitive spirit within the ministry is the lack of geographical limits to parishes in the Protestant tradition. To this factor is added the decline of denominational loyalty. Today newcomers to a community will "shop around" in churches of different denominations.

Other factors that foster a competitive spirit are: the mobile society in which we live, the "voluntary association" mentality of American Christianity, and "the bodies, bricks, and bucks" standard of success for churches. (See chapters 7 and 11.)

The stage is set for fear of intimacy. You don't associate with competitors with whom you are involved in a life-and-death struggle for survival. You are afraid that your competitors may find those chinks in your armor that will give them advantage in the struggle. Also, if a minister is successful, two forces will keep him separated from his peers. First, the successful minister is likely to be boastful in an effort to cover up his feelings of inadequacy. Second, those who are less successful will be envious. Boastfulness and envy are not conducive to intimacy.

Many ministers are afraid to become too intimate with denominational executives and fellow ministers because of the part which they play in placement. Most denominations have placement systems in which the positive recommendations of fellow pastors and denominational executives are a must. And a minister never knows when he may want to move. So there is always that fear of the shove from behind, if the congregation becomes dissatisfied; or that lure from ahead if a larger congregation is looking for a new pastor. Therefore, ministers never discuss the areas in which they need to grow, and certainly not the areas in which they feel they have failed. The façade of being able to walk on water must be kept up.

The Professional Mask. A direct result of loneliness is the professional mask. Many ministers put on masks because after years of loneliness no true emotion exists inside that human shell. Or if any emotion is left, it is not enough to provide warmth, love, compassion, sympathy, empathy—all those qualities which make a person human and make possible human relationships.

Part of my personal anguish grew out of the realization that I was becoming professional and that, likewise, most of the ministers I knew who had been pastors for many years, had also become professional. I cried out to some of my friends—"I don't want to end up like what I see happening to many ministers!" I became even more specific and asked, "Can you tell me the names of any ministers you know who have been ministers for forty years and who are genuine, transparent, warm, human beings?" More often than not, my question was met with stunned silence. My friends found it as difficult as I did to name those ministers who were sincerely beautiful, mature human beings.

But ministers deserve some compassion at this point. Their professional mask comes partly from their loneliness. A mask— a lack of warmth—is often the result of not being able to cope with all of the emotional demands that are made of them. Sometimes the demands are so great that, to avoid the pain of giving everything one has, the minister will say the right words, smile at the right time, appear to be sad in times of sorrow, but all without genuine feeling.

I remember the total exhaustion which I felt one time when one emotional demand was piled on another, and my desire was to run away and hide. For several weeks I had been grieving over the fact that our daughter, our oldest child, was leaving for college. I was feeling a deep sense of loss. During those weeks I also suffered the agony of watching a beautiful eighteen-year-old girl die of leukemia. She was our daughter's closest friend, and a favorite at school and church. The diagnosis of leukemia had been made in the spring, and by late summer there was no hope for recovery. Jane died on Thursday. The funeral was set for Saturday morning because there was a wedding scheduled for Saturday afternoon in the same sanctuary. I was responsible for the funeral service at 11:00 A.M.

and then had to perform the wedding ceremony at 3:00 P.M. At eleven o'clock on Saturday I tried to respond to the grief of Jane's family, the grief of my family, and my own personal grief. At three o'clock I was trying to respond to the joy and happiness of the love which brought two people together to exchange their wedding vows. Then, following the wedding, I was called from the reception and told that one of the church members had died of a heart attack. Would I please come as quickly as possible to the home of the bereaved family?

On Saturday night and Sunday morning we made the final preparations to drive our daughter to college. Of course, I would perform the 11:00 A.M. worship service before leaving. I was numb and remember only that I did get through the service and did preach a sermon. I was drained of emotion, aching from the strain of too many demands in too short a period of time.

I do not consider this experience to be unique. Rather, it illustrates the demands which all ministers face. Yes, it was the most draining experience that I have faced. I wonder sometimes, however, if there have been other experiences in my life that have been just as potentially draining but that I don't remember because I sought for and found the right mask for the right time, and therefore didn't expend as many emotional energies.

Without being too simplistic, the problem is that the minister is called upon to walk on water and he responds to that call only to find he is human and that to meet the situation he must become professional—he must put on a mask. Tragically, he fools no one. He knows, and the people know, that genuineness is absent from those acts of ministry.

Poor Interpersonal Relationships. Low self-esteem, unresolved anger, fear of intimacy, and professionalism all too often add up to poor interpersonal relationships. But other factors also cause many ministers to have difficult times relating to the members of their congregation and/or fellow staff members.

Because a minister is an authority figure, he may become autocratic in his relationships. He may fall into the trap of assuming that his every whim should be viewed as a pronouncement from Mt. Sinai. Moreover, the minister is often encouraged to be autocratic. Some members feel more comfortable with a father figure who will tell them what they should do and/or believe. They look forward to receiving a verbal "spanking" every week. If they can come to church and have the pastor fuss at them and spank them for their shortcomings, they can leave the worship service without the painful process of confession and acceptance of forgiveness. They accept verbal spanking as atonement for the sins which they have committed.

While being autocratic may have some benefits for preaching, it plays havoc with the process of being "fellow workers" of Christ. An autocratic minister does not easily accept criticism and suggestions from the members of the congregation. He is frequently defensive, and when confronted with significant opposition, he often lashes out at those who dare to question his judgment. Such behavior hinders members from offering their suggestions and recommendations to the pastor. Consequently, the ministry of the church is diminished because it becomes a "one-man show." In turn, the spirit of the congregation suffers because there is no opportunity to negotiate differences.

An autocratic minister also has difficulty working with fellow staff members. He views his co-workers as hired help who are supposed to carry out *his* program. Such an attitude discourages the other ministers from developing their gifts and using their skills in ministry.

Poor staff relationships are compounded by the fact that many churches look upon the pastor or senior minister as the only true minister. Generally this view extends to the idea that only the senior minister is truly called of the church and of God to a particular task, that the other ministers are hired by the congregation with the approval of the senior minister. Many churches require or assume that the staff will resign when a new senior minister comes. But such attitudes make it difficult, if not impossible, for the staff to develop a team ministry.

I have mentioned just a few of the more obvious results of trying to walk on water. Because these attitudes can be destructive to a minister's personal ministry, I think it is important for ministers to learn how to join the human race, and for congregations to urge them to do so. Moreover, I would say to the laity, "Without your help as a fellow minister, the battle cannot be won."

The importance of winning the battle to be an authentic human being is well-stated by John C. Fletcher, Associate for Theological Education with The Alban Institute, Inc.:

> Today it is true, without exception in my experience, that the identity and strength of the clergy is the key to the vitality of congregational life. . . . There was once a time when the objective fact of priesthood or rabbinate was enough to carry an individual with low self-esteem through difficult times in the tasks of leadership. Something ought to be done because "Father" or "Rabbi" or "Pastor" wanted it to be done. The role itself was so much more than the person that it overshadowed individual reality. Such is no longer the case. The personal authenticity of the minister, priest, or rabbi is the greatest strength of any congregation. The inauthenticity of the clergy is the greatest weakness of organized religion.[8]

How to Avoid the Temptation to Walk on Water

We all know if a minister tries to walk on water, he will end up drowning. The question that must be answered is, how does one avoid the temptation? Following are some suggestions.

Acknowledge One's Humanness. A great deal of unnecessary grief would be averted if ministers would rejoin the human race. This seems obvious. Ministers are not a class of personality-elite who have graduated from the ills of the common herd and can now disperse oracles to the poor devils who still struggle with ailments of personality. We are all in the swim together. Paul said, "I do not claim that I have already succeeded or have already become perfect. I keep striving. . ." (Phil. 3:12, TEV).

For a minister to be able to accept his humanness he must first be able to see himself as a human being. And most of us know how difficult that can be!

J. R. Dolby presented a talk to the Waco, Texas, Ministerial Alliance, in which he emphasized the human quality of the minister. Using the free association of ideas, he encouraged members of his audience to look at themselves as human beings. First he made it clear that "these ideas are not meant to be logically consistent or accurate. These glimpses of the human psyche are more like dream recall—they are more like vague impressions and feelings put into words." Some of the characteristics which resulted from Dolby's free associations included:

- He listens to all of the fears, mistakes, and loneliness of his parishioners but has no one to whom he can tell his struggles.
- He is a man who cries inwardly and often openly in the quietness of his office because he has so many human weaknesses.
- He is a man trying to play the game of religion but often doesn't know where the ball-park is.
- He is a man who plays so many roles that he doesn't know who he is.
- He is a man who stands behind the pulpit and tries not to let his parishioners know that he often doubts what he is saying.
- He is a man who sincerely wants to know just how the gospel meets man's needs.
- He drinks Budweiser and is a convinced Teetotaler.
- At home he is a lover with itchy fingers and a suggestive pinch.
- He wants to become involved in the cause of those treated unjustly but he is afraid to be too open about it because he is afraid of his congregation's response.
- He is a father who often isn't home.
- He wants to be well known and hopes that the next church will be a little bigger and more prestigious.
- He would like to tell some of his congregation to go to Hell but this would take six months of theological discussion to clarify.
- He tells the congregation to walk in the Spirit and then goes to the office and wonders what it means.
- He is syrupy sweet in his conversation—like a used car salesman.
- He curses under his breath when the chronic neurotic in the church calls while he is entertaining guests and then feels guilty after he treats her so rudely.
- He is a man who has fleeting fantasies of going to bed with the shapely brunette in the choir.
- To a child he is God—the God who lives at the church.
- He is the one who wouldn't even express a little smile if a hole had developed in his waders and his shorts were getting wet while conducting a baptismal service.
- He is concerned about the well-being of this city but is more concerned about a new building for the church. A building for the over-privileged.
- Above everything else he is a human being.[9]

Preach "Confessionally." During the worship services, ministers have more contact with the greatest number of their congregation members than at any other time. Therefore, the ministers' sermons are the perfect vehicles through which they can communicate their own humanness.

When I say "preaching confessionally," I do not mean exposing oneself spiritually each week, but being responsible for personal honesty and openness—sharing difficult experiences and communicating personal questions or doubts.

This suggestion runs counter to much of the advice given to seminarians. Often the admonition is: "Don't ever preach on a subject that you have doubts about." However, if I were to follow this advice to the letter of the law, I would frequently find myself unable to preach.

My experience has shown that confessional preaching can and does bring a positive response from members of the congregation. Specifically, I remember the response of a teenage girl to a sermon on "The Ministry of Doubt" in which I shared some personal stories. As she listened, this teenager was able to relate to some of the doubts I had had as a teenager and to some of the doubts I still had. My admission of uncertainty helped her recognize and work through some of her own doubts which had recently caused her to be mildly depressed.

On another occasion—one of the anniversaries of my ministry—I preached on Paul's admonition to "carry one another's burdens." Part of the application of the sermon was my confession of my need for help from the congregation, not only in seeking to carry their burdens but also in trying to carry my own. I spoke of my vulnerability and humanity. The result was an outpouring of love and concern which I had not felt in many years.

Lest one assume that confessional preaching applies only in the setting of a worship service, let me tell of the time I addressed the local Rotary Club on the subject "I Need All the Help I Can Get." In this speech, I spoke on what it means to be a minister. I was dumbfounded when I looked over to the president of the club, a stockbroker, who was so moved by what I had said that he could hardly dismiss the club.

These observations should not obscure the fact, however, that there will be those who will object and criticize confessional preaching. The minister is the "answer man" for a portion of the laity and at times it is the majority portion. Therefore, when the answer man says he has more questions than answers, it can be troubling for some. For if the answer man doesn't have the answer, to whom shall they go? But this point needs to be made: The laity and the clergy are to go together to the One who has the words of life. It is only when they search together that the idolatry of worshiping a false Messiah—the preacher—can be overcome.

Demand Higher Salaries. Most people realize that ministers are paid low salaries. Studies have shown that finances may be the most important source of stress for Protestant ministers.[10] Also, the study of Southern Baptist ministers by Paul Turner showed that two-thirds felt their salaries from the churches were either much too low or a little too low.[11]

What is to be done about this problem? My answer is that the ministers are to demand higher salaries.

This recommendation is not based primarily on the fact that ministers' salaries are too low. Rather, it is based on the belief that by demanding higher salaries, ministers will force themselves and their congregations to a more balanced view of their humanness. Moreover, they will recognize their need for socially accepted expressions of self-worth and the fact that they are not above the same physical and emotional needs of other people.

In our society, money is a symbol for love and respect, therefore salaries have an impact on self-esteem. "It has become the token of affirmation to persons, institutions, commodities, and life-styles. Corporate executives, for example, revel in their year-end bonus. Are they base, crass, materialistic souls? Yes, just like the rest of us. But they understand something else about that bonus, which clergy have yet to examine. In today's world a boss finds it hard to say to a valued employee, 'Harry, you are a good man, you do good work, I need you, I love you for what you are and what you do.' Instead, he says, 'Harry, here's your bonus.' (Or, 'Sorry, Harry, but we can't give you a bonus this year.') The communication takes place. The symbol of money makes Harry feel valued and productive."[12]

Ministers and their families would have greater self-esteem

if their salaries were in keeping with the training and demands of their vocation. Also, higher salaries would relieve some of the anger felt by ministers and their families over the present wage level—anger that comes from feelings of being used and of being looked upon as families which make little contribution to life and are, therefore, paid accordingly.

I believe that a higher salary would also cause a minister to accept greater responsibility for himself and his family. A minister is forced to face the physical needs of his family and find ways of meeting those needs. The attitude of excessive dependency on "God, the good will of the congregation and merchants" leads many ministers to become dignified chiselers. They will ask for discounts on retail purchases and expect doctors and dentists to charge lower fees. This attitude is a consequence of the belief that the minister is "different."

Of course, many churches are not able to pay an adequate salary because membership is too small. For many years it was assumed that if a church had three hundred members they could provide for a pastor. But today, with the constantly increasing cost of living, the number of members required to provide a proper financial base is climbing toward five hundred.

If, as I have contended, salaries are important, what can be done about the situation in these smaller churches? I believe one answer is for the prospective minister to develop an effective "tent ministry."

I suggest that during their high-school and college years, as they prepare for church-related vocations, more young people could be presented with the need for tent ministries and counseled to develop their skills in non-church-related vocational areas so they will not depend on the church to provide for their basic financial needs. Before entering the seminary, these people could be given the opportunity to consider whether the church-related profession they have chosen is in keeping with their gifts. If so, while in seminary they could be encouraged to combine the basic seminary curriculum with courses related to the needs and special skills required in small congregations. At the time of graduation, ministers who have followed this path will be able to seek positions in non-church-related vocations in areas where they will also be able to respond to the call of a small congregation.

Such development of tent ministries would not only help the smaller churches which have trouble finding and keeping ministers, but would also provide ministers' families with the financial support so many now lack.

Develop Friendships. One becomes truly human through relationships. Conversely, one cannot become human in isolation. There is no real possibility of the clergy overcoming the temptation to walk on water if they do not develop friends.

Friendship means that when one needs help, someone will provide it. It develops when people are willing to admit their limitations and ask for help. Truly, the closest friends I have are people who I have told in words and in actions, "I need you." That is why friendship is so important—and so difficult—for ministers. They assume that the proper ministerial stance is to be self-giving and self-sufficient—always giving help to others but never asking for any.

How can a minister develop friendships? Well, friendships require initiative on his part and help from the congregation. The willingness to take initiative will be strengthened when the example of Jesus is remembered. He needed friends. He asked for help; he asked Peter, James, and John to stay awake and pray with him. Unfortunately, their failure to do so was a painful experience for Jesus.

In *The Listener,* Taylor Caldwell emphasizes the importance of listening if one is to be human. She has something to say to both clergy and laity.

> Man does not need to go to the moon or other solar systems. He does not require bigger and better bombs or missiles. He will not die if he does not get "better housing" or more vitamins. . . . His basic needs are few, and it takes little to acquire them, in spite of the advertisers. He can survive on a small amount of bread and in the meanest shelter. . . .
>
> His real need, his most terrible need, is for someone to listen to him, not as a "patient," but as a human soul. . . .
>
> Our pastors would listen—if we gave them the time to listen to us. But we have burdened them with tasks which should be our own. We have demanded not only that they be our shepherds, but that they take our trivialities, our social aspirations, the "fun" of our children, on their weary backs. We have demanded that

they be expert businessmen, politicians, accountants, playmates, community directors, "good fellows," judges, lawyers and settlers of local quarrels. We have given them little time for listening, and we do not listen to them, either. . . .[13]

Larry Baker, who had been a pastor prior to becoming a seminary professor, makes these suggestions in an excellent article on the loneliness of ministers and their families:

> What shall we do? . . . First, place this issue of friendship on your priority list and face up to the presence of loneliness in your own life. Also, remember that God didn't intend to be a substitute for people. A layperson's words, in a different setting, are applicable, "I'm twenty-seven years old and I've discovered that God and I can't do it alone. I need people!" Again, help the church understand the need of the pastor and his family for friends. Fourth, don't apologize for having special friends. Their selection isn't a violation of democracy. Also, as friendships develop within the church, guard against "using" friends to achieve personal goals. Sixth, explore the possibility of a regular, fellowship-sharing group with other ministers. Also, take the lead in building friendships. It's still true: "A man that hath friends must show himself friendly" (Prov. 18:24).
>
> The need for friends is a very human need. God created Adam then said, "It is not good that the man should be alone." That judgment applies as well to pastor and wife. The Psalmist said of God, "He setteth the solitary in families" (Ps. 68:6); he was pointing to man's need of fellowship and God's provision for it. Jesus himself needed, sought, and established friendships; he had a deep, constant and abiding relationship with the Father, but he was also drawn to other people. Recently I read Emerson's words, "A friend is a person with whom I may be sincere. Before him I may think aloud." All of us—ministers and wives alike—need that kind of friendship as tonic for the soul's loneliness![14]

Accept Professional Help. This advice seems simple and easy to follow. Such is not the case. Loren Mead has said it well: "A particular problem in most congregations is that both the clergyman and the members tend to look to the minister as a *source* of support, not as a *recipient* of support. Not much thought is given to seeing that his emotional needs are met, and often he has difficulty admitting his needs or accepting genuine support even when it is available."[15]

When I was a pastor in Kansas City, our family physician suggested that I get professional counseling. He had been treating me and realized that at that time my depression needed more expert help than he could provide. It was interesting to see how he approached the subject. He said, "You wouldn't consider going to a psychiatrist, would you?" Perhaps assuming that a minister would not consider going to a psychiatrist, he posed the question in such a way that the expected answer was "No." And, as expected, I answered, "No." Not until several years later did I consider seeking professional help.

At first, I had hesitated because I had known I would receive opposition from the members of the congregation. Moreover, I had fallen into the trap of believing I could walk on water and all problems could be solved by "me and God." But this attitude had kept me from growing as a human being.

Now, I realize that a psychiatrist can be of tremendous help to a minister both in his work and in his personal growth. As Dr. Robert Glen points out:

> The great advantage for the pastor of consulting regularly with a psychiatrist is that it enables him to have someone with whom he can discuss freely his feelings about life in general. No puzzling issues—in counseling, parish administration, or in his own family life—can then build up over a prolonged period of time. It is a sense of isolation or alienation that is so frequently the fate of the pastor. He cannot communicate on a professional level with the members of his congregation, but must always maintain his status of pastor. Thus, he often loses his concept of being a human being, whereas, with the aid of the psychiatrist, he can maintain a feeling of being a significant person.
>
> In summary, the pastor and the psychiatrist, as a "professional layman," can work together to alleviate the pressures, and to reinforce the pastor's successes, especially in the area of pastoral counseling. There, the emotional is the source of the problem, blocking the development of the spiritual. In understanding both the emotional difficulties and the strengths of the parishioners, they can be helped toward greater service to the parish, to God, and to their fellow man. Also, in helping the pastor deal with his own

family problems, the frequently seen tragedy of the successful pastor with unsuccessful family life can be avoided.[16]

Develop Good Mental Health Habits. The minister as a human being must find ways to develop good mental health habits. As with physical health, good mental health requires attention, time, and effort.

I agree with Lyn Elder who has suggested that "the most important single thing in maintaining mental health is the practice of inner awareness. This takes time and effort, but it pays dividends. Each day—preferably at the beginning of the day, though it may be repeated throughout—try to feel your own feelings, to recognize your emotions, and to acknowledge them to yourself as honestly as you can."[17]

Much attention in mental health has been focused on ways of coping with stress. One three-year study delineates some of the methods used by three hundred managers from thirteen London, Ontario, companies and reveals that some managers are able to cope effectively with stress while others are not. What are the most successful tactics?

> In terms of the number of stress symptoms reported, the five best coping techniques were: building resistance by regular sleep and good health habits; keeping work and non-work life separate; getting exercise; talking things through with on-the-job peers; and withdrawing physically from a situation when necessary. The subjects with the stress coming out their ears eschewed many of those proven methods for less effective ones such as changing the strategy of attack on work, talking with their spouses and changing to another work activity.[18]

There are several statements in this report which to me are unusually relevant for ministers. Note, first, two of the ways that are considered less effective in coping with stress: talking with spouses and changing to another work activity. As I see it, these are the two methods most commonly used by ministers. Ministers talk over their job-related problems more frequently with their spouses than with anyone else. Moreover, moving from one church to another has been the accepted way of dealing with stress. Until recently, the average pastorate lasted approximately three years. It is true that the duration is increasing, but the reason does not seem to be because ministers are learning how to cope better with stress; rather, it is because they cannot move.

Of the five best coping techniques, I want to emphasize two: getting exercise and withdrawing physically from a situation when necessary.

First, ministers as a group do not give high priority to physical exercise. Dr. Kenneth H. Cooper, an authority on physical fitness who developed the aerobics program for the Canadian Air Force, lectured Southern Baptist pastors on their poor physical condition. I believe his characterization applies to ministers in all denominations.

Second, "stress interruption" is a familiar term to many, but the reality that it describes is implemented on too few occasions by ministers. Yet, those who have gone to Career Development Centers express the need for a moratorium on stress as one of the most important needs of pastors.[19] I am talking about the need to stop and take time away from the ministry—a few hours, a few days, or even a few months—to evaluate where one has been and where one is going. And to insure the fulfillment of this need, study groups of the Presbyterian Church U.S. and U.S.A. have recommended that sabbaticals be provided for all ministers.

The Laity Must Help. Most of my answers have been directed toward ministers. This is natural because I am a minister and I see my shortcomings. However, in the very nature of my answer I seem to be implying that ministers are superhuman, that we can pull ourselves up by our bootstraps without help. We cannot.

The laity must help. And by help I don't mean simply a well-intended statement like, "We have wanted you to come to our home but we know how busy you are." Nonsense. Ministers are busy and lonely, and each characteristic reinforces the other. If a minister is to be truly human, the layman must interrupt the frantic pace of an overcrowded calendar and provide times of genuine human friendship, times which say, "We want to be with you because you are a person—not because you are the parson."

However, one or two or even a hundred offers of help may not be enough to change a personality pattern which is constantly being reinforced. The laity will have to wage a concentrated battle to overcome the minister's tendency to try to be superhuman.

It needs to be added, also, that helping a minister to be human can be an unpleasant experience. No one likes to be around a person who has feelings of inadequacy and low self-esteem, or who fears intimacy and wears a professional mask. Any person who is hurt either physically or psychologically is more difficult to love than someone who is whole. But Christian love is the act of binding up wounds and pouring on oil. And a minister needs all the Christian love he can get.

One of my most memorable experiences of being helped by laymen to be more human occurred during my first pastorate. At least three times a week, and often five times a week, this friend would stop by on his way home from work and we would go and get a cup of coffee. Generally, we talked about matters of common interest and seldom about the church. I must admit that on several occasions I felt that I was wasting time. But in retrospect, I see those times drinking coffee as one of the greatest gifts which I have received in my years as pastor.

In the same pastorate there was a friend who traveled a great deal, and often would ask me to go on trips with him. I remember one Sunday night he waited until after the evening worship service for us to leave. We drove until about 2:00 A.M. before arriving at our destination. As I fought my sleepiness and tried to stay awake, I wished I was at home in bed. Now I look back on that experience as a highlight in my understanding that my friend wanted to have time with me as his friend and not as his pastor.

These two men, who took the initiative over and over again to seek me out and to say, "We like you as a person," helped me see that there is nothing greater than friendship among human beings. I would add that there have been other men and women since then who have contributed to the fighting of my temptation to try to be superhuman. I have been successful in my continuous struggle as a result of the laity who have accepted me as a friend, and I have failed as a result of my pride and of the expectations of the laity who have wanted me to walk on water.

* * *

The temptation to try to be superhuman is real for ministers. The destructive effects are numerous. Some answers to the problem have been suggested here. But the necessity for ministers to accept their humanity has nowhere been expressed as concisely or with as much urgency as in the statement of the apostle Paul: "Yet we who have this spiritual treasure are like common clay pots, to show that the supreme power belongs to God, not to us" (2 Cor. 4:7, TEV). The laity must help ministers live this truth.

Chapter 3

Not Ready for
Solid Food

Paul expressed great concern over the spiritual immaturity of the Christians at Corinth. He wrote, "I had to feed you milk, not solid food, because you were not ready for it" (1 Cor. 3:2, TEV).

We need to share Paul's concern for spiritual immaturity because there are reasons to believe that Christians today are as spiritually immature as those in Corinth. Furthermore, our spiritual immaturity may be one of the greatest threats to the survival of our churches or even to the survival of our society.

It is important, therefore, for those of us who are committed to the church as God's answer to man's need, to probe the question of the spiritual maturity of both clergy and laity. Again, I focus my attention on the clergy; however, I believe that most of what is said about the clergy applies equally to the laity.

EVIDENCE OF SPIRITUAL IMMATURITY

What is the evidence of spiritual immaturity among the clergy? For me, the evidence begins with my personal experience. For years I drew on the spiritual reserve which I had gained as a child, teenager, and young adult through active participation in the life of the church and a half-hearted commitment to systematic prayer and Bible study. Yet my spiritual reserve was never a significant power in my life because I had not been taught to any great degree, either in my church life or in my seminary days, the art of spiritual growth. And my experience with spiritual immaturity does not appear to be unique.

John Claypool, a prominent Southern Baptist minister, uses an illustration from Lloyd Ogilvie to describe his own experience. He writes:

> Lloyd Ogilvie described himself, when just out of the seminary, as a man "with a rudder but no sail"; that is, as a young minister he found himself with worlds of fine concepts and high ideals as to what he should be doing, but the power to put these into practice was lacking. He discovered that his seminary training had given him all sorts of technical competence, but where was the spiritual energy to actualize all of this? There had been times in his life, he reported, when he was overwhelmed with confusion; that is, he had energy but did not possess a vision or plan of what to do with it. At this early point in his ministry, however, confusion was not the problem. He had lots of ideas for what he wanted to do, but the power to act on all of this was not present.[1]

In his book *Creative Ministry,* Henri J. M. Nouwen, a Roman Catholic theologian who has caught the attention of Catholics and Protestants alike with his insight into the meaning of Christian ministry, discusses yet another indication of the spiritual immaturity of the clergy.

The book's theme is "the relationship between professionalism and spirituality in the ministry." Nouwen states, "Perhaps we have to say that one of the main reasons for the many frustrations, pains, and disappointments in the life of numerous Christian ministers is rooted in the still-growing separation between professionalism and spirituality. However, this separation is quite understandable if we look at the development of theological education during the last decade."[2]

He then adds that the routine of spiritual exercises at the seminaries became suspect as ministers began to feel that prayer was an escape into the safety of the interior life and a way of avoiding the burning issues that should stir the Christian conscience. They reasoned, "Let us not close our eyes in order to indulge in nice and gratifying thoughts about God and his mysteries, but let us keep them open to the growing needs of the world around us. Why spend our time in rather dull and fruitless hours of meditation and contemplation when we could use our time better to train ourselves in the necessary skills and techniques that help us to be of real service to our fellow-man?"[3] Therefore, while the seminarians developed greater skills through pastoral training in hospitals, prisons, and special city projects, they neglected the traditional spiritual disciplines of prayer, meditation, and chapel attendance.

Ernest Mosley, a leader among Southern Baptists in the field of pastoral ministries, makes these observations concerning the spiritual immaturity of ministers:

> During many of the ten years of service as a consultant and supervisor of work in pastoral ministries, I didn't focus attention on the spiritual needs of persons in the ministry. I assumed the persons would be growing spiritually if they were committed to Jesus as Lord and to the ministry as their calling. Therefore, I proceeded to speak and write about the work involved in being a minister and how to get that work done. Now I know that my assumption was incorrect. Through the years I've heard comments and engaged in conversations that clearly revealed the desperate need of ministers for the renewal of a relationship with Christ that provides the strength and style for life.[4]

From an entirely different point of view, we also have the testimony of Dr. James D. Mallory, a practicing psychiatrist in Atlanta, Georgia. In a paper presented to a consultation called by the Presbyterian Church U.S.A., he emphasized that theological confusion and spiritual immaturity are, on the basis of his experience in counseling ministers, major reasons for the low morale among ministers.[5]

If one needs any more evidence of spiritual immaturity within today's society, all one has to do is ask any Christian, lay or clergy, "Can you tell me about your prayer life?" The embarrassed reply is, with few exceptions, "Well, it's not what it should be."

CAUSES OF SPIRITUAL IMMATURITY

A major cause of spiritual immaturity is the neglect of spiritual discipline because of resistance to immature views of prayer and worship. John Claypool described his resistance in these words:

> Perhaps the greatest intellectual obstacle that I encountered was the suspicion that prayer represented a regression to an infantile state where one wanted everything done for oneself and did not want to put forth any effort on his own. Unfortunately I encountered some folk in college who attempted to substitute the act of prayer for the hard discipline of work and study. . . . Such action really did turn me off and only deepened my suspicion that prayer was the domain of the weak and the fearful and the lazy. I remember saying defiantly to some contemporaries that no farmer could sit on his front porch and pray and by so doing get a crop planted and harvested. I now recognize . . . [the] gross misuse of the prayer discipline, but at the time it only contributed to making the whole process intellectually suspect to me.[6]

I experienced a similar resistance which slowed the development of the discipline required for my spiritual growth and prayer. During the second World War, I served in the Navy and was personally aware of friends who were killed in battle or lost at sea. I saw the death of my comrades as the inevitable consequence of war, not as God's will. I rebelled, therefore, against the semi-magical interpretations of prayer as shields against bullets, torpedoes, bombs, or other forms of military armament.

I also resisted talk about how husbands or sons were saved by the direct intervention of prayers. I would hear people say, "I prayed for my son every day, and he came home alive." To me, such a position was a direct denial of our human responsibility for the destruction of war. Their words seemed to imply that as Christians we should pray for the safety of our loved ones rather than actively work for peace.

Moreover, I rebelled against the insensitivity expressed in this semi-magical view of prayer. Many other men and women had also prayed for the safety of their loved ones, yet their friends and relatives had been killed. To me, those who testified to the power of their prayers were expressing a high degree of spiritual pride and callousness. They were convinced of their spiritual powers, and insensitive to the heartache of those who had lost loved ones. But by expending my energy in rebellion against such attitudes, I neglected my own spiritual growth.

A second cause of spiritual immaturity is lack of training in spiritual disciplines. This has been true for both clergy and laity.

Fortunately, in the past few years there has been an increased interest in prayer. A news story in the *Kansas City Times* on July 21, 1979, reports a dramatic growth in houses of prayer and adds that "Patricia Crewell, editor of the current *House of Prayer Directory*, says the directory lists nearly twice as many houses as a year ago."

Unfortunately, the kind of spiritual training provided by these houses of prayer has been the exception rather than the rule for most Christians. Even though prayer groups in churches and periodic studies of books on prayer have always existed, serious, disciplined training for the contemplative life-style is hard to find.

It is also true that, contrary to the assumptions of lay people, the clergy has not received rigorous spiritual training as a part of their seminary curriculum. Seminaries have placed little if any emphasis on spiritual training during the past several decades. However, I believe that situation is changing, and Glenn Hinson reflects the concern which is now present in the seminary community. He writes:

> To yield full dividends, given the aim of total formation, the burden for spiritual formation falls upon the total educational experience in which the student is involved. I am in complete agreement with a recently concluded report on spiritual development sponsored by the American Association of Theological Schools when it asserts that *"in a student's experience of the entire spectrum of seminary life he is being spiritually formed or malformed."* It follows from this that the total shape of the community in which he is educated affects and influences his spiritual growth. I concur also when this same report goes on to place the burden of spiritual formation upon the faculty. It firmly avows, *"If any one thing has emerged from our study of seminaries, it is the conviction that the spiritual development and formation of students begins with and depends on the spirituality of the faculty."* The faculty must decide what the seminary envisions as its educational task.[7]

A third cause of spiritual immaturity is the failure of ministers to admit their spiritual problems and ask for help. When a minister arrives at his first church, members assume he is spiritually mature. At least this was my experience. I remember being called to comfort a parishioner whose mother had died. As I walked into the room, the attending physician, who was a devout Christian and probably more spiritually mature than I, immediately turned to me as a spiritual expert. I felt uncomfortable both because of my spiritual immaturity and because the doctor assumed I had a maturity I did not possess.

Such pressure causes a minister to be slow to ask for help as he faces spiritual problems. When they face a crisis in their spiritual lives, most ministers seek to solve it by themselves. A study made by the temporary Commission of Continuing Education of the United Presbyterian Church showed that at least 50 percent of their ministers have had a serious crisis in their faith. Of this group, 83 percent indicated they resolved the crisis without the aid of any outside help.[8] While admiring the desire of these ministers to solve their spiritual crises by themselves, I find it difficult to believe that such spiritual self-medication or self-surgery can be very effective. In fact, I wonder if it may leave some serious scars.

Yet another cause of spiritual immaturity is simply the nature of our society. A contemplative lifestyle goes against the grain of our culture—a culture which puts a premium on activism. As William Hulme states, "Despite the Church's emphasis on justification by grace, our society is held together with justification by works."[9] He adds, "The Protestant world does not place much value upon meditation. From a functional point of view it seems a waste of valuable time. To those who wish to meditate, we give our blessing—so long as their numbers are small. We can take a few oddballs in any crowd. They receive our awe but not our emulation. Meditation is a symbol for the superfluous."[10]

An important warning against a serious obstacle to spiritual maturity was voiced by John Henry Jowett, a ministerial giant of the early twentieth century. He wrote movingly of "The Perils of the Preacher." His words, written nearly eighty years ago, need no elaboration.

The first peril which I will name, and I name it first because its touch is so fatal, is that of *deadening familiarity with the sublime.*

You will not have been long in the ministry before you discover that it is possible to be fussily busy about the Holy Place and yet to lose the wondering sense of the Holy Lord. We may have much to do with religion and yet not be religious. We may become mere guideposts when we were intended to be guides. We may indicate the way, and yet not be found in it. We may be professors but not pilgrims. Our studies may be workshops instead of "upper rooms." Our share in the table-provisions may be that of analysts rather than guests. We may become so absorbed in words that we forget to eat the Word. And the consummation of the subtle peril may be this: we may come to assume that fine talk is fine living, that expository skill is deep piety, and while we are fondly hugging the non-essentials the veritable essence escapes.

I think this is one of the most insidious, and perhaps the predominant peril in a preacher's life. A man may live in mountain-country and lose all sense of the heights. And that is a terrible impoverishment, when mountain-country comes to have the ordinary significance of the plains.[11]

Another formidable obstacle to spiritual maturity is that which William Hulme calls the "nice prayer." The "nice prayer" is that public prayer which is expected from ministers at potluck suppers, father-and-son banquets, Rotary clubs, and countless community gatherings. Because the minister is leading others in addressing God he is necessarily concerned about the wording. Such prayers "are politely worded and abundant with thanksgivings and eulogies to the Deity. Often they carry a punch line that contains a hidden or unhidden moral."[12]

The problem is that these "nice prayers" can carry over into a minister's private prayer life. When this happens our prayer life may become superficial and dishonest. As Hulme says, "Most of us have stored-up hostilities toward God, or at least toward providence, but our *good* prayers rarely express it. It is rather difficult to express hostility in the carefully chosen words and soothing tones of public prayer. Yet our biblical heritage is something else. The prayers of the prophets and even of the psalmist are not always *nice* prayers. In fact, we hesitate to use some of them in our public worship because of the hostility they express. Yet, they are honest prayers."[13]

I would contend that the honesty of the prophets and psalmists was one element that helped make them spiritual giants. In our private prayers we must try to have the same honesty as the biblical writers. We need to learn how to express resentment and anger at life and even at God.

I have suggested several causes of spiritual immaturity, but probably the most painful reason to admit is lack of discipline and motivation. I have already spoken of how we are influenced by our society to be activists, and therefore tend to place a low priority on the contemplative life. But we need to admit and confess that we have not developed a hunger and thirst for spiritual maturity. According to Hulme, "The pastor needs to recognize the ambivalence in his frequent lament that he cannot find the time for a disciplined devotional life. He needs to do the same with his other lament that he cannot find the time for calling. What we consistently put off due to the press of other demands, we either value lightly or are resisting. While it seems to one that he is a prisoner in these matters, the fact remains that the prisoner may be in love with his chains."[14]

Our spiritual immaturity is real and the reasons for it are also real. Therefore, spiritual maturity will not come easily or quickly. To grow spiritually we must be able to answer "Yes" to the question "Is spiritual maturity important for the minister?" Then we must ask the question "What are the steps to spiritual maturity?"

THE IMPORTANCE OF SPIRITUAL MATURITY
FOR THE MINISTER

There are two reasons why a minister needs spiritual maturity. First, a minister must be above all else a person who belongs to Jesus Christ. Second, a minister must have maturity to meet the demands of the pastorate.

Elizabeth O'Connor, who has interpreted so insightfully the meaning of spiritual growth, writes in *Call to Commitment:*

We are not called primarily to create new structures for the church in this age; we are not called primarily to a program of service, or to dream dreams or have visions. We are called first of all to belong to Jesus Christ as Saviour and Lord, and to keep our lives warmed at the hearth of His life. It is there the fire will be lit which will create new structures and programs of service that will draw others into the circle to dream dreams and have visions.

To understand this is to be thrown back upon those disciplines which are the only known gateways to the grace of God; for how do we fulfill the command to love, except that we learn it of God, and how do we learn it of God, except that we pray, and live under His word and perceive His world?[15]

Ministers, therefore, cannot hope to serve unless they are constantly striving for spiritual maturity. It is when our lives are filled with God's spirit that ministry takes place.

Henri Nouwen affirms the relationship between ministry and spirituality in these words: "Ministry is not an eight-to-five job but primarily a way of life, which is for others to see and understand so that liberation can become a possibility."[16] This terrifying responsibility which Nouwen places on the minister must be accepted. This, to me, is not a denial of the priesthood of the believer; it is an affirmation of the meaning of ministry and of the Christian life. We are to be witnesses in our daily actions that the new life in Christ is a reality.

I turn to an even more explicit and beautiful passage written by Nouwen. These words offer a unique and insightful characterization of the spiritually mature minister, and they portray the ideal toward which every minister should strive.

Ordination means the recognition and affirmation of the fact that a man has gone beyond the walls of fear, lives in intimate contact with the God of the living, and has a burning desire to show others the way to Him. Ordination does not make anybody anything but is the solemn recognition of the fact that this man has been able to be obedient to God, to hear His voice and understand His call, and that he can offer others the way to that same experience. Therefore, the minister who wants to make celebration possible is a man of prayer. Only a man of prayer can lead others to celebration because everyone who comes in contact with him realizes that he draws his powers from a source they cannot easily locate but they know is strong and deep. The freedom that gives him a certain independence is not authoritarian or distant. Rather, it makes him rise above the immediate needs and most urgent desires of the people around him. He is deeply moved by things happening around him, but he does not allow himself to be crushed by them. He listens attentively, speaks with a self-evident authority, but does not easily get excited or nervous. In all he says or does, he proves to have a vision that guides his life. To that vision he is obedient. It makes him distinguish sharply between what is important and what is not. He is not insensitive to what excites people, but he evaluates their needs differently by seeing them in the perspective of his vision. He is happy and content when people listen to him, but he does not want to form cliques. He does not attach himself to anybody exclusively. What he says sounds convincing and obvious, but he does not force his opinion on anybody and is not irritated when people do not accept his ideas or do not fulfill his will. All this shows that his vision is what counts for him and that he strives to make it come true.[17]

The second major reason a minister must have spiritual maturity is to be able to meet the demands of the pastorate. Walter Wagoner, an astute interpreter of seminary life, writes: "There are few experiences so revealing of the future staying power and growth of a parish minister as his habits of worship and devotion; and if such habits are not cultivated during the seminary years, there is every expectation of personal bankruptcy as a pastor. Worship is the native air of those who *really* believe in God. Nothing else will cleanse, fortify, and redeem with anything near the power of worship. It is literally a *sine qua non* for the minister, for all Christians."[18]

There are at least four facets of the pastorate that demand spiritual maturity. I recognize that to a lesser or greater degree these four facets of the pastorate are present in the life of every Christian. However, I name them in relationship to the pastorate because it has been at these points that I have found my spiritual immaturity exposed and, as a consequence, have realized my need for spiritual maturity.

The first facet that demands spiritual maturity is the pastor's daily need to set priorities for maximum use of the time available to him. As a generalist, the pastor is faced with many functions—teaching, preaching, crisis ministry, pastoral visitation, evangelistic visitation, administration, counseling, community activities, and denominational activities—each of which could become a full-time job.

Several years ago I read that Paul Tournier began each day by setting aside one hour for prayer and meditation. He wrote how difficult this was for him when he first started. He confessed that on the first day he was sure he had spent at least one hour in prayer, but when he checked his watch it had been only five minutes. As time passed, however, his ability to meditate and pray grew. He said one of the most important things he gained from that hour of prayer and meditation was the opportunity to permit God's spirit to give him guidance and wisdom in setting priorities for the day and in allocating his time and strength.

In fact, Tournier's experience was an impetus for my being more disciplined in my time of prayer and meditation. I find that while praying and meditating I am able to set priorities and to find the strength, and a measure of peace, in being able to say "no" to many of the demands on my time. Moreover, without the strength I receive from prayer, I find it impossible to pursue those difficult tasks which are often the most important.

A second facet that demands spiritual maturity is the difficulty of maintaining enthusiasm when there is no evidence of success. By the very nature of ministry, it is practically impossible to see success in the sense of having brought to completion a given task. When one is working with people it is difficult to tell what impact a sermon, a counseling session, or an evangelistic visit may have had. Therefore, one must find strength through spiritual maturity to carry on without the usual, visible gratification.

The nature of the spiritual maturity which is needed in the pastorate was pointed out by Harry Emerson Fosdick. He wrote that Romans 8:28 was one of the most important passages in Scripture. It is when one has a spiritual maturity to believe that "God works in everything for good" that one is able to live the lifestyle of a servant and continue to serve without demanding evidence of success. If God is at work in everything, success is guaranteed. Therefore, there is no need to constantly demand evidence of success through such things as increases in numbers of people, budgets, and buildings.

Spiritual maturity is also required to develop skills in interpersonal relationships and to maintain open and candid relationships with members of the congregation. Moreover, the pastor's ability to serve depends on his ability to love people—to be actively concerned for all people, including those who oppose him. And this kind of love comes only from God.

I was called upon by a deacon to visit a church member

who was to undergo a very delicate and dangerous surgical procedure. The deacon asked that I go by the hospital to pray with the church member and give him emotional and spiritual support. The problem for me on that occasion was that, only three weeks earlier, the man who was to undergo surgery had headed a group of members who were going to call for my resignation. I felt the charges that had been made were not true and the tactics that had been used were secretive and underhanded. As it turned out, the business meeting took such a turn that the group decided not to make public their charges.

I was angry and hurt by what had taken place. Now I was being asked to help a man who I believed had spread false and vicious rumors. Reluctantly, I agreed to go to the hospital. When I was walking down the hallway, I felt a surge of anger welling up inside of me. But I realized that I had enough self-control to go into the member's room and go through the motions of praying and expressing concern. I did not believe, however, that this is what I was called upon to do. I stopped in the hallway, and for some five to ten minutes I prayed silently, asking for help to forgive so that I could be honest in my prayers and concern. I believe God's spirit helped me minister to that man.

Although all people are, at one time or another, hurt by friends and associates, there is a difference for the minister. The difference is that he is called upon to serve those who have hurt him. A business friend put it well when he said, "I was deeply disappointed by a client who called off a business deal at the last minute." He went on to say, "I had spent a great deal of time in preparation for the business venture." Then he added, "The difference between me and you is that I won't have to see that person again. However, you are called upon to minister to those who have let you down." I appreciated the insight of my friend. Yes, a minister does need spiritual maturity to deal with interpersonal relationships.

The fourth facet of the pastorate that demands spiritual maturity is the need to overcome the pessimism that comes from being let down by those you work with. Members of the helping profession are familiar with the "burnout" syndrome. Pessimism and cynicism are twin pitfalls for those who work with people. Because human beings are at times irresponsible and deceitful, it is possible to get to the point where you look with a jaundiced eye at all people. This problem is doubly serious when you work with a voluntary organization.

The lack of dependability of some people and the frustration of impotence to accomplish certain tasks persistently trouble the pastor because he has no power over members of his congregation other than that which comes from trust or moral persuasion. And these sources of power are not sufficient to correct situations where church duties are given low priority or where church members demonstrate irresponsibility.

To meet the burnout syndrome ministers need spiritual maturity. They must have the ability to see that this is God's world, that he is active and present in this world. He is the ruler and Lord of history. Matters of ultimate consequence are in his hands. God will be the ultimate victor. Therefore, we are to carry out our task and leave the ultimate outcome to God. This, as I see it, is not a "cop-out"; it is the recognition that while man does affect consequences, even when he is irresponsible, he never dethrones God.

John Killinger has written a beautiful statement on the meaning of prayer which speaks to the temptation to give in to pessimism and cynicism.

> We see the world as a wilderness and not as a paradise. We behold the mud instead of the stars. Or, in religious terms, we experience the absence of God instead of his presence. . . .
>
> The problem is with us. We lose the ability to discern his presence. We forget how to pray. The paradise reverts to wilderness.
>
> How to see again! That is what we want. How to live everyday as though the world were paradise and not wilderness, as though all of life were filled with the miracles of God!
>
> That is what we desire more than anything else—to see the miracles again! Well, you can. You really can!
>
> All you have to do is learn to pray. It's that simple. Prayer develops a whole new consciousness, a whole new way of looking at the world. By putting you in touch with God, amid your various circumstances, it enables you to see the paradise around you.
>
> I know, because I am beginning to see it again.[19]

SOME STEPS TO CHRISTIAN MATURITY

It would be irresponsible to emphasize the need for spiritual maturity and not to suggest some steps to achieve it. However,

I am not writing a book on prayer and the contemplative life. Therefore, my statements will only suggest steps which have been helpful to me.

If it is true that both clergy and laity are called "first of all to belong to Jesus Christ as Saviour and Lord, and to keep our lives warmed at the hearth of his life" then our first step must be to take the example of Jesus seriously and seek to follow it daily.

In the beginning of Jesus' ministry, Mark states that "in the morning, a great while before day, he rose and went out to a lonely place and there he prayed" (Mark 1:35). Later in Jesus' ministry, Luke notes that "in these days he went out into the hills to pray; and all night he continued in prayer to God" (Luke 6:12). It was after he had gone up the mountain to pray, taking with him Peter, James, and John, that he experienced the transfiguration (Luke 9:28). And it was because it was his custom to go to the Mount of Olives in the evening to pray that Judas knew where he could be found (Luke 22:39).

The biblical record makes clear, therefore, that prayer was an essential part of the life of Christ. Our first step to spiritual maturity takes place when we follow his example in our prayer life.

A second step to spiritual maturity is persistence. It is axiomatic that no physical or musical talents can be developed without hours, weeks, months, and years of strenuous preparation. The persistence required of an athlete who would compete in the Olympic games is well-known. No less a determination will suffice for spiritual growth.

Persistence is required because emotions fluctuate. The one constant fact about emotions is that they are never constant. Because prayer and meditation involve our emotions there is a temptation to neglect spiritual exercises during periods when God appears to be absent. The great saints have understood the reality of the "Dark Night of the Soul" and have written of their experiences. As I have understood it, their one common answer to the "Dark Night of the Soul" has been that of persistence.

The use of devotional resources is the third step which is needed for growth in the contemplative lifestyle. The first resource that comes to mind is the Bible. Many Christians find this their first and most valuable source for spiritual growth. I have not found this to be true for myself. My problem has been that as I read the Bible I am constantly looking for sermon topics or ideas for devotional talks. Therefore, I find it difficult to permit the Scriptures to speak to my needs. I find, however, that devotional materials based on passages of Scripture do speak to me. I also find that books which guide in searching for great truths in Scripture are helpful. For example, I have recently studied Bernhard Anderson's book *Out of the Depths, the Psalms Speak for Us Today.* I have found this book to be of great help because it leads the reader to go to the Psalms with an openness to their message seeking new understanding.

Books on prayer are indispensable devotional resources. These books are sources of intellectual understanding as well as stimulation for the spirit. Harry Emerson Fosdick's *The Meaning of Prayer* was one of the first books to have a significant impact on my prayer life. One of the latest books to have such an impact is John Killinger's *Bread for the Wilderness, Wine for the Journey.*

Other devotional resources are found in the manuals for spiritual growth. One example is Glenn Hinson's *A Serious Call to a Contemplative Life Style,* a stimulating book which opens up new vistas of the spiritual life. While Hinson declares that the book is "essentially a book about problems rather than answers," he is too modest in his claims. The book provides answers by addressing problems. Moreover, the Appendix entitled "Selected Devotional Reading" is a ready source of excellent aids for the serious student of prayer.

A fourth step to spiritual maturity is participation in prayer retreats. These exercises are coming into their own. For many years silent prayer retreats were the domain of Roman Catholics. Fortunately, many of us who are Protestants have recently had the opportunity to learn of new dimensions of prayer and gain meaningful insights from and with Catholics through interdenominational prayer retreats.

My experience at these retreats leads very naturally to a fifth step, namely, involving the laity in one's program of spiritual growth. Every pastor can attest to the strength received from visiting the "saints." In most cases these are men and women who have faced serious trials and tribulations and have overcome them through their faith in God. In one of my pastorates the acknowledged spiritual giants in the congregation were a father and mother who had given much of their lives, without bitterness and resentment, to a son who was born with cerebral palsy. They cared for this son day and night. Yet, they never complained and always had time to care for those in physical, emotional, and spiritual need. My relationship with this family was a source of great spiritual growth. Every pastor needs to permit such mature Christians to teach him how to grow spiritually.

Another way to involve the laity in one's program of spiritual growth is to encourage and participate in church services in which laymen play leadership roles. In one church where I was pastor, the devotional at the Wednesday night prayer service was given by men and women from the congregation. Those services offered me an opportunity to learn and grow spiritually.

Involving laymen in a minister's spiritual growth is important for at least two reasons. First, a minister needs more time for learning. He spends too much of his time teaching. Second, he needs to see how God's spirit works in the lives of all, clergy and laity, who seek to truly depend on him for guidance and strength. Sometimes ministers can fall prey to the belief that clergy have a corner on spiritual matters.

I recommend keeping a spiritual diary as a sixth step to spiritual growth. *Markings,* by Dag Hammarskjöld, has been an inspiration and challenge to many—a challenge because the journal demonstrates a depth of searching which few achieve. My own diary has often helped me clarify my feelings and see evidence of God's guidance. My diary bears out that which I have long contended—God's guidance is seen primarily in retrospect. In rereading my diary I find questions and prayers expressed in times of decision-making, when only a vague apprehension of God's leadership existed along with a stronger question: "Is this what God would have me do?" Now I can look back and see where God guided me. This is in no way to say that all of my major decisions have reflected God's guidance. Far from it. It is merely a recommendation to keep a journal as an aid to spiritual growth.

A final suggestion relating to spiritual maturity is a recommendation that each minister personalize his or her devotional life. It is helpful as one seeks to live a disciplined devotional life to follow suggestions from those who have learned the art of prayer. However, it is also important that one not be chained by the methodology of other Christians. I have found that my own approach has changed over the years. Some practices which I carry out today would have made me very uncomfortable years ago. Specifically, I find it meaningful to go into the sanctuary early Sunday morning, or sometimes late Saturday night, and kneel in prayer. For reasons I cannot explain, I would not have been comfortable doing this fifteen years ago.

Paul Tournier offers an interesting example of the importance of personalizing one's devotional life. He writes, "One day, almost a year ago, I realized that I was doing myself harm because I had begun to read the newspaper before my morning meditation, the time when God was asking me to listen to Him before listening to the world. Rectifying this was simple, but it was enough to brighten again the climate of my life.

"I have just read these last words to my wife. She immediately answered: 'It is just the opposite in my case; I listen first to the radio news and that thoroughly wakens me; after that I can meditate to some purpose.' So each one must sincerely seek his own way of making contact with God."[20]

William Hulme offers advice based on his own experience and directed to the specific needs of the pastor: "The time prior to the supper hour is of distinct advantage for the pastor or any man whose work consumes a great deal of emotional energy—even as it is obviously not the best time for the housewife. A break for rest and meditation and committing the day's events to God at this time makes it possible for the pastor to join the family circle with a refreshed spirit. Otherwise he may be with his family in the body while his mind belabors the problems of the day. The minister who attempts to join himself to his family table directly from his work involvement is exposing his stomach to indigestion and the family atmosphere to tension."[21]

*　　*　　*

I have in my office a prayer attributed to Martin Luther which has been helpful in directing me to God as I attempt to carry out my duties as a pastor and seek to grow spiritually. The prayer reads:

> Oh Lord God, Thou hast made me a pastor and teacher in the church. Thou seest how unfit I am to administer rightly this great responsible office; and had I been without Thy aid and counsel I would surely have ruined it long ago. Therefore do I invoke Thee.
>
> How gladly do I desire to yield and consecrate my heart and mouth to this ministry. I desire to teach the congregation. I, too, desire ever to learn and to keep Thy Word my constant companion and to meditate thereupon earnestly.
>
> Use me as Thy instrument in Thy service. Only do not Thou forsake me, for if I am left to myself, I will certainly bring it all to destruction. Amen.

Chapter 4

In the Wrong Line

I asked my friend a simple question, "How was your trip to Africa?" He answered enthusiastically, "The most wonderful experience I have ever had. It lifted a tremendous load from my shoulders. I can do my work as a pastor with a new sense of happiness. After all, the work of a missionary is the same as that of a pastor. You preach, you try to help people, you meet defeat, and you feel frustrated over lack of response and apathy."

I was puzzled by this answer. I couldn't see the connection between learning firsthand about the problems faced by missionaries and finding a new satisfaction as a pastor.

It was not until later in our conversation that I began to understand. My friend told me the story of his call to "full-time Christian service." When he was a teenager, he went to a church camp. During his last evening there, a missionary spoke to the campers and made an appeal for "full-time Christian service." After he finished, the missionary instructed those who believed that God was calling them to be missionaries to form one line, and those who believed that God was calling them to be pastors to form another line. My friend truly believed that God was calling him to be a missionary, so he stepped into what he thought was the appropriate line. Needless to say, he was quite surprised when the counselor said, "Son, I'm glad you have been called to be a pastor." It seems my friend had stepped into the wrong line.

The young man was dismayed to learn of his mistake. But the counselor did not ask any questions. He just told him that his pastor would receive a letter telling about the decision and would help him in any way he could. Between the boy's embarrassment and the counselor's failure to listen, the mistake was not mentioned. His decision was announced to the church, and members were asked to give their support. There was no opportunity for turning back.

All through college and seminary, he thought of telling someone about the "wrong line," but he was ashamed to talk about it. Moreover, he felt that possibly it had been God's spirit that had led him into the line for pastors.

He lived with questions and doubts for twenty-five years. Relief came only when he found that the work of the pastor and that of the missionary were the same. He realized that the overriding question was not whether one was a missionary or a pastor, but whether one was faithful to the task at hand. He concluded, therefore, that as long as he was faithful as a pastor, he did not have to worry any longer about having chosen the wrong line.

My friend's agonizing experience may be unique in that he believed he had stepped into the wrong line. However, the questions, doubts, fears, and anxieties related to the meaning of God's call are part of the experience of many Christians, both clergy and laity.

As has been the case with other forms of religious experience, we have been slow to investigate, to question, or to try to understand the nature of God's call. Moreover, the problem has been compounded by poor counseling, the ego-needs of the counselor, the unawareness of the ego-needs of the one called, the failure to determine who did the calling—God or the subconscious—pressure from other people, and theological confusion as to the meaning of God's call. These questions are not new but the present crisis in the ministry demands that we examine the assumptions which have characterized our actions.

BIBLICAL AND HISTORICAL TEACHING ON CALL AND ORDINATION

Has God called me? Every committed Christian has faced this question, and the answer is an unequivocal "Yes." Every

Christian is called of God—called to salvation and to servant-hood. And some Christians are called to carry out special tasks for God's purpose of redemption.

The Bible uses the idea of call in three ways. The first and most important is God's call to salvation. The second is God's call to service. The third is God's call to carry out special tasks or functions.

In the gospels Jesus calls sinners to repentance and the weary and the heavy-laden to come to him for rest. This picture of the ministry of Christ makes clear that call is related to God's offer of salvation. God took the initiative. He called Abraham to be his instrument and promised, "Through you I will bless all the nations" (Gen. 12:3, TEV). God sent his Son, that "whoever believes in him should not perish but have eternal life" (John 3:16). Or, as Paul states it, "God was in Christ, reconciling the world to himself, not counting their trespasses against them" (2 Cor. 5:19).

This basic biblical truth is often presented by using the word *call* and its cognates. In fact, Paul employs some form of the term more than forty times in his writings. Henlee Barnette has written, "Each time the terms *kaleo* (verb, 'I call'), *kalein* (present infinitive active, 'to call'), *klēsis* (noun, 'a call'), and *klētos* (adjective, 'called') are used in a theological sense, they refer solely to the call of God to salvation, which includes service."[1] K. L. Schmidt substantiates this view by pointing out that in the writings of Paul, *calling* assumes a technical meaning as a synonym for salvation—redemption.[2]

We may conclude from the biblical evidence that God's call reaches every person—it is his offer of salvation. When a person responds to that call, the response is not to a particular vocation, but to a particular life—the life of being a part of "God's own people" (1 Peter 2:9).

This leads to the second biblical meaning of the word—"service." In 2 Corinthians 5:19, Paul adds to the good news that "God was reconciling the world to himself" the reminder that through Christ, God was "entrusting to us the message of reconciliation."

Jesus was forthright in stating the purpose of his call when he told his first disciples that they were to be fishers of men. In 1 Peter, the call to service is linked to God's purpose as revealed in the Old Testament and is applied to all Christians, the body of Christ: "But you are a chosen race, a royal priest-hood, a holy nation, God's own people, that you may declare the wonderful deeds of him who called you out of darkness into his marvelous light" (1 Peter 2:9).

There is yet another biblical meaning implied in the word *call.* God has called individuals to perform special functions to help carry out his offer of salvation. In the Old Testament, Moses was called to lead the children of Israel out of bondage, give them the Law, and help forge them into a nation. Similarly, Isaiah, Jeremiah, Amos, and many others were called to per-form special tasks. In the New Testament, the picture is the same. Jesus called out disciples and sent them on special mis-sions. Barnabas and Saul were called to leave Antioch and proclaim the good news that the Messiah had come.

In many instances, those who were called to special tasks were so designated through some special action of the church. For example, Saul and Barnabas were sent out on their mission-ary journey by the laying on of hands (Acts 13:1–3). The appointment of "the seven" was likewise by the laying on of hands (Acts 6). Paul admonished Timothy not to neglect the "gift you have, which was given you by prophetic utterance when the elders laid their hands upon you" (1 Timothy 4:14).

These rites of designation for special tasks became the basis for the church's development of the rite of ordination. And it is the rite of ordination which has divided Christians into two groups—the clergy and the laity. Even today there is a temptation to assume that only those who are ordained are truly called of God.

Ordination has been interpreted in many different ways. However, it is possible for the purpose of this discussion to isolate two streams of thought. The first is the position held by most Roman Catholics and the second is that held by most Protestants. (However, while the Protestant position, in theory, is often the opposite of the Catholic position, in practice there has been little difference.)

The Roman Catholic position, which had originated by the middle of the second century A.D., makes a clear-cut distinction between clergy and laity, between sacred and secular callings. The key to this distinction was the development of an official clergy with bishops, possessing the sole right to ordain other clergy and to rule the church.[3] By the early part of the fourth century, Eusebius records that there are two callings in the church. First, there is the calling for those who would be perfect, which means separation from the world. Second, there is the calling for those who remain in the world. To these, there is attributed a "second grade piety."[4]

During the Middle Ages, the gap between sacred and secular callings widened. Only the clergy was considered to have a religious calling. In the Western church, this distinction was emphasized during Communion in which the priest partook of both elements, while the laity received only the bread. A further distinction was made with the establishment of celibacy for the clergy in the eleventh century. Later, the Encyclical *Unam Sanctam* of Pope Boniface VIII (1302) drew another sharp line between priest and layman. No doubts were left that the laity was intended to have a second class status in the church.[5]

The Roman Catholic separation between clergy and laity is further underscored by the teaching that ordination is a sacrament. The Council of Trent defined ordination as a sacrament instituted by Christ which conveys the Holy Spirit to the person ordained. Like baptism, ordination is held to impart an indelible character. Therefore, a cleric, if degraded, does not lose the gift of Order and on restoration is not reordained.[6]

The Second Vatican Council sought to narrow the gap between clergy and laity by emphasizing the responsibility of all Christians to proclaim the gospel. This emphasis has led to renewed vitality of the laity in many Catholic parishes. However, some Catholic clergy have opposed giving the laity added responsibilities.

A case in point was the five-year struggle (1974-1979) at Good Shepherd Catholic Church in Washington, D.C. The focal point of the struggle was the parish council. The parish council, which had been favorably established after Vatican II, was elected by church members to help the clergy make decisions regarding parish life. But the formation of a new diocese brought a new bishop who took steps that led ultimately to firing the parish council. After a long and bitter dispute, steps toward reconciliation were taken by a new pastor.[7]

So the role of the laity is a question in flux in Roman Catholic teaching and practice. However, the fact that ordination is still considered a sacrament keeps a definable gap between clergy and laity.

The position of Protestants is quite different. And the most significant differences in thought can be found in the answers to these two questions: (1) Does the layman have a status equal to that of the ordained clergy? (2) If a person is once ordained, is that person always ordained?

There is little evidence in Scripture for the answers to these questions. Therefore, we must look to the historical teachings of the church.

The answer of the Reformers to the first question is "Yes." Both Luther and Calvin emphasized the doctrine of the priesthood of all believers. Luther declared that "there is really no difference between layman and priest, princes and bishops, 'spirituals' and 'temporals,' as they call them, except of office and work, but not of 'estate' . . . for they are all of the same estate."[8]

Henlee Barnette points out, "Unfortunately, Luther's view of the universal priesthood was never really implemented. As Georgia Harkness says, it was 'stillborn.' Spiritual immaturity on the part of church members who had been kept in this state by the church for centuries, the preaching office requiring trained men, and ordination—which created a dividing wall between clergy and laity—were some of the reasons why the clergy remained in a dominant position in the church."[9]

What Barnette says of the time of the Reformation is still true today. The clergy remain in a dominant position in Protestant churches. The first task for those of us in the Protestant tradition, therefore, is to take seriously our belief in the priesthood of all believers. Only then can we have a solid foundation on which to build a clear and sound relationship between clergy and laity in which both enjoy the same status.

Does ordination confer an indelible character upon a person? If one is once ordained, is he always ordained? The answer of the Reformers was "No." Martin Luther expressed it best: "That fiction of an 'indelible character' [is] a laughingstock. I admit that the pope imparts this 'character,' but Christ knows nothing of it; and a priest who is consecrated with it becomes the life-long servant and captive, not of Christ, but of the pope, as in the case nowadays. So I cannot understand at all why one who has been made a priest cannot become a layman. . . ."[10]

This position has not been fully implemented by Protestants. There has been and still is a gap between belief and practice. John Leith, a noted Presbyterian teacher, describes the belief and practice in the Reformed tradition in this way: "There is in principle no reason why ordination may not be laid aside, at least in Reformed theology. God who calls a man to the ministry of the Word may call him to a different ministry. In practice, however, there was from the beginning a strong conviction that the ministry was a lifetime vocation, that those who entered it did so with this understanding, and that the laying aside of ordination was desertion. This understanding of the ministry became part of the ethos of the church."[11]

Once again, part of the task of Protestants is to close the gap between belief and practice. Until that gap is closed, there will be confusion on such matters as how to view clergy who leave church-related vocations and what to do about ordination when a person moves out of the clergy role. Even in light of the present confusion between belief and practice, it can be said that in the Protestant tradition there is nothing to prevent a person from either leaving a clergy role to become a layman or from laying aside ordination when one leaves a clergy role.

IMPLICATIONS FOR FULFILLMENT IN MINISTRY

Several important implications, which are directly related to fulfillment in ministry, can be drawn from this brief outline of the biblical and historical teachings on the subjects of God's call and ordination.

As I see it, there are three major clusters of problems associated with call and ordination. And it is impossible for either clergy or laity to find fulfillment without some help in finding answers to the questions raised by these problems.

The first cluster includes the questions: *Is there a qualitative difference between the call of the clergy and of the laity? How should clergy and laity relate to each other?*

Protestants affirm that clergy and laity are co-workers. All Christians are equally called. There is no distinction of status between clergy and laity. Leith says, "There is no higher calling than the call to be the church, and in this call all the people of God share alike. Christians are equally Christian, and there is no higher order of existence."[12]

The recovery of this biblical view of call could mean new spiritual vitality within the church and a new surge of enthusiasm for carrying out the ministry of reconciliation. Greater attention could be focused on the biblical doctrine of gifts and of helping one another discover these gifts.

There are congregations like The Church of the Saviour in Washington, D.C., that have renewed their interest and vitality in the ministry by focusing on Paul's teachings about gifts in 1 Corinthians 12.[13]

Adoption of the stance that all Christians are equally called, that they are all co-workers, allows the clergy to step down from their pedestal and more fully develop their own gifts. Healthy relationships between clergy and laity permit the clergy to recognize the gifts among the laity and stop trying to carry out all the tasks in the life of the church singlehandedly.

Furthermore, the laity can begin to look at themselves as responsible ministers and find the ways in which their unique gifts can be used in ministry to God and others. In this spirit of full Christian equality, the goal of the laity will be to develop their gifts, not to try to become a reproduction of the ideal pastor. The ideal layperson will be seen as one who has fully developed his potential and not as "a clergyman writ small."

Unfortunately, this attitude of equality will not be easy to achieve. It is not unusual for clergy and laity in the Protestant tradition to try to deny their heritage and biblical teachings. Many clergymen are infatuated with their position and authority. Often, they are threatened by the thought of equally sharing their authority with the laity. The laity, in turn, are sometimes slow to accept the responsibilities inherent in equality. They plead the pressures of their vocations as the bases for demanding that the clergy accept the lion's share in Christian service.

When clergy and laity accept equal status, the responsibilities within the life of the church can be more clearly defined and more equitably distributed. The primary functions of the clergy—preacher, teacher, and pastor—can be retrieved from the deluge of secondary functions. And the congregation can require greater accountability for those tasks.

Reflecting on my experience in the ministry, I remember how uncomfortable I felt when as a young pastor I was called to the hospital to pray for someone who was critically ill. I often wondered why the family did not call on spiritually mature friends to help them in their time of need. But as I protested this practice to my friends, I was told that a pastor was a clearer symbol of God's love and mercy than a layperson was. Unfortunately, this view relegates the laity to the level of spiritual eunuchs, impotent to bring God to man and man to God.

When all Christians accept their priesthood, there will also be less pressure on dedicated Christians to go into the parish ministry. At the present time, a number of men and women who are unsuited for the parish ministry enter seminaries because they believe the only way to become fully committed Christians is to go into church-related vocations.

I had a seminary classmate whose experience typifies the trauma which so many suffer when their call to the ministry is based on their belief that it is a higher calling, rather than on the solid recognition of their gifts.

Joe was in his early forties and had been a practicing dentist for fifteen years. When he became dissatisfied with his role as a layman, Joe's pastor interpreted his dissatisfaction as an indication that God was calling him into "full-time Christian service." Without serious consideration of Joe's gifts, his pastor advised him to go to the seminary. Joe sold his practice and enrolled in seminary. It soon became obvious that he could not handle the academic pressures. Moreover, in his homiletics class he found that he could not organize his thoughts into a sermon, nor could he get up before an audience without becoming panic-stricken. Before long, Joe was in a serious state of depression. Thankfully, the supportive dean of students recognized Joe's trouble and helped him realize that what he had interpreted as God's call to a church-related vocation was based largely on the false assumption that to be a first-class Christian he needed to be a pastor.

In contrast to Joe's plight, there is the record of the lives of men and women such as Dag Hammerskjöld. In his book, *Markings,* Dag Hammerskjöld makes clear his call to be a "priest." His parish was the United Nations, and his ministry was to men and women from the four corners of the world who were seeking to attain the goal of peace.

Carlyle Marney, who was a leading American clergyman, described the situation well when he wrote:

> We Christians have been given a mighty weapon—the conviction that the Man Christ can make us whole, and that men who are being made whole can create a well society aiming to keep the world out and to bring the world in. The Christian church has been a failure at both. We have neither kept the worldliness out nor have we brought the world in. Relevant Christianity requires the healing of the inhabited world of men, and this demands a new priesthood: a priesthood that believes in the redemption of the world, not the redemption of the church. For centuries the church has refused to see the need to put a priest at every elbow. No professional clergy can do what the church is called to do. . . .
>
> Now we are serious here, and we want the gospel. What shall we do? We must recover the priesthood of every believer or we can't *do* at all. We must discover that we really are "priests to each other," for every man needs a priest at his elbow.[14]

To combat their relegation to a lower status, both by themselves and the clergy, some laymen have attempted to establish their equality by organizing into lay-leadership groups. My experience with these groups has been largely negative. I have known of many congregations which have strong lay movements that express anti-clerical sentiments. In practically every case, the witness of the church was weakened by in-fighting, power struggles, and elbowing for the upper seat.

I affirm that the priesthood of believers means that the gifts of each priest are to be used in the ministry of reconciliation. Therefore, the task at hand is not to organize the laity over against the clergy, or the clergy over against the laity, but for all "priests" to be reconciled to one another and to use their individual gifts so that "the whole body . . . makes bodily growth and upbuilds itself in love" (Ephes. 4:16).

When we put into practice the priesthood of all believers,

the ministry of reconciliation will become a more significant reality in our times. Clergy and laity will stand side by side as equal partners, called unto salvation, called of God to service.

The second cluster includes the questions: *What does it mean to be called to a church-related vocation? Are there criteria which can be used to determine if one has gotten into the "wrong line"? Or is the question of God's call to "full-time Christian service" a subjective experience which does not lend itself to objective standards? What part should the community of Christians play in presenting and authenticating the call to a church-related vocation?*

It is important that people have a clear understanding of whether or not they have been called to a church-related vocation. Those who are sure there has been an authentic call find staying power in time of difficulty. They do not run every time a mouse roars.

James Blevins gives an example of the confusion which exists in the minds of many as they seek to understand their call to a church-related vocation.

A student who was doing poorly in Greek came by to see his seminary professor. "What seems to be the problem, Joe?" the professor asked.

"I just can't catch on," he replied. "In fact I'm failing all my courses. It's not that I don't try. Look at my textbook—it's all torn from throwing it against the wall. I just hate study and the whole seminary."

"Do you have outside commitments which are taking up your time?" inquired the professor.

"Yes," Joe said, "I'm pastor of a weekend church. But I hate it—in fact, I hate to preach. Every Sunday, I despise going into the pulpit."

"Why in the world then are you at the seminary, Joe?" the professor said in surprise.

"I feel called to preach," Joe replied in a quiet voice.[15]

Blevins' example would be humorous if the trauma and pain weren't so real. What hospital would admit as a candidate for surgery residency a person who fainted at the sight of blood, didn't like to study anatomy, and hated to perform operations? Yet men and women with no gift for ministry are admitted to many seminaries because they insist that they have been called of God to a church-related vocation.

Too little time is spent determining whether one's call is from God, from a significant other, or from subconscious needs. This lack of attention can be attributed in large part to our belief in the private nature of religious experience. As a general principle, most Protestants do not believe that it is the task or the responsibility of the Christian community to help an individual evaluate personal experience. When the question of God's call is raised, we do little more than listen. We seldom take the time or have the skills to investigate the meaning of the experience. To express it in biblical terms, we have overlooked the explicit injunction to "test the spirits."

There is no denying that it is a difficult task to evaluate the religious experience of another person. But the failure to do so is the failure of love—that is, the failure to be willing to pay the price and to take the risk involved in examining the nature of God's call to church-related vocations.

The setting in which most of us were called into full-time Christian service was one which involved many outward and inward pressures. Whether it happens at summer camp, youth revival, or some other setting, the invitation to follow God's call usually includes several potentially destructive forces. Among these are the need to please authority figures, the idealism of youth to help the lost and needy, and the pressure on the minister or missionary to have a successful service. As a colleague said, with a tinge of bitterness, "My pastor felt that he had carved another notch on his gun when he talked someone into becoming a minister."

The impact of our subconscious on our religious decisions is a question which most of us know too little about. Pastoral counselor Everett Barnard says, "Apparently we either do not believe in an unconscious mind or else we do not understand its functioning. Consequently, we delegate to God responsibility for its functioning and emanations. For instance, a man strangled his wife to death. When he was asked why he did it, he replied, 'God told me to do it.' Many calls are the creations of the unconscious mind, and these are automatically assumed to be the voice of God. So there are callings of false gods as well as of true God, and they continue to bring men into the ministry."[16]

Barnard also raises a crucial issue: "Can it be that we are not concerned enough that an individual may fail in his ministry if he enters it from the wrong motivation?"[17] If we are concerned, then all those involved in the religious experience must be sensitive to the person's motive and to whether the call is genuine or false. The concern must begin with the family, involve the members of the local church, and include adequate vocational guidance at various stages of development. Included in the concern of all must be the ability to accept in love rather than judgment a person who becomes aware of a pseudo-call.

What happens when a clergyman finds that his call has been a pseudo-call or at best a mixed bag? Must he immediately resign his ordination and leave the ministry? Not necessarily.

With the aid of friends and/or skilled counselors, such individuals must work through their feelings as well as gain a better understanding of themselves. It is possible that they will conclude that their gifts and personality do not permit them to survive in the ministry. On the other hand, such ministers may find that they are able to make a deeper and more conscious commitment to a church-related vocation. In either case, the individual must be able to depend on the love and support of the Christian community.

There are no foolproof ways of determining whether a person has been called to a church-related vocation. This fact is brought out by the inability of some men and women to function in their church-related vocations even though they have received personal counseling, passed psychological tests, and received the best educational training available.

However, the best safeguard for successfully identifying an authentic call to a church-related vocation is a responsible and responsive Christian community which participates in the whole experience of investigation of call. And on some occasions it may require the "calling out" of individuals who have not felt that they have been called to a church-related vocation.

There are several notable examples among Baptists of men

who were urged, against their personal feelings, to enter the preaching ministry, including John Bunyan and George W. Truett. Neither felt that they had been called to preach, but both responded to the pleas of fellow Christians. The total Christian community would have suffered if the members of their congregations had not assumed their responsibility of "calling out the called."

All Christians have the right to expect the Christian community to which they belong to work with them in determining their gifts—their calls. There should be no hesitancy on the part of the Christian community to say, "I believe your call is to a church-related vocation," or, "I believe you are mistaken in your call to a church-related vocation."

I remember with great regret my failure to express my honest feelings concerning a young man who was a candidate for an overseas assignment. Because the young man felt so strongly that God was calling him, I did not openly state my reservations. Later, his assignment ended in disaster for both him and the church he served. Although I do not know that my objections would have been enough to have kept the young man from receiving the assignment, I do know that I did not act responsibly.

The Christian community also needs to be responsive. By this I mean that all Christians, laity and clergy, need to show love and understanding. As I mentioned before, my friend struggled with the question of the "wrong line" for twenty-five years because he did not feel that he could talk to anyone about his mistake. I recognize that, to a certain degree, my friend was accountable for his problem, but I also contend that there is too little responsive love in most congregations. Those who are struggling with questions about God's call to church-related vocations should feel such love from a community of Christians that they can feel comfortable sharing their struggles with others.

When there is love and, as a result, the freedom to test God's call to a church-related vocation, there is less potential for getting into the wrong line. The community will speak the truth in love, and thereby make possible decisions less burdened with guilt, with the desire to please others, and with the host of other false motivations that are often mistaken for God's call.

Sometimes this lack of love that I described shows itself in the response of the Christian community to ex-pastors. An ex-pastor in Houston reported that most congregations greeted him with coolness if not with suspicion. In failing to show love to ex-pastors, the Christian community penalizes those who are following God's call to leave a church-related vocation. A greater injustice is done to ex-pastors who left their vocations for the wrong reasons. They are not given the forgiveness nor the support which they need in their darkest hours.

Where there is love, there is the possibility of healing and forgiveness for those who have acted out of the wrong motives. Love can rescue and restore the fallen.

The third cluster includes the questions: *Is the call to a church-related vocation a lifetime call? Is it possible to be called from a church-related vocation to a non-church-related vocation? Is ordination irrevocable? Can it be set aside either temporarily or permanently?*

I first became aware of these questions when I was a child. My parents were missionaries in Brazil, and I got the distinct impression from those about me that God's call to foreign missions was a lifetime call. Therefore, when a missionary did not return from furlough, he was considered a deserter who was to be looked upon with both pity and reproach.

As Morris Ashcraft, professor of theology at Southeastern Seminary, has said, " 'Full-time Christian ministry' is a term not found in the New Testament. It seems to mean, in the language of today, that one will spend one's working time in the ministry and will receive a salary for so doing. God does call particular persons for special ministries. These persons perform their ministries under the leadership and power of the Holy Spirit. But in the New Testament there is nothing about 'full-time' as opposed to 'part-time,' or 'ordained' as opposed to 'un-ordained,' or 'life-long' in contrast to 'short-term.' "[18]

There is, therefore, a need for those in the Protestant tradition to reexamine their practice. There is nothing in our understanding of biblical evidence and historical heritage to label as deserters those who leave a particular assignment such as foreign missions or who leave a church-related vocation.

John Leith has stated, "The general expectation in the church that the ministry is a life-long vocation may imprison men today, just as Luther said Roman doctrine imprisoned them in the sixteenth century."[19]

There are those who believe that many ministers take too lightly God's call to a church-related vocation and therefore abandon their call without much thought. My experience has been the opposite. I find that there has not been enough openness to the possibility that God is calling one to another vocation.

I can personally attest to this. Like many other pastors, I faced a midlife crisis in which I struggled with the question of leaving the ordained ministry. I felt a great deal of pressure from those about me. In one instance a respected layman said, "I don't know how a person can live with himself when he leaves the ministry." After much struggle I came to the conclusion that there was no reason to believe that leaving the ministry would mean that I was turning my back on God. Upon reaching that conclusion, I was able to tackle, without the burden of fear and guilt, the question of whether my gifts were best suited to the parish ministry. The question of gifts becomes obscured when one begins from the unwarranted premise that the parish ministry must be a life-long commitment.

In times such as I experienced, laymen can be of tremendous help. They are in the position to evaluate and to ponder whether a minister has the gifts needed for the ministry. If he or she has the gifts for a church-related vocation, the support of the laity will alleviate a tremendous burden and make possible a stronger clergyperson. If he or she does not have the gifts for a church-related vocation, it is a very cruel practice to permit the minister to continue to struggle alone without the love and advice of laity.

What I am suggesting is not easy. It is difficult to tell a minister that he is wrong in believing that he has the gifts for ministry. But to confront a person and then support that person during a time of self-examination and possible relocation is an act of love. I have found that much of the bitterness that results from leaving a church-related vocation could be avoided if the minister had the proper support from the laity, other ministers, and church executives.

Moreover, I believe the question related to leaving particular assignments and setting aside ordination should be based on the broader questions of the value of the individual. For example, some foreign missionaries have found that their children are not able to cope with the cultural shock of returning to and living in the United States. Therefore, the choice confronting the missionary is, will I return to the assignment to which I was called, or will I remain in the States with my children? To me, the answer is to be found in the value of the individual. Parents have the responsibility to stay with their children.

The question confronting ministers comes in many different ways. There are times when the variety of demands on ministers may cause them to be destructive in their relationships to members of the congregation and/or members of their families. If a minister can find no satisfactory ways to cope with the destructive patterns apart from resigning or laying aside his ordination, then I believe such steps should be taken.

I would emphasize that in making a plea for ministers to examine the nature of their call and to be open to other calls, including the call to a non-church related vocation, I am not minimizing the importance of God's call, nor am I suggesting that the call be taken lightly. Rather, it is just the opposite. The awareness of God's leadership offers tremendous staying power. It provides strength and comfort in times of difficulty.

What is needed is not a non-biblical concept of call to a church-related vocation that imprisons a minister for life, but a conviction that God's call and leadership are constantly being revealed, and therefore one must be open to the guidance of God's Spirit. This understanding of God's call as an ongoing relationship will not only give greater strength to meet difficulties, but will make it possible for the minister to correct past mistakes and to be open to future direction.

Of course, it is easier to write about laying aside ordination than it is to do it. Our culture worships success. The person who becomes an ex-pastor is labeled a failure, whether this is true or not. Therefore, there is the pressure to remain in a church-related vocation even in the face of continuing evidence that it would be within God's will to enter another vocation.

The following observations by Frank C. Williams, director of the Midwest Career Development Center, put the question of the laying aside of ordination in a proper perspective:

Our experience here at the Center and my experience as a Ministerial Relations chairman would lead me to express the concern that we need a concept of the call that recognizes that God may call a man "out" of the ministry in precisely the same way that we feel He calls men "in" the ministry. If this were incorporated into our systems, it would enable men to set aside their ordination if they felt called by God to undertake secular work with the realization that they would not be closing the door forever on their ministry and that, if, after a few years in secular work they felt called back into the ministry, they could come back into the institutional church to resume their ministry. One might even be bold enough to suggest that they could come back into the church even better prepared for ministry as a result of their stint outside the institutional church.

In support of this concept, the United Presbyterian study found a significant number of men who held secular jobs prior to a late entry into the ministry indicating that their experiences in non-church occupations were extremely helpful in preparing them for their pastoral ministries.[20]

*   *   *

One of the keys to fulfillment in ministry is to remember that all Christians are equally called. Christians are equally Christian, and there is no higher status in the body of Christ. The laity must take the leadership to achieve this status of equality between clergy and laity. The clergy, being human, are not going to relinquish their centuries-long status of superiority without the aid of the laity. Moreover, we must take seriously the fact that God can and does call individuals in and out of church-related vocations.

When both clergy and laity can live out these truths, there will be fewer traumas related to getting in the "wrong line." And most important of all, there will be greater fulfillment for both laity and clergy as we serve as ministers of reconciliation.

====================

Chapter 5

A Crumpled
Note

The young man was driving home from work at the proper speed when suddenly the sun blinded him. Seconds later, there was a terrible crash. His car smashed into a parked truck which had not been driven completely off the pavement. The doctor said he had a fifty-fifty chance of making it.

For hours the young man's family had been asking why had this accident happened, why had God permitted it. For six hours I struggled as best I could to express love while at the same time feeling deeply inadequate because I could not speak the same theological language.

When I arrived home from the hospital about midnight, I was tired and emotionally drained. I went to the refrigerator, where my family left notes for one another, to see if there were any messages. There was only one, and it had been crumpled then pressed out. The message had been written by me: "Sorry, I won't be home tonight. I have to go to the hospital because of an emergency. Hope to see you before you go to bed." But the message implied within the crumpling of the note was from my son. It was a message of anger and frustration. The "church" had once more destroyed our plans for a quiet evening together.

When my children were small, there were many expressions of anger and frustration that I didn't notice. Now they are grown, I can see in retrospect what I didn't see at the time. I can even see that, at times, they hid their anger because of love for me. They chose not to "lay" any more on me than that which I already carried. Such love lightens the burden of the father, but does not alleviate the pain nor remove the resentment of the children.

STRESS IN THE MINISTER'S FAMILY

I believe that the minister's family is in need of help. This applies to all—minister, spouse, and children. Because the divorce rate among the clergy is well below the national average, a false impression that all is well with the families of the clergy has developed. And even with the increase of divorce among the clergy, there still seems to be a belief that clergy marriages are less vulnerable to problems. This is not true. Ministry is a strain even on a strong marriage. Although some of the problems and pressures present in the minister's family are unique, many of them are shared by all families. Unfortunately, the clergy is often less willing to admit problems because such an admission could jeopardize their job. For this reason, many sores have festered within ministers' families, causing great pain and leaving many scars.

James L. Cooper, reporting on his work as coordinator of counseling services for the Baptist General Convention of Texas, stated: "About one-third to one-half of those [pastors] seeking help . . . were concerned with marriage problems. Many others came because of family stress, financial problems, a lack of job security or uncertainty about their future. Again, much of the latter was brought on by the expectations of the congregation, especially on the role of the pastor's wife and other members."[1]

Edgar Mills and John Koval found from their research "that the minister's own marital problems are among the most difficult for the clergymen to handle. The intimate relationship between work and family roles in the ministry suggests that seminary and continuing education should take seriously the training of couples to handle the inevitable marital stress."[2]

Laile Bartlett, author of *The Vanishing Parson,* states: "The United Church Study found that 54.9 percent of the wives of ex-pastors preferred, or were even eager, to leave the church;

only 12.2 percent wished to stay. In the Unitarian Universalist Survey, not one was found who wanted to go back. The United Church researchers conclude their lengthy discussion of marriage and family factors by saying: 'It may seem we have labored the point of showing the influence of family problems, but it appears that ex-pastors scarcely recognize the significance of their family systems in making career decisions.' "[3]

But this chapter is not about marriage counseling or how to build stronger ministers' families. Help for finding answers to problems may be implied, but will not be spelled out. It is my hope that through an experiential approach—expressed with help from my wife and children—both clergy and laity will gain a better understanding of what happens within the "parsonage."

SOURCES OF STRESS FOR CLERGY FAMILIES

A number of factors contribute to the stress found within clergy families. Some are more important than others. In an attempt to draw a complete picture of the pressures a minister's family faces, however, I have described eight of the most prevalent problems, including some of lesser importance.

1. *The church's insistence on a successful family.* The minister is under pressure to have a highly successful family life. Frequently, the statement in 1 Timothy 3:5 "For if a man does not know how to manage his own family, how can he take care of the church of God?" (TEV) has been interpreted as meaning the minister must have a family with no problems— a perfect family.

Laile Bartlett further illustrates this truth: "Dr. Thomas Osborne, a psychologist in Wheaton, Massachusetts, says that unlike all other professionals, the clergyman and his family are supposed to reflect the 'should do's,' while the rest of the world goes about with 'do do's.' As a layman explained it to a pastor's wife: 'We pay you *not* to have problems.' "[4]

Such pressure puts a terrible strain upon the minister and his wife at all times, but a particularly difficult situation develops when they are having problems. Tradition insists that the wife should always attend her husband's services. So she must go to church and act as if nothing is wrong. Even worse, she must sit and listen to her husband preach and try to receive some spiritual benefit from the service. The husband, in turn, feels defeated and insecure. He must put on a facade and preach, knowing that his wife is in the congregation.

The demand that the family be perfect also makes it difficult for a minister and his wife to seek marital counseling. To seek help is to acknowledge there is something wrong. Because it is not widely accepted for ministers to admit there is anything wrong, they often try to wish away their problems. But problems that are ignored do not go away; they only get worse.

Wallace Denton, a well-known minister and the director of the marriage counseling center at Purdue University, points out two results of the pressure to maintain a successful home:

> In the first place, some ministers and their wives feel trapped in a marriage that is filled with the kinds of conflict, anxiety and personal destructiveness that would otherwise lead to divorce were he not a minister. Feeling trapped and being unable or unwilling to build a better relationship they resign themselves to a bad marriage.
>
> They become marital hypocrites trying to project the image of a successfully married couple . . .
>
> A second result of the minister's marital vulnerability is that either he or the wife may use this vulnerability to blackmail the other into the desired behavior. Thus, one pastor threatened his wife who was considering filing for divorce, "Go ahead! If you do my ministry is over and there is nothing else I can do and support you this way, so don't plan on much support." On the other hand, I have known of situations where the wife either overtly or covertly used the threat of "exposing him" as a way of gaining leverage in the relationship. Because of this vulnerability, each is literally in the position to exploit and blackmail the other.[5]

If a minister should get a divorce, the result is often disastrous. Generally, a minister must resign and seek employment in a non-church related vocation. So to the trauma of divorce is added the trauma of starting a new career. One pastor commented that the "Christian army is the only army that kills its wounded."

In addition to the pressures it places on ministers and mates, the expectation of perfection affects the children. Children often feel they are responsible for their father's vocation. This is an intolerable pressure, especially for young children. It can result in some withdrawing and being afraid to say anything about their family life. The *PK,* "Preacher's Kid," learns to be silent, to repeat nothing, to share nothing, for fear that he or she might share the wrong thing and unwittingly cause embarrassment to the family or trouble from the many powerful people in the church. Other children will do their best to hide their activities from their father, mother, and church members. They develop a pattern of deception in their relationships with others out of love for their parent, the pastor.

One PK expressed her feelings to me about the need for a model family in this way: "There are churches which are more Old Testament oriented than they are New Testament oriented. These churches are riddled with guilt; they have never quite accepted the grace of atonement. In good Hebrew tradition, they feel driven to offer up a sacrificial lamb—a spotless sacrifice acceptable to God. These Christians believe that it is necessary to find one model Christian family to offer to God. What better choice than the preacher's family? After all, they are being paid to be professional Christians. It becomes necessary to have a model of the Christian father, a model mother, a model first grader, a model teenager. Who better to expect all this perfection from than the preacher's family? This kind of pressure to develop perfection no matter how young or how rebellious the child can be devastating to a preacher's family. Churches, like all groups of people, develop mysterious corporate personalities. This unexplainable phenomenon makes some churches easier to work in than others."

The insistence on having a successful family can have some benefits. Many divorces in our society are entered into hastily and leave unneccessary scars. But the pressure to stay together rather than divorce encourages some couples in the ministry to work on building a more meaningful relationship. Fortunately, some churches are also growing more tolerant of counseling for ministers and their spouses.

2. *The minister's need for a supportive family.* One of the primary tasks of the minister is to motivate family units to be involved in worship, to participate in the educational activi-

ties of the church, and to give time, talents, and monies to the ministries of the church. The minister tries "to practice what he preaches." As a result, he consciously and unconsciously puts pressure on his family to set an example for the congregation. This pressure is over and beyond the pressure from the congregation to have a perfect family.

The pressure from the minister is often more subtle and more damaging than the pressure from the congregation. It is more damaging because he is using his family as a means to an end—that of saving face, of not appearing to be a hypocrite. It is more subtle because the minister believes in what he is doing and believes the involvement of his family is valuable for them. His actions are a mixture of love and self-preservation, therefore he may not be fully aware of what he is doing.

The pressure from the demands the minister places on his family can lead to anger within the spouse and children. Anger, in turn, blocks communication and promotes strained relationships.

After I had presented this issue to a group of young ministers, one asked, "How do you deal with this problem? I don't want to pressure my children and spouse, but I do want them to be in church." I replied, "I don't know. I thought I was being very open with my children when they were young, but I realize, both through comments from my children as young adults and from examination of my actions, that I exercised far more pressure than I intended. The only answer that I know is to be constantly aware of the problem and seek to overcome it."

There is a bright side to the minister's family involvement in his vocation. When kept in proper bounds, it provides an avenue of communication between husband and wife not found in other vocations. There are some vocations, particularly in the field of science, that are so specialized that husband and wife have no opportunity to share in the struggles, defeats, or successes of the spouse's work.

3. *The search for identity.* Can a minister's family be themselves? Can the minister's spouse be his or her own person? Are the children accepted on their own merits without undue pressure to play certain roles? My answer to all of these questions is "No!"

Some would say that change is taking place and it is easier than it used to be for a minister's family to be themselves. I have found that there is more talk about change than there is actual change. The role expectations for a minister's family are real and rigid.

It is often assumed that the pressure to conform to certain roles is only from the congregation. Not so. The pressure comes from both the clergy and the laity. The minister at times expects his wife to be either an assistant pastor or the person in the congregation who is most involved in all activities. And this pressure often extends to the children. The solution to this problem must be found in cooperation between clergy and laity.

The search for identity for a minister's wife begins at the time she announces that she is going to marry a minister. Immediately, the wife-to-be is cast as a different kind of human being. One minister's wife reports that responses to her announcement were a mixture of amazement and morbid curiosity, followed by statements such as: "I'd never marry a preacher."

A similar pressure exists for the wives of men who become ministers after having pursued another vocation. Many such women tell how, after their husbands began new careers in the ministry, they often found that attitudes of their new friends conflicted with those of their old ones. My observation has been that their adjustment and search for identity is even more difficult than that of the wives who knew their husbands were going to be ministers, because they must exchange an established identity for a new one which may not be as comfortable for them.

Being related to as if she has no name is a major problem for a minister's wife. Many introductions go something like this: "I want you to meet our pastor's wife." No name. My wife has remarked that she often thought of hanging around her neck a large sign which read: "My name is Marjie Bratcher."

In a similar vein, Pauline Trueblood, the wife of noted churchman and author Elton Trueblood, voiced her feelings when she wrote, "It has been my privilege to converse with many wives in my travels with my husband. I am always on the fringes of every public occasion which we attend, meeting the other women who are also on the fringes. We all know what it is to have our husbands introduced, with the opportunity of making a reply, while we are introduced in a manner which assumes that we are unable to make any response at all. We rise and smile. Personally, I should rather be ignored. If I could say even a few words I should feel more like a human being."[6]

Just as they present obstacles in other areas of ministerial life, the expectations of the congregation can be a formidable barrier to the development of a personal identity for a minister's wife. The minister's wife is expected to do certain things, and she often becomes the subject of criticism if she doesn't live up to these expectations. One wife complained that she enjoyed playing the piano, but it became a sore spot and a chore for her because the congregation assumed that doing so was the role of a minister's wife.

Most ministers' wives are vulnerable to implied criticism. A familiar example of this takes place in the first few months of a pastorate. Members who attend church sporadically are apt to say to the pastor, "I haven't met your wife yet." Often, these statements are less an indication of interest in his wife than they are implied criticism of the fact that she has not become acquainted with all of the members, whether they have attended church or not. Marjie has frequently felt this pressure.

Another expectation—that the minister's wife will be an associate pastor—dies hard. The advice given to new pastors, most often by those not in the pastorate, is that they should express clearly to their congregations that which can be expected from each, the minister and his wife. Supposedly this will avert future problems. Not so. Five and six years into the pastorate, when it had been made clear that Marjie did not make pastoral calls with me, I still heard comments like, "I expected Mrs. Bratcher to come with you."

The sensitive minister is conscious of the pressure that these expectations place on his wife. He is prepared to support her in front of church members and permit her the freedom to develop her own identity. The basis for the involvement of a minister's wife in the work of the congregation should be the same as that of every other member—her God-given gifts.

Whether her gifts are those fitting an associate pastor or a quiet, supportive wife, she should be permitted the freedom to function in the role for which she is best-suited.

Yet another difficult problem for the minister's wife is coping with the assumption that she is aware of all church activities. This problem, in its simplest form, involves church members cornering the minister's wife on Sunday morning to find out the details of such functions as the Stewardship Banquet. This kind of inquiry is an intrusion and can be irritating. But the inquiry which is inexcusable and most difficult to handle is the one related to church problems. Such an inquiry imposes on the family pressures which should remain on the job. For example, during one stressful time in the church when I happened to be out of town, a deacon called Marjie to discuss a tension-filled meeting about which she knew nothing. His insensitive action caused her unneccessary pain and stress.

Certainly, the problem of identity for the spouses of women clergy is equally as difficult. According to a recent article in *The Washington Post*, "One clergywoman, whose husband is not ordained, reported that her husband 'doesn't have a peer group' in some social situations. Among their circle of clergy friends, she said, 'When we go someplace, I am with the wives and he is with the men'—clergymen with whom he has little in common."[7]

However, even more difficult is the child's search for identity. Children don't have the maturity nor the coping mechanisms to combat some of the pressures which they face. Their identity is linked with that of their father. They are PK's. As one PK observed, "You do not hear of DK's [Doctor's Kids] or TK's [Teacher's Kids]."

And the term *PK* seems to carry several expectations. First, the PK is expected to bolster the youth program. It is assumed that most young people will rebel against forced attendance to youth functions. However, such an option is not granted PK's. The kid is expected, as a role model for other young people, to be "an unpaid bulwark in the youth program." Second, the PK must always set a good example. My children can attest to how often a childish prank was rebuked with the words: "You should be ashamed; your father is a preacher!" Third, PK's are perceived both as goody-goodies and as the wildest kids in town. These mutually exclusive roles are assumed without any thought of contradiction.

The PK's search for identity is made more difficult by the fact that the minister's home is largely a fatherless one. Even understanding this condition is shared by families in other vocations, however, does not erase the problem of the weak father-child relationship. Many PK's search for father substitutes in Sunday school teachers, school teachers, or any male that has prolonged contact with them.

The identity problems of the PK are felt most strongly at the crucial junctures of adolescence and young adulthood. One PK said that he developed two "faces"—one toward the church and the other toward his peer group—and easily accepted the dichotomy. Having been involved in church activities since a child, he found it natural to function in the church environment and put up a front for the adults in the church. However, his desire for social acceptance led him to adopt the different "face" which he showed to his peers. Eventually, peer pressure and rebellion against church standards led to experimentation with alcohol and drugs. Living such a dichotomy leads to involvement in the life of the church with little or no real commitment to the church or its teachings. Moreover, the rebellion strains relationships with parents and with siblings.

Another PK said that she had three alternatives open to her in adolescence—all-American youth, rebel, or introvert. Because these three roles are such natural tendencies, it is easy to fall into one of them without any real thought or expression of one's real beliefs or feelings. It becomes imperative in young adulthood to learn who one is—to establish an identity—lest an artificial role continue into middle age when there is greater potential for disaster. For example, the "all-American youth" who found it easier to follow the expectations of the congregation may learn in middle age that he or she has not yet defined a personal value system. But middle-age rebellion against youthful conformity may have serious consequences due to family and vocational responsibilities.

When the PK leaves home as a young adult the questions of identity are reopened. Some PK's mask their identity when in college because they are not comfortable telling their friends that their father is a minister. This denial is not a denial of their father, per se, but a desire to search for an identity unencumbered with the role of their father.

College and/or the first years of a vocation can be times of both relief and anger. Relief that one can work out his or her identity is generally accompanied by anger inherent in the search for identity and increased by the restrictions of earlier years. This anger can cause young adults to blame all of their problems on the father and his vocation. It is a dangerous point at which they may drift away from the family.

Another PK I spoke with concluded an overview of her experiences by saying, "Preacher's kids are many things to many people. They are sermon illustrations; they sing alto with soprano voices when the choir is short; they lead in prayer everywhere in the world. They are not real people, and above all, they are not real children. 'Surely there are some positives!' you cry. Perhaps. Some PK's follow their parent's footsteps, becoming preachers or marrying preachers. These PK's have built-in advantages in finding their first job; they already know the rules. They build on the experiences of their parents and then pass their own experience on to their children. If they choose out of sincere conviction, these PK's are ahead of the game; if they simply follow the line of least resistance, they are in for trouble. The rest of the PK's who were lucky—those who went through the experience without running to alcohol or drugs, those whose parents understood and supported them—are far more sensitive to other people's plights, are far more responsible to their jobs, are far more analytical about the world than their secularized counterparts. Perhaps these traits too were forged by the many pressures of being a PK. But whether they were lucky or unlucky, PK's carry their labels with them to the grave."

On the positive side, the minister's family is constantly being exposed to the teachings of the church. Whether through Bible study, youth groups, or worship services, the minister's children are taught Christian values. Although, as I stated earlier in this chapter, it is possible for church attendance to become a way of life which has little impact and it is also possible in adolescent rebellion to disassociate oneself from the Christian lifestyle, my observation of adult PK's is that they espouse Christian values. As a minister, I find many PK's actively involved in the organized church. This is not to say that there aren't scars which leave many of them reluctant to have anything to do with the organized church. But I believe that minister's children as adults are more likely to be person-oriented, freer of prejudice, and more desirous to live by the ethic of love, faith, and hope than their counterparts in the same age group.

4. *Neglect.* A minister is under pressure from himself and from the congregation to neglect his family. Innumerable demands are made on his schedule, and there are subtle temptations to deny his family the time that is rightfully theirs.

A description of these conditions and the anger involved is found in a story about the wife of an Anglican clergyman. "When she married, she said, she had high-minded visions of entering with her husband into the great work of converting the world. 'But here I am (seven years later),' she said, 'surrounded by four children, tied to the house, expected to turn up at every cat-hanging, feeling like a widow as my husband is always on duty.' Her conclusion is unequivocal. 'Clergymen,' she said, 'ought to be celibate because no decent right-minded man ought to have the effrontery to ask any woman to take on a lousy job. It is thoroughly un-Christian.' "[8]

Part of the blame for this condition must be laid at the feet of the minister. As mentioned, he is often placed on a pedestal as being all-wise and all-helpful. Such rarified air is very exhilarating. Therefore, he becomes a workaholic to enjoy the benefits of being on the pedestal. In other words, the minister becomes a workaholic to receive positive strokes from the congregation. But the positive strokes then substitute for the companionship he would normally receive from his family.

The minister often succumbs to the temptation of using the many demands of the ministry as an excuse for not giving himself to his wife and children. Laile Bartlett reports that "one study found that a surprising number of men, now divorced, admitted that they had used 'the demands of the parish' as an excuse to escape from a dull or problem marriage."[9]

Similarly, Louis McBurney, a psychiatrist who counsels church professionals, speaks of the minister's children as "The Forgotten Begotten."[10] And a PK expresses the situation in this way: "A minister's family undergoes many of the same pressures which exist in any family headed by a dedicated professional. In many ways, it is a fatherless family. With deacons' meetings, committee meetings, Tuesday night visitation, special consultations, Wednesday night services, and Sunday services, the father is rarely at home. This is also complicated by the fact that if there is any leisure time taken by a minister, it does not coincide with the leisure times of the children. The preschool child is not as aware of this fact since his time is not regulated by school or work. Nevertheless, the child is aware that his father is not always at home when the fathers of playmates are at home. As the child grows older, school begins to regulate his time. The father-child relationship is then put under a greater strain."

Many ministers can be faulted for having the immature belief that if they are doing God's work, God will take care of their wives and families. There is no biblical evidence to support such a view; however, the feeling that God provides a special protective shield and/or companionship for the minister's family while he is away doing "the Lord's work" is prevalent. Such a view spells *neglect!*

There are other factors within the minister's work which contribute to neglect. One of them is emotional exhaustion. Counseling, crisis ministry, and pastoral visitation are emotionally draining. Therefore, when a minister arrives at home he has little emotional support to give his family. One wife expressed it this way: "He gives all the good stuff out there." Another said, "I get the crumbs."

The ubiquitous telephone also contributes to this problem. Because of its convenience, the minister finds it difficult to separate work from home. As long as there is the telephone and there are emergencies, real or imagined, a minister's work is only one ring away. A quiet family night can easily be interrupted not only once but many times. One of our sons used to become enraged, and rightfully so, at the constant telephone calls from a particular emotionally unstable woman. She used to call my wife at the most inopportune times. I do not doubt that Marjie and I permitted unnecessary interruptions from this young woman, but it is not easy to know when to cut off a conversation with someone who is distraught. Moreover, the damage is already done when the phone rings, and this is something one has no control over.

Another view from a PK relates to the neglect and anger

caused by the problems of others: "Ministers typically do consultation work and listen to the problems of many people. At times, the minister's only outlet for the pressures caused by dealing with these problems is the family environment. The conditions or problems of church members are the topic of conversation at the dinner table or at other times of family gathering. This entrance of other people's problems into the intimate family circle can cause feelings of jealousy and guilt. The PK may have such thoughts as, 'Boy, they care more about other people than they do about me,' or, 'So many people have problems and I don't deserve what I have.' A feeling of resentment can arise, and the child may drift away from the family and look elsewhere for affection."

I have already suggested that neglect has an impact on the relationship between the minister and his wife. Wallace Denton calls one of the potential marital problems "dry rot" and describes it in this way:

> I grew up on a farm. We grew lots of potatoes. Some of our sweet potatoes would often rot by simply dehydrating without any smell and wither away leaving a dried up shell behind. My father called this the dry rot.
>
> After I got into marriage counseling, I noticed that marriages rot much like those potatoes. Like the white potatoes, some end up in a big, dramatic stink which may or may not be accompanied by divorce. Other marriages, however, seem to quietly dehydrate. Without any fanfare, the vitality in the relationship is dissipated and the marriage left intact but sapped of the meaning, vitality and intimacy that once characterized it.
>
> Dry rot is a silent, erosive, corrosive process which subtly moves in on all marriages, and if not dealt with, gradually dries up the springs which nourish the relationship. The marriage then becomes unable to meet the deepest needs of husband and wife. The dry rot causes a spark between the pastor and his wife to grow weaker and weaker. Each takes the other for granted, though one or both may hardly be aware of it. A kiss becomes a mere ritual, or perhaps even non-existent. Sex becomes so routinized that even though it provides some satisfaction, it leaves one or both partners feeling vaguely unfulfilled.
>
> I find ministers and their wives who are suffering from marital dry rot are often very busy people. She is busy with the children, doing church work, involved in community activities. She feels

rushed, rushed. On the other hand, he is working seven days a week, preparing sermons, keeping an eye on the church budget (not to mention his own), pumping enthusiasm into lifeless committees, mediating conflicts of feuding parishioners, and getting the building program going. He too feels rushed, rushed.

The days go by with a blur. The months blend into years and the years are numbered by the churches of which he has been pastor. Now if you and I ask this couple whether they are unhappily married, they would say no, and they are not—but more importantly neither may they be really happy with the marriage. They are existing. It is a decent existence, but still an existence.[11]

When neglect in a marriage is caused by a commitment to church work, the wife finds her anger difficult to deal with. One minister's wife says, "I wish it *were* another woman. I could go pull her hair out!" Another remarks, "The church at times can become a formidable mistress at whose altar the husband or the minister often serves. A woman married to a minister must deal with this, as harsh as it may sound. She must be able to alert her husband when this tendency pulls at him. Who can stand against the 'bride of Christ'? Only a human man and a human woman, dedicated to each other, and then only with the help of Christ."

Neglect can be combated. The minister, however, must take the initiative and place a higher priority on his home than on his vocation. Ernest Mosley clearly substantiates this point in his book, *Priorities in Ministry*. He lists the minister's priorities in this order: Christian Person, Married Person, Parent Person, Church Member Person, Employed Person, Community Person.[12]

Having determined his priorities, the minister must then take practical steps to implement them. Marjie and I made several attempts to combat neglect in our home. In a lecture to seminary students she explained: "Time is of the essence for the minister in his work, and to make conscious efforts to be an attentive father is truly difficult. We always had a family night once a week—not always on the same night of the week, but one night each week. We took our children on trips with us, we made holidays special, and we even had 'car-nics' in cold weather—just jumping in the car with our lunch and driving away from the scene. But I still heard, 'Mom, why can't Dad be with us on the weekend just like other kids' dads?' Well, some things just can't be explained to kids and some scars are left by *all* parents no matter how hard they try."

In addition to the efforts described by Marjie, one practice I followed after the children were in school was marking the school holidays on my calendar as days off. This made it possible to have uninterrupted time together as a family.

To combat neglect in the marriage relationship, both husband and wife must consciously make meaningful contact. I quote again from Marjie's lecture: "In all marriages, honest communication must exist between the man and wife. This is essential in the minister's home. The deadening sameness of one meeting after another, one demand after the other, one reminder after the other that the minister must be superhuman, can soon wear down a couple's lines of communication. They must have a 'clearing house time' each day to face each other and say, 'Hey, wait a minute. I'm here and I need you.'"

5. *People, people, people.* A minister's family is constantly surrounded by people. This condition is a mixed blessing.

One of the greatest advantages is that of having "readymade" friends whenever one moves to a new community. Wherever I have served as pastor, my life has been made easier by these friends. They show up on the day of the move with sandwiches, salads, cakes, and pies, ready to lend a helping hand. They offer invitations to dinner, concerts, ballgames, cookouts, fishing, hunting, and picnics. And there are those "natives" who show you the "ropes" to survival in the community. It would take a separate book to recount all the gracious things which have been done for me and my family. But in all candor, I must say that there are disadvantages as well as advantages.

One disadvantage is the lack of privacy. A minister's family lives in a "goldfish bowl." The actions of each member of the family are scrutinized by each member of the church. Although much of this interest is well-meaning, it becomes an impediment to normal family living. Often, the total impact of this situation is overwhelming.

Another disadvantage is the required attendance at numerous church-related social engagements. These activities are hy-

brids—part fun and part work—so even the social life of the
minister's family is related to his work. There is precious little
time or place for the family to interact as a single unit.

One of my sons expresses his experience in this way: "As
an infant, the PK is immediately thrown into a highly socialized
world. There is not only a family to learn about, but beyond
that there is an entire congregation to be dealt with. This
larger group of people exists as a constant for the rest of his
life. The individuals in the group may change with time or
as the result of a move from one church to another, but the
congregation is always present."

This type of experience has its advantages. But the total
impact is one that overwhelms a child. The PK has no "territory" which is his or her own. There are always *PEOPLE,
PEOPLE, PEOPLE.*

It would be unfair if I did not add that progress is being
made at this point. Although I have heard many "parsonage"
stories (i.e., of church members walking into the house without
knocking, etc.), I have not personally experienced this type
of pressure. Currently, I find that people are becoming more
sensitive to a minister's needs, and that the minister's home,
whether a parsonage or not, is becoming more and more his
castle.

However, a minister's family must make conscious efforts
to ensure privacy for each member of the family individually
and for the family as a unit. This privacy is essential to survival
in a setting that is crowded with people.

6. *Loneliness.* It is ironic that the minister's family is surrounded by people yet suffers from loneliness. Wallace Denton
has listed this as the number one problem in his article "Family
Conflicts of the Modern Minister." On the basis of his counseling experience with ministers' families, he writes:

> One of the problems which I have noted over the years with
> the minister and his wife is that they often seem to have no peer
> group to whom they can relate. Another way of saying this is
> that it appears to me that many ministers and their wives have
> no group that they regularly interact with where they simply are
> Bill and Mary. Though most ministers seem to develop close rela-
> tionships with some parishioners, even in these groups his role

as "Reverend Jones" and her role as "the minister's wife" lurks close at hand and tends to obscure the other side of their lives as Bill and Mary.

The loneliness which is regularly reported by ministers' families is directly related to this problem. For loneliness has its genesis not in the absence of people, but in the absence of meaningful and intimate relationships with people.

The lack of a peer group with whom he can let his hair down and give expression to the non-minister side of himself seems to me to be related to fear. As the leader, the minister and his wife are afraid to get too "chummy" with the parishioners whom they lead.

However, since most of the social contacts of the minister and his wife are with parishioners, it presents a real problem as to how they can meet their needs for intimacy. With whom can they share their inner concerns, their doubts, their gripes? Where does the minister meet his need to relate to another human being eye to eye?[13]

But the problem of loneliness is not an easy one for the layman to grasp. I remember my cousin and his wife visiting our family. We talked about some of the problems that we were facing at the time, one of which was loneliness. The next evening Marjie and I were taken to an excellent restaurant and then to a boat show as guests of some members of the church. At the boat show we met my cousin and his wife. He pulled me aside and, with a laugh, said, "What's this loneliness all about?" How do you explain that, even though you are treated graciously, being the guests of church members is not necessarily the same as friendship? This is not to say that church members can't be friends; often they are. But to church members, the minister and his wife are still "Reverend and Mrs. Jones."

A consequence of this loneliness is the emotional drain that a minister and his wife feel because they turn to each other for the support they should receive from friends. A pastor friend of mine told me that his wife awakened him in the middle of the night and said, "I've had it. I can't continue to carry your load and continue to carry my load. I want out of this marriage." In describing the confrontation with his wife, the most distressing statement he made was, "I didn't even know that we had any troubles."

This example is not atypical. The study by Mills and Koval shows that in times of stress, ministers rely heavily on the support of their wives.[14] Therefore, I would give all ministers one bit of advice: Don't make your spouse your unpaid psychiatrist. To do so will overburden him or her and place a terrible strain on your marriage relationship.

Both minister and spouse need confidants—people with whom they can be perfectly honest. At times church members can serve as confidants, but not often. In most cases it is necessary to go outside the congregation to find a confidant; and it is not unusual for the confidant to be a counselor or a psychiatrist or another pastor—someone who can skillfully help with problems associated with loneliness.

A perennial problem facing the minister's wife is the lack of a pastor. One minister told of his experience. "My wife couldn't relate to me as her pastor—I am her husband." Yet she needed a pastor, just like any other church member. So she found another clergyman to whom she could turn for counseling and occasionally attended services at that pastor's church. "At first, I found it hard to accept," he shared. "But then I thought about it—about how all these years she had been denied a pastor. Now I think it's kind of neat!"

7. *The minister/parent as an authority figure.* Every parent is an authority figure, and men and women in many vocations are authority figures. However, there are few, if any, vocations in which the authority of the vocation and the authority of the parent combine to have an impact on the children as great as that of the minister.

The primary difference for the minister is the fact that he must exercise his vocational role of authority in the presence of and in relation to his family. The children of the minister, therefore, seldom see him outside the role of authority. As a parent he is an authority figure. At home, when he responds to a phone call that is reporting some crisis situation, he is an authority figure. When the children go to church and see their father preaching, he is an authority figure. And children find it difficult to cope with this constant exposure to the pressure of authority.

A PK writes: "A question can arise in the mind of the young child, exactly who is that man speaking from the pulpit?

A connection can be made at an early age between the father in the pulpit and the Father in heaven. In my case, this led in part to an inability in later years to react directly to my father. I grew up believing that everything my father said was the gospel of truth. Self-defense was virtually impossible since what my father said had to be right and I was naturally in the wrong."

The minister, as a parent, must consciously try to assert his humanity. His ability to admit mistakes, ask for advice from his children, listen to their needs, demonstrate his need for his family, and remove his "clerical collar" when he is at home can relieve some of the pressure and encourage open communication.

For similar reasons, ministers also need to learn how to have fun and specifically how to have fun with their families. Robert Kemper, a pastor and an editor for *Christian Ministry,* claims that clergy should work less and have more fun. He says most ministers have a high work addiction and a low pleasure anxiety. While preaching salvation by grace, they live their lives on the premise of salvation by works. Such a practice leaves little room for fun and relaxation.[15]

I must confess that one of my mistakes in relationship to my family was the failure to create more fun together. Sure, we had fun, and lots of it, on long trips and excellent vacations. But, I never did learn the art of relaxation and fun through such father-child activities as building projects, tinkering with automobiles, going fishing, etc.

In this section, I have consciously combined the need for having fun with the problem of authority because learning to have fun with one's family is the best antidote to the smothering authority which is inherent in the role of minister/parent.

8. *Sexual transgression.* Every marriage is potentially beset with the problem of sexual transgressions. It seems the moral climate of our day is more conducive to extramarital affairs than it was a generation ago, and the minister's family is not immune from these pressures. In fact, evidence points to the fact that wandering affections are a major problem.

When lecturing on "Fulfillment in Ministry" at Midwestern Seminary, I spoke on the problems and pressures encountered in the minister's family. In my lecture I did not mention the problem of extramarital affairs. One of the students, a veteran pastor and chaplain with over twenty-five years of active ministerial experience, asked why I made no reference to sexual transgressions. I replied that I did not know of any studies on the subject and had hesitated to draw conclusions from my own observations and knowledge. My friend suggested that I was making a big mistake because based on his experience as a chaplain, he believed this was the number one problem for the minister's family.

I do not know that I would agree that wandering affections are the number one problem, but upon reflection I realized that it is a serious omission not to focus on this problem as it applies both to the minister and the minister's spouse.

Because until recent years most married ministers have been men, I will approach the subject from the viewpoint of the male minister and his spouse. But wandering affections are not limited to the minister. From my knowledge it appears that the minister is more vulnerable to sexual transgressions than his wife, but the problem exists for both.

Ministers are continually thrown into close emotional and physical proximity to women parishioners. Most of the church volunteers with whom he works are women. Moreover, his duties in counseling, pastoral instruction, and crisis ministry place him in situations which can have strong sexual overtones.

To these pressures is added the pressure that comes from the attitude of many women parishioners. As one woman stated, "When I'm with a clergyman I can feel free, because I have the feeling that he's in charge of the morals."[16] I interpret this to mean that this woman believes the minister is superhuman! While most ministers have high moral standards, the record is clear that they are not immune to sexual transgressions.

Two examples can help illustrate the nature of the problem as related to pressures faced by ministers.

George was a highly aggressive minister. He was known in his community as a man of charm and boundless energy as well as the pastor of the fastest-growing church. But some of the ministers who knew him believed that he was often unethical in his approach to prospective members, that he was not above "sheep-stealing." Some even felt that he exuded an attitude of spirituality which was phony. However, because George was so successful, many of the criticisms from fellow ministers were looked upon as sour grapes.

Rumors of sexual improprieties began to circulate. Yet there was no specific evidence, and again the criticisms were put down as unfounded gossip kept alive by disgruntled ministers.

The first real indication of a problem came when a woman parishioner from George's church went to another minister for counseling. She confessed the affair that she was having with her pastor and asked for help. Further investigation disclosed that this was a pattern in George's behavior which had been going on for several years. He was forced by a church executive to go to a psychiatrist for counseling and treatment. The psychiatrist reported that, in his opinion, George bordered on being a sociopath and should immediately be relieved of his ministerial duties.

As a pastor I would interpret this behavior, which is not unique, to be the sexual aberration of a person whose standard of ministerial success is that of the "million dollar round table" (see chapter 8 on "Ministerial Success"). Such a pastor gauges his success by the number of sales he makes (i.e., the number of baptisms, church additions, and the growth in attendance). People become objects to be manipulated for the purpose of success. It is only a small step from the manipulation of people for one's ego needs to sexual promiscuity.

Joe's case depicts a different set of circumstances that led to a sexual affair. Joe was on his way up, climbing the ladder of ministerial success very rapidly, when he was called to a large church where the former pastor had been very popular. The "honeymoon" period was brief. Joe kept running into one obstacle after the other. It seemed the members had not worked through their grief of losing the former pastor and were constantly, although unfairly, comparing Joe to him.

Joe became depressed over his troubles and went to a counselor for help. The counselor assured him that the problems within the church were not his fault, but neither was he going to be able to solve them in a short period of time. Since Joe's depression was strong evidence of his emotional strain, the counselor recommended that he change pastorates.

After Joe made the decision to move, two or three churches

appeared interested in him but at the last moment called someone else. This added to his distress. At the same time, a woman
from the church who worked closely with Joe expressed concern over his obvious depression. In need of someone to talk
to, Joe began confiding in her, telling her more and more
about his feelings of anger and frustration. The parishioner
was very supportive and in time, a sexual attraction developed
which led to an affair. When the official board gained knowledge of his affair, Joe was asked to resign.

There were indications that Joe wished to be found out.
His actions had caused some of his co-workers to be suspicious
of his relationship. When analyzing his behavior, it is hard
not to believe that subconsciously Joe used the affair as a way
of getting out of a difficult situation.

Dr. Wayne Oates, one of the most noted figures in the field
of pastoral care, has suggested to me in a private conversation
that he believes that many ministers enter into affairs to escape
the ministry. He theorizes there are ministers who cannot opt
out of the ministry and enter another vocation because of immature views of God's call. Therefore, these men place themselves in situations in which they are forced by the church
to leave the ministry.

I'm not suggesting that these examples reflect the only or
even the major problems. Rather, I'm suggesting that the minister has the same pressures as other men, and maybe more.
Thus, the problem is real and of major significance for
ministers.

As I stated above, the problem of extramarital affairs extends
to the minister's wife, although to my knowledge the problem
is not as widespread.

However, in these situations I have found two recurring
characteristics. First, the root problems are neglect and loneliness. Second, many times the sexual involvement stops short
of sexual intercourse.

The first time Jane called me, she asked to talk to me anony-
mously. I agreed, even though my practice has always been
to refuse to enter into any lengthy discussion with an anonymous caller. As I look back on the incident, I recognize that
there was something in Jane's voice that expressed anguish
and a need to remain anonymous.

Jane confessed she had become attracted to her next-door neighbor. He and his wife were good friends of both Jane and her husband. The two couples saw each other on an average of once every two weeks for bridge and an informal evening of recreation. Because Jane's husband was so involved in his work, the bi-weekly bridge game was essentially the only social and recreational life which she and her husband had.

Jane went on to say that she found herself attracted to John, the next-door neighbor, and that this attraction was reciprocated. John started coming by during the daytime with some excuse related to their bridge games. Their sexual attraction manifested itself in embraces, kissing, and physical closeness. Because both Jane and John felt uncomfortable and guilty about these meetings, they had decided to stop seeing each other, but they were not successful in carrying out this resolve. It was at this juncture in their relationship that Jane called me for help in severing her relationship with John.

In response to Jane's plea for help, I indicated that she needed to have the one-on-one support and assurance of forgiveness which I felt inadequate to give by phone. I asked her if she attended church. She said "Yes." I then asked her if she would feel comfortable speaking to her pastor. She hesitated a moment, and then replied, "I can't. My husband is my pastor."

That first conversation with Jane ended abruptly when she saw her husband driving up. But subsequent calls provided opportunities for confession, assurance, and pardon.

It was on either the third or fourth call that Jane said, "I want to tell you my name." I replied, "It is not necessary, if you are not comfortable in doing so." Her answer was, "I believe that I can feel a more complete sense of forgiveness if I tell you who I am." Then she disclosed her identity.

Since that occasion I have known of other ministers' wives who have had the same type of involvement as that of Jane's, and also some who have had involvements marked by sexual relationships. Unfortunately, most of those involving sexual relationships led to separation and divorce.

Whatever the reasons and whatever the involvement, my observations lead me to conclude that the impetus for extramarital affairs originates with the minister and his wife not facing honestly the pressures which come with the ministry. As in any other marriage, attention must be given to the pressures in our society and the major pressures of the specific vocation if husband and wife hope to achieve the fulfillment which is available to them.

*   *   *

The ministry is a strain even on a good marriage. Would my family have been stronger if I hadn't been a minister? I don't know. What I do know is that my family has scars as well as good points. Some of the scars could have been avoided if I had been more aware of what was happening. Some of the scars are just part of the territory and I probably could have done nothing to prevent them.

My goal in this chapter has been to alert both clergy and laity to the realities of life in the parsonage so they can be prepared to change those destructive pressures which come with the territory of being a minister. When there are fewer family scars, there will be greater fulfillment in ministry.

Chapter 6

Where Do I Go
for Help?

· One of the most serious obstacles to fulfillment in ministry is the inability to find and receive help in time of trouble. This was the problem which Karl West faced (see chapter 1). Until recently, there has been both a failure on the part of the clergy to understand their need for help and a failure on the part of the church to provide help for the clergy.

When I graduated from the seminary, I assumed that I would not need any further systematic help. My attitude reflected the view held by the seminary community: Graduates had received sufficient training and resources to last their entire ministry. (I should mention that, fortunately, this view has since changed.)

But soon after accepting my first pastorate, I found that I needed help and I realized I didn't know what kind or where to seek it. I was very lonely and often frightened. Furthermore, I was not aware that my predicament was one encountered by many other ministers.

Mills and Koval, in the study cited previously, found that "two-thirds of the ministers report self-steps to resolve stress, while only one-third report seeking out colleagues, superiors, lay people and family informally to help. Among the latter, only one-seventh sought help from fellow ministers or denominational superiors." They concluded that "since apparently ministers have a relatively low tendency to seek help from each other in stress (but . . . a high willingness to accept help from each other), emphasis should be placed upon creating opportunities to build strong supportive relationships among them in which support can happen naturally."[1]

Ministers, however, cannot be blamed totally for not developing a support system. As Dr. Edward Golden, professor of behavioral science at Drexel University, points out, denominations have been slow to see their responsibility.

Most of the major denominations have merely called, trained, and retired their personnel with only minimal support in between the conclusion of their training and retirement. As the First Annual Meeting of the Department of Ministry of the National Council of Churches reported, the Church has been morally irresponsible in the management of its manpower. As young people are recruited and called into the ministry and dedicate their lives to their God and His Church, the Church must also dedicate itself to these young persons to assist them in developing their potential so as to fulfill their lives professionally and personally. . . .

Probably I reflect the years of working with those who have been professionally employed in the Church and who for many reasons find themselves bitter, beaten, and behaviorally ineffective. As a result of a lack in a total management approach to personnel support, increasing numbers of clergy are awakening to the realization that they have been had! . . . The typical pastor and professional worker feels no one cares for him and his development. The ministry today is a lonely profession, and for good reason. Harry Levison, when he was at the Menninger Foundation, reported that the ministry is probably the most besieged professional group in America.[2]

Such neglect has taken its toll on the lives of ministers. The authors of *Ex-Pastors* state:

Many persons in the church have not taken seriously the ex-pastor. Many who do get him into focus think of him in terms of betrayal, or they say, 'He should never have gone into the ministry in the first place.' However, instead of being betrayers, these ex-pastors feel that they have been betrayed by the church system which recruited them on flimsy grounds, trained them inadequately, placed them unwisely, gave them courage to preach prophetically, then proved unwilling or unable to help them when in trouble, and then let them go with scarcely an afterthought.

We can easily become defensive and say that things are not that bad. But the feeling of pain and anger on the part of those who have dropped out is no more distorted than the abysmal attitudes taken toward them by others in the church system.[3]

But it is not enough to draw a picture of the problem. There is a growing realization on the part of the ministers and of the denominations which they serve that help must be sought and provided. The question is, What kind of support does the minister need?

Edgar Mills gave an excellent definition of a minister's support system and enumerated its important functions.

The concept of a *"support system"* is an old one but it is little understood. The principle is very simple: when a minister feels shaky about his work or himself, there are certain resources available to support and strengthen him. In some respects, each of the factors I have discussed constitutes part of the minister's total support system: the increase of his competence, the opening of opportunities for advancement, and the availability of appropriate rewards are supportive. Moreover, he trusts God, and he leans upon that trust as upon a supportive staff. But I am thinking now of another very significant function which is familiar to every working man and yet is only beginning to be provided in any systematic way. The most powerful support system consists of people one can trust in times of unusual stress. For this system to function, a minister must be able to recognize and admit the stress points of his ministry, he must know whom he can trust, and such people must be alert to his possible need for support. . . .

I am convinced that there are at least three functions which ministers need to find available in their human support systems: There is the *head-patting* function, consoling and encouraging in the midst of discouragement; there is the *problem-solving* function which helps him analyze the stress and develop strategies for dealing with it; and there is the *feedback* function which gives him straight, absolutely trustworthy data about himself and his work.[4]

These functions can be provided in many different ways; however, I believe a minister's support system should include four groups: Ministers' Peer Groups, Helping Professions, the Congregation, and the Denomination.

MINISTERS' PEER GROUPS

Many ministers have found their vocational salvation in peer groups. While these groups vary in format and in the goals which they are seeking to achieve, it is possible to distinguish two major categories. The first is the sharing group. The main goal of this group is head-patting—consoling and encouraging in the midst of discouragement. Its rationale is that every pastor needs a pastor. Professional growth groups constitute the second category. In these groups the stated goal is to develop professional skills. These groups, to use Mills's functions, provide problem-solving and feedback with head-patting as a by-product.

A typical testimony for the value of a peer sharing group is that given by Emmett Henderson:

> A year ago nine ministers in northeast Georgia established a Ministers' Colleague Group. Following this year's experience we have concluded that ministers can minister to ministers. We have learned that we do not have to go spiritually hungry. We can feed each other. We have learned that we do not have to be professionally lonely. We can be brothers to each other.
>
> One member of our group observed, "Since my youth, I had heard that a pastor has no pastor. Yet I did not realize the significance of that statement until I became a pastor. Furthermore I had grown up with the superman concept of the minister which made it difficult for me to express my weakness and woes."[5]

These groups have filled the void of loneliness which most ministers feel. But ministers have to meet two conditions which contribute greatly to the success of peer sharing groups.

First, every participant needs to make a covenant with the other members to be present at each session. If he or she cannot be present, then the group should be notified before the meeting. This demand for accountability keeps a participant from "copping out" when he or she is afraid to face the group because the sharing went further than expected. It is at such times that the participant needs the pressure of accountability to return and receive the support of the group in spite of painful and embarrassing revelations. If the participant is not held accountable, the group can never truly become an avenue of significant support.

The group should be warned that some members may abuse the requirement of accountability and that when this happens, the group will need to be sensitive to the situation. I remember one group where a participant shared very personal feelings of inadequacy and fear. He did not return to the group for three weeks nor did he notify the group that he would not be present. When he returned, the group openly expressed their feelings of hostility and resentment toward his behavior. But because these feelings were expressed within a setting of concern, the offending member was able to accept what was said. Moreover, what was said helped this minister to see the seriousness of his emotional condition. He withdrew from the group with the blessings of the other members and sought professional help.

Second, it is important that a peer sharing group be inter-denominational. Because it is usually easier to share one's feelings with someone who does not pose a threat to one's standing in the denomination, openness comes more quickly and in greater depth in an inter-denominational group. Moreover, such a group composition makes it clear that most of the stresses ministers feel cut across denominational lines. If all of the participants belong to the same denomination, it is possible for the individuals to say, "Woe is us. Our denomination is terrible. Nobody knows the trouble we've seen."

Other factors which facilitate the development of such groups can be learned in actual practice and in fact should reflect the needs of the particular group. For example, most groups in which I have participated have met once a week from September through May. This makes it possible for participants to drop out, if they find that their circumstances have changed, without the group feeling a sense of rejection. This plan also avoids the disruptions brought on by summer vacations and permits the disbanding of a group that didn't achieve its purpose.

Professional growth groups have not been as popular as peer groups and are more difficult to maintain. There are at least three reasons why this is true. First, emotions are more strongly felt than is the need for professional growth. Second, the proliferation of excellent continuing education opportunities causes ministers to feel they do not need to be involved in week-by-week professional growth. Last, many ministers fail to set priorities. The demands on the parish minister are so many and so varied that he or she may believe there isn't time to sharpen one's professional skills. The end result is that too many ministers reach middle age showing little indication of professional growth.

In spite of the problems which militate against professional growth groups, there are many resources for those ministers interested in participating in one. One of the best is the "Group and Guided Study Programs for Ministers and Laymen" developed by Dr. Richard P. Murray of the Perkins School of Theology in Dallas, Texas.

Ministers' peer groups provide an easily available source of support. The basic requirements are for the minister to admit that he cannot walk on water and to trust fellow ministers to provide love and guidance.

ASSISTANCE FROM HELPING PROFESSIONS

There has been a shift recently in the attitudes of both ministers and laymen toward professional counseling for ministers. Some years ago it was not unusual to hear the statement, "I won't ever turn to my pastor for help if he or she has to go to a psychiatrist for counseling." Moreover, many ministers and laymen took the view expressed by a pastor, "What can a psychiatrist or a psychologist do that Jesus of Nazareth cannot? They (the Counseling Committee) are trying to sell us something our divine Lord has offered us absolutely free . . . God is the best counselor I know. We don't need a psychiatrist, we need God. A minister can go to God and get the counseling he needs."[6]

Fortunately, some of these views are changing. An indication of this change is seen in the acceptance of Dr. Louis McBurney's book, *Every Pastor Needs a Pastor.* Dr. McBurney, a board-certified psychiatrist and founder of Marble Retreat in Marble, Colorado, a center for church professionals, observes that ministers are human, like everyone else, and can benefit from psychiatric care and counseling. As a member of the Board of Directors of Marble Retreat I have heard nothing but compliments about the book. However, there is still a wide gap between the acceptance of Dr. McBurney's ideas as set forth in his book and ministers' acceptance of psychiatric care. Ministers' resistance includes fear of acknowledging one's humanity as well as apprehension that parishioners may find out and react negatively to the fact that their pastor has sought psychiatric help.

I can testify to both the fears and the benefits of receiving psychiatric help. Even though I still find it difficult to admit to members of my parish that my wife and I have had psychiatric care, I can acknowledge the value of such care.

Psychiatric care can meet all three functions listed by Mills—head-patting, problem-solving, feedback. I find my sense of self-worth strengthened through counseling; I receive excellent insights into the actions and attitudes of many of my parishioners, which help me diffuse conflict situations; and I find it invaluable to have a psychiatrist with whom I can discuss some of the problems in my congregation. My ministry through interpersonal relationships has become more sensitive and of greater benefit to everyone involved as a result of the psychiatric help I've received.

A side benefit to this has been my sharing on a professional basis information regarding patients of the psychiatrist who were also members of my church. I would be less than honest if I did not admit that besides the benefit which I provide the psychiatrist, I receive an added measure of head-patting as we work together as colleagues.

SUPPORT FROM THE CONGREGATION

In many ways this is one of the most important and also one of the least utilized facets of the minister's support system—important because the congregation can provide all three functions of the support system, under-utilized because many ministers are afraid to get too close to their congregation.

Head-patting is structured into the life of most congregations. At the close of each worship service, parishioners who wish to give their evaluations of the service and sermon seek out the minister. Unfortunately, the fact that this has become a ritual has caused many ministers to overlook its value. It's true that probably 90 percent of the comments are the same each week. But it's also true that at each service there are individuals who received a needed word of comfort or encouragement and who desire to express their sincere appreciation.

Harry Emerson Fosdick used to pray before each service that God would use his sermon to help at least one person. His prayers were answered a hundred fold, not only because of God's power but also because Dr. Fosdick was a conscientious minister of the Word. A minister does not have to become either drunk with or cynical about standardized compliments. If he is a conscientious preacher like Dr. Fosdick, he will pick out those genuine expressions of appreciation that provide legitimate head-patting.

Several years ago I started a file which I labeled "Eulogias" (praises or blessings). I used a Greek term rather than an English one, trying to camouflage the file's true contents in the event that someone found it. You see, I had the misconception that it was wrong to accept positive strokes for the good that I did—that I would become too proud and arrogant. However, painful doubts about my self-worth led me to establish the file in which I keep sincere statements of appreciation for things I have done. A note which I particularly prize came from a teenager whom I called after he was in a car accident. The telephone call was made out of a sense of concern but also of duty. I gave little thought to the value of what I was doing. Yet, several weeks later, I received this letter:

> In the phone call you gave me, I found more help and comfort than anything else. I don't know why but through you somehow I always feel God's presence. Keep up the good work, little things mean a lot to people. God bless you.

I have a hunch that ministers would experience greater fulfillment in ministry if they were able to accept more head-patting from their congregation. An ex-pastor told me that one reason he had decided to return to the parish ministry was that in his years as an ex-pastor he had learned how to receive positive strokes. Later contact with him revealed that he had indeed learned how to accept head-patting and that he had a sense of joy in his ministry which he had not experienced in previous years.

The congregation is also the logical place to begin problem-solving, since it is the largest source of occupational stress for most ministers. Mills and Koval report:

> The largest source of occupational stress for ministers is their job in the local congregation—nearly two-thirds cite it as a cause. Almost 30 percent of all ministers specify this as growing out of personal or ideological conflict with parishioners. Eighteen percent also report frustration, overwork or lack of achievement as stress-producing, and another 19 percent describe conflict within the congregation, financial or community troubles of the church, or staff problems as sources.
>
> Implication: Although more intensive study needs to be made of the stress due to relationships in the parish, this is clearly a point at which a clergyman needs maximum skill. Human relations training, conflict management and organizing skills can be taught but often are extremely expensive or difficult to obtain. Many ministers point out that parish work makes demands for which seminary did not (or could not) prepare them. The effective handling of difficult relationships in the local church appears to be one such demand, remediable only by intensive effort by pastors, schools and denominations.
>
> A second implication is that, because stress tends to arise locally, there should be ample resources to deal with it locally.[7]

Problem-solving can begin with open and honest discussion with the power structures in the congregation. To achieve this a minister must first identify the formal and informal power structures which exist in any congregation. Quite often the informal power structures are the strongest, and when this is the case, they are more difficult to deal with than the formal.

I have found that the informal power structures can include such diverse groups as: the leading families, the president of the women's group, the Christian education committee, the finance committee, a Sunday school class. Such informal power structures cannot be ignored. Neither should they be given the position of an official group by receiving undue attention from the minister.

On the other hand, it is not always easy to involve the formal structures in problem-solving. These groups consist of volunteers who are not always present at appointed meetings and are inclined to delegate problem-solving to the pastor and/ or staff. Specifically, in Baptist churches, I have found that the deacons are not always eager to take the time necessary to resolve problems. This is not due to a lack of interest as much as to the basic attitude that as volunteers they do not have the emotional capacity or the time to devote themselves to the taxing process of goal-setting and ministry definition. Moreover, the pastor is viewed as the developer of ministries and concepts. The role of the deacons and congregation is either to approve or disapprove what the minister recommends.

In spite of these limitations, open and frank discussion with the deacons and the congregation is invaluable to problem-solving. One pastor who had a long and distinguished career was asked the secret of his success. He replied, "I never missed a deacons' meeting." This is not only good practical advice; it is also in keeping with the meaning of the priesthood of believers.

Feedback from the congregation in an organized fashion is a procedure which has come into its own. There are innumerable resources available to facilitate such procedure. One of the first which I encountered was in Donald P. Smith's book *Clergy in the Cross Fire.* [8]

I should add that feedback is a continuing process in every parish. The minister needs to provide avenues for feedback which will be comprehensive and periodic. This feedback helps correct problems, strengthen existing ministries, and develop new ministries. If such a provision is not made, the minister will receive feedback, often reflecting the frustration of parishioners who cannot or will not be heard, through brush fires, pot shots, and irrational criticisms.

A case in point was a lady who appeared before the pastor-church relations committee of which I was the chairman. She told the committee her pastor should resign because on at least two occasions he had sung a solo in the morning worship service. While this may have been a painful experience, I do not believe it was sufficient cause to dismiss the pastor. The problem was that she did not have an effective channel for feedback—a channel where she could both voice her concerns and find help to clarify her criticisms—therefore, she focused on a minor irritant. But her objections were of no real value to her, to the committee, or to the congregation in determining the actual problems and finding solutions for them.

It may appear to be a contradiction to say that support from the congregation is one of the most important and also one of the least utilized facets of the minister support system, but there are valid reasons why this is true.

The congregation is both a clientele for a minister and an employer. This arrangement places both the minister and the congregation in an awkward position.

The members of the congregation consider their pastor to be a professional and as such to be endowed with certain gifts and skills. In turn, the congregation views itself as being composed of "lay" people (non-professionals). In our society the non-professional may be critical of certain aspects of the services of a professional, but the non-professional does not assume the right to advise or offer solutions to problems faced by the professional. For example, a patient may come to the conclusion that his physician is not providing the best medication, but the patient would never assume the prerogative of joining with other patients and voting on what medication to give. Only other physicians are considered to have that skill. So there are times when the congregation is reticent to become too deeply involved in problem-solving because it believes that the minister as a professional has all the answers.

On the other side of the coin, the congregation is the employer of the minister. In the employer-employee relationship, usually the employer reserves the right to judge employees' performances and to fire an employee if his or her performance does not meet established standards. In this setting the employee seeks to please his employer. Moreover, the employee does not divulge self-doubts about competence nor volunteer any information about shortcomings. In the same way, the congregation, while at times refusing to accept responsibility in problem-solving, will exercise its right to discharge the minister—the employee. In turn, the minister—the employee—is afraid to be too open in discussing felt needs.

I've experienced both situations described above. At times

I've felt anger toward deacons as I tried to relate in a leadership style which implied collegiality. The deacons desired more "thus saith the pastor." Conversely, I have also found myself in the position of employee, particularly when my viewpoints were contrary to those of the majority of the deacons and/ or the congregation.

The answer to this dilemma lies in both clergy and laity understanding and accepting their collegiality as ministers of Christ. The approach which I believe is essential at this point has been discussed in chapter 4, "In the Wrong Line."

DENOMINATIONAL SENSITIVITY

An indispensible part of the minister's support system is sensitivity on the part of denominational executives. I agree with Edward S. Golden that "The church has been morally irresponsible in the management of its manpower." And I can identify with the statement "Ex-pastors feel they have been betrayed by the church system which recruited them on flimsy grounds, trained them inadequately, placed them unwisely, gave them courage to preach prophetically, then proved unwilling or unable to help them in trouble and let them go with scarcely an afterthought."

In defense of denominational executives it should be said that the size of most denominations makes it difficult if not impossible to maintain a pastoral stance. This is certainly true for Southern Baptists. They have grown so rapidly in the last fifty years that the average minister is not well known by those in denominational positions. Moreover, the mobility of both the minister and denominational personnel militates against long and lasting friendship.

Another cause of neglect by the denomination is the oversupply of ministers. Most denominations are not threatened by the loss of even a significant percentage of its ministers. For example, it is estimated that in the early 1970s Southern Baptists were losing approximately 1,000 ministers a year from the parish ministry. This astounding figure went unnoticed and when publicized received little response. The point is that when you have an oversupply of troops it doesn't really matter how many are maimed, wounded, and/or killed, provided there are enough recruits to keep the army at optimum strength.

It is also true that administrators are concerned with the welfare of the institution, which is as it should be since this is their task. However, remember that the concern for the welfare of the institution often interferes with the concern for individual people within that institution.

Again, in fairness to denominational executives it should be pointed out that institutional myopia also afflicts ministers. They are responsible for the parish, and they too fall into the trap of using people and placing the health of the parish above the welfare of the individual members.

Part of the solution to this dilemma can be found by viewing the church as a community, not as an institution. From this vantage point all involved will be more open to "carry one another's burdens." The key issue is active concern (love) on the part of denominational executives for ministers and active concern on the part of ministers for denominational executives.

Denominational personnel can provide much needed help in all three functions of a support system.

Head-patting. Low self-esteem is a painful reality for many ministers. In turn, this low self-esteem often results in anger and resentment against the congregation they serve and the denomination of which they are a part. For this reason, denominations need to provide encouragement and recognition for those who are ministering in difficult and discouraging situations. Specifically, there is the need to recognize ministers serving in small congregations and congregations in transitional areas. Such ministers seldom see a pastor search committee or receive recognition through denominational positions.

A denominational executive told me of a meeting which he held for pastors who were serving churches in transitional communities. The purpose of the meeting was to indicate his awareness of their needs and to permit them to share their feelings with him. They did, but not in the way he had expected. Instead of praise and thanks, he received anger and resentment. Their pain was so great that the first time they received any recognition, their true feelings boiled over. Fortunately, this denominational executive was mature enough to accept their feelings and wise enough to see that the meeting was a success rather than a failure.

Problem-solving. The denomination is in an excellent position to provide help in problem-solving. Two examples are: help for new pastors and help for pastors who have run into conflicts.

Research has established that the first major crisis in the life of a minister takes place three to five years out of the seminary. Allen P. Wadsworth, who made a study of graduates of Southeastern Baptist Theological Seminary writes: "The occupational data indicated that the mean time for leaving the pastorate and entering secular employment after seminary education was three years and nine months." [9]

There is a need, therefore, for all denominations to provide head-patting and problem-solving support similar to that which took place in the Young Pastor's pilot project of the United Methodist Church. This program was built around small cluster groups which included a pastoral consultant. The very existence of the program gave young pastors the assurance that their denomination had not forgotten them. Other benefits were: stress interruption, sharing frustrations and triumphs with peers, development of strong ties with peers, and professional growth under the guidance of the consultant.

There is an urgent need to provide problem-solving for minister-church conflicts. The denomination is in an excellent position to provide help in several ways.

First, the denomination can identify and train consultants who would be available to provide guidance for ministers and churches who are unable to resolve their conflicts. There are indications that congregations and ministers are open to such help. Even among Baptists, who have often made a fetish of their independence, there is a willingness to accept outside help.

Second, the denomination can establish halfway houses and/or retraining centers. When ministers are forced to resign, many have no place to turn. This is a particularly difficult problem for those living in a parsonage. One minister I knew moved in with his in-laws for six months while seeking relocation. He was fortunate that he had a place to go. How much better it would have been, however, if the denomination had provided a retraining center where he could have received support, counseling, and whatever retraining he might have needed. Such centers can also be of great value to men and women who want to prepare themselves for bi-vocational ministries.

Feedback. Many denominations have made organized attempts to encourage pastor search committees to define their expectations and goals with prospective ministers and to incorporate these goals and expectations in a covenant. This is an excellent step forward. However, another step needs to be taken. Periodic reviews of the congregations' and ministers' expectations are needed. These reviews can provide excellent feedback for both ministers and congregations. But it has been ascertained that these reviews have a better chance of succeeding when a third party is involved. The denomination can help by making available men and women capable of guiding a church and its minister through such a process. (For an in-depth discussion of the importance of covenants between a congregation and a minister and the importance of parish consultants, see chapter 7.)

*   *   *

An effective support system is a must if ministers are to find fulfillment in ministry. The good news is that this support system can be attained with the help of peers, the congregation, helping professions, and the denomination.

Chapter 7

Not Called to
Catch Flies

A deacon once said to me, "Ed, you can catch more flies with honey than with vinegar."

I thought, "But I was not called to catch flies."

Our discussion had been prompted by a sermon I had preached on race relations in which I had urged the church to accept as members all who professed faith in Christ regardless of race and color. As we talked, it became clear that we had different perceptions of the role of the church. We disagreed over the nature of the church and the role of the minister. My friend claimed that the role of the church could be more fully achieved if I did not preach on controversial subjects. I should attract the congregation with comfort (honey), not challenge them (vinegar). I did not (and do not) agree with this view. I believe that the task of the minister includes *both* comfort and challenge.

My experience is not unique. This conflict over the nature of the church is the experience of every pastor. In *Clergy in the Cross Fire,* Donald P. Smith points out that the cause of the problem is twofold—role confusion and role conflict. He states:

> From the first moment a young pastor steps into the pulpit or presides at a board meeting he is caught in the cross fire of conflicting expectations for the ministry. . . .
> If ministers preach on social issues, someone is sure to tell them

to "stick to religion." If they don't, someone else will slip away from the church because they aren't relevant. On the one hand, they may be confused over why they are in the ministry and where their priorities lie. On the other hand, they may have developed a very clear picture indeed of the way they are going to spend their lives and of what they are going to do for the world. If they move confidently in one direction, someone is almost certain to rise up and challenge their right to do so. If they fail to move, some will get restless because they are drifting. They are supposed to be paragons and experts in everything. To fall short in any aspect of their ministry is to become a target for criticism, even though their performance in other areas may be outstanding. And so the impossible demands of universal expertise may lead to feelings of inadequacy, self-derogation, and guilt.[1]

How serious are the problems of role confusion and role conflict? What are some of the causes? What are some of the answers? These are the three questions that will be dealt with in this chapter.

THE SERIOUSNESS OF THE PROBLEMS

The seriousness of role confusion and role conflict is well-attested. Samuel Blizzard brought the problems to the forefront in his classic article, "The Minister's Dilemma."[2] Subsequent studies by Paul Turner, Jeffrey Hadden, Donald P. Smith, Mills and Koval, and the researchers of *Ex-Pastors* affirm that confusion and conflict are all-pervasive and destructive conditions.

Paul Turner in his study of a selected group of graduates of The Southern Baptist Theological Seminary states that "role confusion is perhaps the greatest hazard in the ministry today."[3] Hadden in his book concludes that there are four major crises facing the church. Two of these are: "the crisis of meaning and purpose of the church" and "the crisis of identity for the Protestant clergyman."[4]

Role confusion and role conflict cause the clergy to have a high level of job-related tension, low job satisfaction, and low self-confidence. In turn, the laity, left confused by these characteristics, resort to withdrawal or open conflict. Many become disillusioned with the effectiveness of the parish ministry and look to other institutions for their arena of service.

Smith gives some clear and convincing arguments as to why these problems need to be examined and their solutions need to be found:

> Role conflicts are likely to be most harmful when role senders are very close to the focal person; are dependent upon him; have high power over him; and exert high pressure on him. Most, if not all, of these conditions prevail in the relationships of many pastors to their church officers. Kahn found that when conflict occurs under these conditions, the typical response of most people is to withdraw either behaviorally or psychologically. This may relieve the stress temporarily, but in the long run withdrawal is likely to prove self-defeating, since it leaves the conflict unresolved and, as we shall see, often causes a series of other related conflicts.[5]

The researchers for *Ex-Pastors* found that many of the men who dropped out of the pastoral ministry found role confusion a burden too great to bear. They add, "The pastor struggling and suffering with this problem must not be left to solve it alone."[6]

Indeed, it can be said without fear of exaggeration that role confusion and role conflict are major problems related to fulfillment in ministry. The task at hand is to identify some of the causes and some of the answers.

Causes of Role Confusion and Role Conflict

The pervasiveness of role confusion and role conflict indicates that these problems have many causes. But, as is the case with all complex problems, there are no simple ways to define or analyze all of them. Nonetheless, in an attempt to shed some light on the nature of these problems, I will discuss briefly seven of the major causes.

First, there are differing and often conflicting expectations regarding the nature of the ministry. Take the example of our Lord. One of the first questions he faced had to do with the nature of his role as the Messiah. Following his baptism we are told that he went into the wilderness where he fasted and prayed. During this period of time he was tempted; and his temptations were all related to his role as the Messiah. At the time, there were differing and conflicting views about the role of the Messiah. There were those who saw the age of the Messiah as the age of material plenty. Others saw it as a time of liberation from the occupying forces of the Roman Empire. Yet others saw the Messiah as coming to give a position of special privilege to the Jews. Jesus struggled with these differing views, and when he left the wilderness he had a clear concept of his role: the Messiah was to be the Suffering Servant.

The problem which Jesus faced is likewise faced by ministers today. Role confusion pervades the entire church. Niebuhr, Williams, and Gustafson in their classic study published in 1956, *The Purpose of the Church and Its Ministry,* reported: "The contemporary Church is confused about the nature of the ministry. Neither ministers nor the schools that nurture them are guided today by a clear-cut, generally accepted conception of the office of the ministry, though such an idea may be emerging."[7] I would add that the study made nearly twenty years later by Jeffrey Hadden shows the problem has not been resolved.

Not only is there not a clear-cut, generally accepted conception of the ministry, there are many differing conceptions. A study for the American Catholic Bishops came up with fifteen distinct conceptions of ministry prevalent in the American church today. These divisions are described as "not theoretical, not bureaucratic. They exist in people who are the congregations."[8]

Second, another cause for role confusion stems from the very nature of Christian ministry. The biblical model presents several roles, including: prophet, priest, evangelist, pastor, teacher. The two most often used by ministers are prophet and priest—to challenge and to comfort. Confusion for ministers arises as they try to decide which of these tasks is more important in addition to when and under what conditions they should challenge and/or comfort.

This difficulty was made clear to me in a preaching mission led by Dr. Edward Steimle in Waynesboro, Virginia, in 1970. At that time I was still very much caught up in the social activism of the sixties. Much to my surprise, and I would add consternation, Dr. Steimle suggested to the participating ministers that the times called for us to proclaim the message of 2 Isaiah: "Comfort ye, comfort ye my people." I did not immediately agree but upon further reflection realized that he was right.

This incident also taught me that ministers need to discern "the signs of the times." They must not become locked into one stance. They must constantly evaluate the needs of the congregation to determine when to comfort and when to challenge.

Third, a reason for role confusion is that the demands of the institutional church and the needs of our society have been added to the biblical role models. As the roles multiply, it becomes difficult to know when and how to give priority to the various roles. James Smart expresses it this way:

> What is a minister? He is an evangelist. He is a preacher. He is a priest. He is a religious administrator. He is a social reformer. He is a director of worth-while enterprises for the community. He is a species of amateur psychiatrist. He is an educator. He is an interpreter of life somewhat in the fashion of a poet. He is the voice of the community's conscience. He is the custodian of the values of democratic civilization. He is a man of superior wisdom and virtue whose task each week is to show men and women how to live more wisely and virtuously. Is it any wonder that young ministers, and some not so young, find themselves dragged in a dozen different directions as they try to fulfill the claims of the ministry?[9]

Another cause of role conflict is conflicting views of the nature of the church held by clergy and laity. Jeffrey Hadden has identified the comfort-challenge polarization in the church as a clergy-laity conflict. He writes:

> Herein lies the basis of conflict between clergy and laity: The clergyman's new theology has moved him beyond the four walls of the church to express God's love in concern for the world, while the layman comes into the sanctuary of God to seek comfort and escape from the world. Clergy have come to see the church as an agent that should be challenging the structures of society

that lead to injustice in this life, and to utilize the forces of love and political power to bring about a new social order. This development has left the majority of laymen bewildered and resentful. For them, the church is not an agent of change, but rather a buffer against it.

Thus, in a very real sense, what has emerged is a house divided. Laity have one church—a church that they want and need; a church largely confined to four walls, their friends, and a salaried comforter. From the church they draw love and support, which they pay for with cash and consume when they need it. But this church has become a source of increasing frustration. Their comforter is increasingly telling them that the rules have changed and that they are to become producers of love rather than consumers. But the frustration for the clergy is equally great, for the old church will not free him to enter the new.[10]

This statement by Hadden has helped me identify the pressures which I have felt as a pastor more than any statement I have read. A very influential member told me one time that he did not like to hear sermons on problems facing the world. He believed that these problems needed to be confronted, but not at church. When he came to church he wanted to be comforted and inspired. This attitude has been a strong undercurrent in every church which I have served as pastor.

My own orientation as a clergyman is similar to that of most pastors I know. I was taught at seminary and have accepted as a true norm of ministry that the task of the church is to express God's love and concern for the world. Therefore, the church is to be involved in challenging structures in the society that lead to injustice and trying to use the forces of personal persuasion as well as political power to bring about changes in the social order. The themes of justice, righteousness, and mercy as expounded by the eighth-century biblical prophets are to be central in the life and ministry of the church.

The comfort-challenge polarization between clergy and laity leads to debates over the policies, programs, and ministries of the church, and over the amount of money to be contributed and spent. Authority and control are generally established by the purse strings. Often, members will withhold gifts unless decisions are made that affirm their individual wishes. Because the church is a voluntary association, the minister is vulnerable to the laity's wants and wishes. Therefore, when the rift be-tween the clergy and laity widens, the result is usually conflict.

Besides these differing views of the nature of the church held by clergy and laity, there are differing views held by the clergy and denominational executives. Such conflicts may not be as much of a day-to-day occurrence as those with the laity; however, they are just as real and as much a source of anxiety.

National leaders are concerned that the church be world oriented and deeply preoccupied with the problems of society. The judicatories closer to the church are conscious of institutional success and the need for more money and more members.

The minister agrees with the concerns of denominational executives, both national and local. However, his priorities are: the success of the parish as an institution, and meeting the needs and crises of the individual members of the parish. Therefore, conflict is inevitable.

Because the denominational executives have the power to affect the distribution of denominational rewards, which vary from placement to recognition on a given commission or board, differences can also cause significant anxiety for pastors.

Many pastors find that positions on various boards and commissions are part of the head-patting in their support systems. I have tried to be responsible in exercising my responsibilities in the positions I've held, but would be less than honest if I did not admit that I look forward to these meetings as interruptions from stress and opportunities to gain new perspectives on church-related problems. A colleague expressed similar feelings and indicated that at one particular stressful time these board meetings were the source of her emotional salvation.

Sixth, the conflict between internalized norms and externalized pressures in the minister's situation is another source of problems. A young minister accompanied each turn of the handle of the mimeograph machine with the statement "I know I was called to preach, I know I was called to preach." He was called to preach, but there was a need for a church bulletin for the church service on Sunday. His role conflict was the result of what he believed he should do (internalized norms) and what he had to do (the external pressures).

One of the most often repeated criticisms of seminary training is that it does not prepare the ministers for the demands of the parish ministry. At the seminaries students learn the preacher-scholar mode. This role is internalized by the students and accepted as one of the primary norms for the practice of ministry. Unfortunately, the seminarian does not also internalize the role of administrator. In part, this failure is the fault of the seminaries because they do not emphasize such a role in their curriculums. But it is also the fault of the seminarian who does not see the need for taking the courses in administration that are offered.

I remember the very self-deprecating pattern which I developed in my first pastorate. When I arrived home each evening my wife would ask what I did that day. I would reply, "Nothing." What I was saying was that I didn't accomplish that day what I felt was important. I did not spend all morning studying as I thought I should have. I did not have uninterrupted time to focus on my sermons, and so I was not following the pattern of a preacher-scholar. Rather, I was swamped with demands of administration and of institutional survival that I was not trained to perform and which I considered to be unimportant. By continuing to say that I was accomplishing nothing, I lost a sense of joy and self-worth. My problem was the result of a conflict between what I believed should be the priorities and the priorities which could not be denied if the parish was to survive.

The internal-external conflict is also rooted in the differences between the gifts of those who are attracted to the ministry and the demands of the parish ministry. Many ministers are not able to cope with their role as leader of a voluntary association. They are ill-suited to the managerial or executive roles demanded in the parish. Tom Brown concluded from his counseling while he was director of the Northeast Career Center that "probably half of all ministers are ill-suited to executive endeavors, being by nature introverted, curious, and meditative rather than extroverted, judging, and conclusive." He added, "They try to play the executive role, nevertheless, or feel like failures for not playing it . . . and soon reach a point of complete and desperate frustration, feeling like NOBODY."[11]

A seventh cause is the internalization by either the clergy or the laity of mutually incompatible values and expectations. A typical minister may experience a struggle between ministering to the personal needs of parishioners and ministering to those of his family. Or a congregation may wish to grow but believes that any stewardship, evangelistic, and outreach programs will diminish its high spiritual standards. The problem is not that the expectations are wrong; the problem is that in each case each expectation is held as an absolute. When you try to cope with opposing absolutes you have conflict.

One way to demonstrate this conflict is to ask ministers to write down the number of hours which they believe they should spend on each of the roles which they must perform. In my experience, when this type of test has been given and when the answers have been tallied, the minimum number of hours which were to be spent on vocational pursuits have ranged from a low of 80 to a high of 130 hours per week. Yet these same ministers held as an absolute the belief that their families should receive first priority. With these kinds of mutually incompatible internalized expectations the only possible outcome is inner conflict, guilt, and lack of self-worth.

ANSWERS TO ROLE CONFUSION AND ROLE CONFLICT

Even such a brief review of the causes makes clear that it is not an overstatement to say that role confusion and role conflict are perhaps the two greatest hazards to fulfillment in ministry for both clergy and laity. It becomes imperative, therefore, to offer some suggestions for solutions.

To begin with let me point out that it is neither possible nor desirable to eliminate all role confusion. Samuel Blizzard wrote, "The ministry is a free profession with diffuse role definitions in a voluntary institution. Diversity of role performance and lack of clarity is to be expected."[12] In fact there is every reason to believe that if one model were established for ministry and this model were forced on all ministers, the very heart of ministry would be destroyed, for ministry must always be open to the needs of the particular people at the particular place and time in which they find themselves. So the first task is to dispose of the myth that the solution can be found in the statement "Let's get the role straight, inculcate it in the clergy, and see that the laity understand it."[13]

It is just as impossible and inadvisable to remove all role

conflict. Unfortunately, most ministers look upon conflict as bad and their reaction is to try to pour oil over troubled waters.

It is true that conflict can be destructive. It is also true that apathy is worse than conflict. Conflict shows that there is life, while apathy means eventual death. But the failure to deal constructively with conflict has led many congregations to a state of apathy where both clergy and laity have withdrawn from active confrontation, and consequently from constructive dialogue and solutions. The goal is for clergy and laity to live in creative tension as they work together in finding those roles which most aptly depict the mind of Christ in their particular time and place.

Having recognized that it is impossible to eliminate all role confusion and role conflict, what can be done so that these realities will not continue to be two of the greatest hazards to fulfillment in ministry?

First of all, the minister needs to define for himself the nature of the ministry, or to put it another way, a minister needs to be an *actor* rather than a *reactor* in a role definition.

There are several excellent definitions of the role of the minister. Thomas Mullen defines the role of the pastor under five headings: The Equipping Ministry, The Builder of Community, The Catalytic Agent, The Pastor as Teacher, and The Man of Truth.[14] Ernest Mosley defines the role of the minister as involving three basic functions: proclamation, care, and leadership. The pastor stands before the people as one declaring the Word of God. He stands with them providing guidance, counsel, and care. And he works among them providing leadership to the church's growth and mission.[15]

Each minister must determine for himself the role definition which best meets his understanding of the Bible, the teaching of the church, and the context in which he carries out his ministry. This definition is to be used for personal clarification and for communication and negotiation with the laity. It should be solid enough to give clarity and fluid enough to permit change on the basis of new truth and changed circumstances.

My definition of my role as minister has included the five areas of preaching-teaching, crisis ministry, change agent, outreach, and administration. More recently I have thought of my role under the rubric of "Resident Theologian." I have not discarded the other functions, but I have come to believe that there is a greater need for Christian apologetics. This need, as I see it, has resulted from an increased interest in spiritual matters plus a decrease in the understanding of the Christian message.

In stating that a minister needs to be an actor rather than reactor I am not placing all of the responsibility for role definition on the minister. I *am* saying that the minister needs to take responsibility for having a clear role definition. And for ministers to have clear role definitions, theologians, seminary staffs, and church executives need to place greater emphasis on defining the purpose of the church and its ministry. The question is too important and the truths to be brought to bear on the subject are too complex and varied for the task to be left up to each minister working independently of the total community of faith. Rather, each minister must be supported by the total body of Christ as he seeks a clear definition and direction to what he does.

"Know thyself" is good advice for every minister and a second answer to role confusion and role conflict. It is axiomatic that no two people are alike. Moreover, if we accept that the diversity of our gifts comes from God, we are obligated to have a clear concept of the nature of these gifts—to know who we are.

The well-known saw which tells of the minister who said he enjoyed everything in the ministry but preaching, visiting, and administration did offer some insights into his gifts. One might wonder, however, if his gifts were suited to the parish ministry. Each minister does need to know his gifts in preaching, visiting, and administration, as well as in a dozen other areas.

How can a minister know himself? The three most likely means are personal introspections, feedback from friends and associates, and the help of professional counselors. Among the professional counselors most able to help ministers in understanding their gifts for ministry are those who have skills in ministerial career assessment. The development of the Career Assessment movement has been a boon to ministers, and they should avail themselves of these services several times during their career.

Unfortunately, many ministers are slow to examine their strengths and weaknesses. Hadden points out a temptation that is particularly relevant to ministers; one to which they often succumb.

> For example, when there is no other professional around to question the justification of his activities, the minister may find it easier to take on a motif of busyness that is psychologically rewarding to him and acceptable to his congregation, but which neglects many of the long-range problems of the church. Filling his life with so much activity that he never has the time to be troubled with the question "why," is the path of least resistance. While this may be functional for the immediate needs of the individual, it is dysfunctional for the larger task of reinterpreting the essential meaning of the faith and the role of the minister in contemporary society.[16]

This kind of role definition can be described as the "crowded date book" role, often used but totally ineffective in getting to know oneself.

A third step is to clarify the nature of the American parish church. Conflicts can be minimized if one begins with a clear picture of the nature of the parish church in American society. Thomas Campbell makes an urgent plea for all those who are in the parish ministry to recognize that the church in American society is a voluntary organization and this view must be taken seriously.

He further contends that the parish minister must recognize the forces in our history and culture which have pressed towards "privatized" religion:

> If one grants that there will be a pluralism of religious groupings in the culture and that there will be a separation of church and state, there is a strong press for religion to have its primary relation to the private concerns of life. Just exactly how a pluralism of religious bodies will exert force for social change except through the indirect influence of transformed individuals is very difficult to say.
>
> The press toward "privatized" religion present from the very earliest years of our country has been strengthened by the growth of industrialization and bureaucratization within the country. Peo-

ple begin to see life as evermore specialized in its various areas of concern, and religion is more and more pressed into the area of private concern: home and family, personal ethics, and individual relations to the Divine Presence.

The American context is very much one of voluntary churches concerned primarily with private religious experiences.[17]

I do not argue and I do not understand Campbell as arguing that this is the biblical pattern for the church. Rather, it is the American pattern. Therefore, the minister must start with this realistic view of the American church and seek to minister within it with the least amount of destructive conflict and with the greatest amount of effort directed toward positive change.

Closely related to this third step is the need to have a realistic view of the role of the pastor in a parish church. Two statements, one by John Biersdorf and one by Reinhold Niebuhr, helped me at this point.

Biersdorf gives a simple but beautiful illustration. He notes that students have been taught that eighth-century prophets should be looked upon as models for their ministry, but have seldom been told that Amos's independent economic base was an essential aspect of his prophetic activities.[18]

The point as I understand it is that one must be slow in condemning the parish minister for not being exactly like Amos while still holding up Amos as one of the models that we should not neglect.

Reinhold Niebuhr approaches his insight from a different standpoint. In his book *Leaves from the Notebook of a Tamed Cynic,* he wrote:

> No amount of pressure from an itinerant "prophet" can change the fact that a minister is bound to be a statesman as much as a prophet, dealing with situations as well as principles. In specific situations, actions must be judged not only in terms of absolute standards but in consideration of available resources in the lives of those whom the minister leads.
>
> It may be well for the statesman to know that statesmanship easily degenerates into opportunism and that opportunism cannot be sharply distinguished from dishonesty but the prophet ought to realize that his higher perspective and the uncompromising

nature of his judgments always has a note of irresponsibility in it. Francis of Assisi may have been a better Christian than Pope Innocent the III. But it may be questioned whether his moral superiority over the latter was as absolute as it seems. Nor is there any reason to believe that Abraham Lincoln, the statesman and opportunist, was morally inferior to William Lloyd Garrison, the prophet. The moral achievement of statesmen must be judged in terms which take account of the limitations of human society which the statesman must, and the prophet need not, consider.[19]

A fifth answer is to develop covenants between minister and congregation followed by periodic goal setting and review. One of the most effective ways of clarifying the role expectations of both the church and the minister and thereby minimizing conflict and avoiding a mismatch is for a covenant to be entered into at the time the congregation calls a minister. The recommendation made at the general assembly of the Presbyterian Church U.S. (in the spring of 1974) expresses the importance of such covenants: "In order to institute real partnership and to free both Ministers and churches for mission, Ministers and churches must be enabled and required to form their relationships with each other on the basis of negotiated covenants. The pulpit nominating committee must discuss frankly with the Minister the congregation's goals, expectations, and projected divisions of responsibility between Minister and people, as well as the length of term of the call."[20]

An initial covenant is not sufficient. It is impossible in an initial covenant to adequately describe the nature of the gifts of the congregation and that of the minister. It is absolutely necessary that there be periodic and frequent reviews of the covenant in the form of evaluation and goal setting. A congregation and its leadership change very rapidly and often very radically in a mobile society; and it is possible for a covenant to become completely out of date within four to five years simply because there are new leaders and new needs in the congregation.

Sixth, ministers should make use of parish consultants who have specialized skills in organizational development. Whenever conflict arises due to role confusion and different role expectations, expert outside assistance may be the only solution to the conflict.

The Episcopal Church in Project Test Pattern carried on an extensive study in the role of consultants in solving role conflicts. The results of this program were reported in *New Hope for Congregations* by Loren Mead[21] and *Congregations in Change* by Elisa L. DesPortes.[22] These studies confirm earlier studies by Higgins and Dittes that it is possible with the aid of outside consultants to close the gap between the clergy and laity related to expectations and understandings of the purpose of the church and its ministry.[23]

Many excellent instruments have been developed so that ministers and congregations can go through the process of solving conflict in the churches. However, the results from Project Test Pattern have shown that third-party consultation can increase the rate and the effectiveness of change.

Finally, ministers should maintain a stance of consultation and negotiation between the clergy and laity. Hadden observes that the clergy "seem to operate on the assumption that laity are an immovable force that must be worked around and not with."[24] Such an attitude breeds destructive conflict. For there to be a minimizing of conflict, the clergy must see the laity as equal partners, that is, implement the doctrine of the priesthood of the believers. This stance of equal sharing of authority, coupled with trust, will provide a climate for consultation and negotiations. I like to describe this stance, using Paul's words, as "speaking the truth in love."

*   *   *

Role confusion and role conflict can form an unholy alliance to block fulfillment in ministry. It need not be so. There are ways to respond to these issues in such fashion that potentially painful experiences will lead to greater fulfillment for both clergy and laity.

Chapter 8

Blacktopping the Parking Lot

"One pastor said, 'The goals of my ministry are the salvation of mankind and the coming of God's kingdom on this earth.' When reciting his accomplishments on the way to achieving these goals, he boasted, 'We have blacktopped the parking lot of the church and redecorated the inside of the parsonage from top to bottom.' This minister had no difficulty in seeing the relationship between his proximate and ultimate goals, and thus he saw himself as a great success. But many pastors find difficulty in this which the simpler thought lines of the more naive generation did not encounter."[1]

I do not know if I qualify for the category of a *less* naive generation, but I certainly do qualify for the category of the many pastors who find difficulty in understanding success in ministry.

A THEOLOGY OF AMBITION AND SUCCESS

Failure to achieve success in ministry is generally defined as a situation in which both clergy and laity have used inadequate models to measure success. This is a major part of the problem. For me, however, it begins with the question of whether or not ambition and success are sub-Christian. Or, to put it another way, is there such a thing as Christian ambition and success?

Ambition and success have always had negative overtones for me. This is not by chance. The dictionary definitions of these words stand in opposition to the teachings of Jesus. For example, the dictionary gives two definitions for ambition: "an ardent desire for rank, fame, or power" and "a desire to achieve a particular end."

Success also has two basic definitions: "a degree or measure of succeeding, attaining a desired object or end" and "a favorable termination of a venture; specifically, the attainment of wealth, favor, or eminence."[2]

These definitions make clear the quandary of the Christian. There is no doubt that Christ had certain "desired ends" for himself as well as for his followers. However, his desired ends are not the same as those described in the dictionary—"the attainment of wealth, favor, or eminence." The teachings and life of our Lord point us to the ends we are to strive for as his followers. Concerning himself Jesus said, "The Son of man came not to be served, but to serve, and to give his life as a ransom for many" (Matt. 20:28); "I have come that they may have life, and have it abundantly" (John 10:10); and "For this I was born, and for this I have come into the world, to bear witness to the truth" (John 18:37).

Jesus was no less explicit about his desired ends for his followers: "As the Father has sent me, even so I send you" (John 20:21); "You, therefore, must be perfect, as your heavenly Father is perfect" (Matt. 5:48); and in the parable of the sheep and goats (Matt. 25:31–46) Christ enumerated specific acts of kindness to be done to "the least of these my brethren"—visit the sick and those in prison, feed the hungry, clothe the naked, and give drink to the thirsty.

If these desired ends are to be achieved there must be ambition, but ambition is suspect when it is seen only as "an ardent desire for rank, fame, or power." As Christians we are aware of the teachings of Jesus; we are to desire service. Therefore, Christians often find themselves in a quandary as to how to view ambition. Is ambition a quality which must be suppressed because it leads to the wrong ends, or is ambition a power which must be accepted as a gift from God to be encouraged and directed to Christian ends? Is there such a thing as Christian ambition?

Before answering that question I want to point out that ambition and success are major factors in fulfillment in ministry. Pastors leave the ministry because they feel they are not successful. Churches fire pastors because they are not successful. We cannot underestimate the importance of success. As Nathanael Guptill writes, "Success is the personal fulfillment that every human being who does not opt out of life altogether must seek if he is to maintain either his sanity or his integrity."[3]

In a diary where I record both my activities and feelings I have entries for one eight-day period that illustrate my problem which I believe is also the problem of many other ministers.

> After the first Sunday I was on cloud nine. There was good attendance at church, excellent response to the sermon and a spirit of enthusiasm in the congregation. The following week I counseled with a woman whose husband had attempted suicide; visited a family that had bitter feelings towards the church; received assurance from a family which had been hurt in a church conflict that they had overcome their resentments and were going to reunite with the church the following Sunday; visited a widow and her sister; counseled a couple that were living together and were being hurt in the process; arranged the fiftieth anniversary celebration for a couple that did not have any family to take note of this important event; visited in the hospitals; prepared my sermons; carried out my administrative tasks. The following Sunday the attendance was down and those who had promised to join the church did not. On Monday I was a basket case. I berated myself for wanting to be successful. I told myself that ambition was wrong and that I should learn to be impervious to not reaching goals which I longed for.

My problem was twofold. First, I had succumbed to the standards of success in the ministry most often used by clergy and laity—increased attendance and increased church membership. Moreover, I failed by not finding joy in my role as a servant—a sign of spiritual immaturity. Second I had berated myself for having ambition and wanting to be successful. I condemned ambition as sub-Christian and sought to eliminate it by self-flagellation. It took me a long time to come to a clear understanding that ambition is a God-given gift and that the issue is *how* ambition is used.

Jaroslav Pelikan did a great favor by describing Christian ambition in his address "Toward a Theology of Ambition." Because his insights are so valid I will rely on his presentation for most of what I have to say on Christian ambition. Dr. Pelikan affirms that the doctrine of the Trinity "contains within it the basis for a positive reinterpretation of ambition as a theological imperative." The Christian affirmation that God is "Father, the Almighty, the Maker of heaven and earth" does not mean that God has completed his work of creation. "On the contrary, the pattern of his creative activity is to endow his creatures with a capacity to actualize their potential and then to allow them to develop toward their fulfillment. Human history, then, is not a Punch-and-Judy show in which God pulls the strings and we are merely puppets. It is a genuine life-and-death struggle in which the outcome truly hangs in the balance and in which therefore human responsibility and human initiative really matter."[4]

God gives us power whereby we can exercise, to significant degree, control over the forces of history. We are not simply objects of God's creative operation; we are also active participants in the creative process. We are endowed by God with a potential, and the achievement of that potential is ours to realize. "It is a sin to suppose that we have created ourselves and that by our cleverness we can disenthrone the Sovereign of the Universe. But it is no less a sin to deny his gifts by wrapping them in a napkin and burying them. *Therefore the moral corollary of the theological doctrine of creation is not only Christian humility, but also Christian ambition, the acceptance of the possibilities that God has placed before us and into us and the resolution that these possibilities shall not be allowed to lie fallow.*" (Italics are mine.)[5]

Ambition is at the very heart of the Christian life. However, ambition can be a double-edged sword. Ambition has led clergy as well as laity to lie, steal, and use other people. In fact, one of the most common destructive expressions of ambition among the clergy is their manipulation of people to achieve ego-gratification.

Pelikan points out, however, that God's redemptive work in Jesus Christ removes some of the risks of ambition. "The picture of Christ as Lord and Savior is central to any theology of ambition, for his saving work, by making our human achievements unnecessary for salvation, serves to make them possible in a new way."[6] As a Christian, to be able to stand before God, I do not have to be perfect or proper, and I do not have to be successful.

"What would happen if Christians really believed this and acted upon it? Would the church be the heavy-footed institution that it is if the liberating power of Christ dominated its counsels and determined its plans? When I am faced with two alternatives—one of them safe but conventional, the other imaginative but risky—I have now been emboldened to run the risk. Christian ambition is different from other ambition in that it does not have to achieve its goals and can therefore decide upon its goals *because they are worthwhile rather than because they are attainable.*" (Italics are mine.)[7]

A third step in understanding the meaning of Christian ambition is to consider the role of the Holy Spirit. The Nicene Creed speaks of the Holy Spirit as "the Lord and Giver of life." This means that the Holy Spirit is the source of human good and the giver of gifts. Whenever the divine power of God enters into our lives it does not abolish our nature but sustains it. "The doctrine of the Holy Spirit as the Lord and Giver of life means that all our natural endowments and ambitions can find their fulfillment in him. He elevates the whole range of human talent, completing what we in our weakness cannot complete in crowning our nature with his grace. . . . The grace of God is not so paltry that it needs to cut man down to size in order to be visible. *No, God the Holy Spirit delights in acting as a lure, to call forth from each of us the best he can be and do; and then the grace of the Spirit will carry us the rest of the way.*" (Italics are mine.)[8]

Ambition, far from being a curse, is a gift of God. The Holy Spirit delights in acting as a lure to call forth from each of us our best. It follows, therefore, that as Christians we are to use the gift of ambition. The goals of our ambition and our ability to realize, at a feeling level, that we do not have to be successful to be saved will remain crucial to our effective use of this gift.

As I stated above, Jesus was explicit in stating the goals

for himself and his followers. These goals can be summarized in one word—service. Our ability to serve, to be servants, is success.

To achieve success as servants we must do two things. First, we must analyze our present standard of success and reject inadequate models. Second, we must find guidelines based on success as servants which can also be applied to the everyday tasks of the parish ministry.

INADEQUATE MODELS

If we can agree that ambition is a God-given quality and it is put into focus by a theology of ambition, then the first hurdle in defining success in ministry has been overcome. The next hurdle is to determine the desired objects or ends which we are seeking to attain.

At this point we run into problems. The goals which our society espouses are often antithetical to those of our Master. Moreover, both clergy and laity have been highly influenced by our culture's standards of success.

To clarify the issue of desired ends, I want to give some examples of culturally influenced models which are inadequate for measuring success in ministry. Moreover, I want to point out the effect that these models have on ministry.

Larry Baker, professor at Midwestern Baptist Theological Seminary and formerly the pastor of the First Baptist Church in Fayetteville, Arkansas, suggests that the two most prevalent models of success for ministers are: the executive model and the million-dollar-round-table model. To his suggestions I would add the model of the president of the corporation and the model of the crowded calendar.

The executive model measures success by the size of the church, the complexity of its organization, and the size of the staff. The million-dollar-round-table model measures success by the number of sales the minister makes—the number of baptisms, additions, and Sunday school participants. The model of the president of the corporation measures success by how effectively he can keep the stockholders happy—he leads the church members into believing they are the greatest group of Christians this side of heaven. But the crowded calendar is a model which is particularly appealing to ministers.

The following scenario is everpresent when ministers meet, particularly if the pastors are friends and have not seen each other for several weeks or months. As the pastors get ready to leave they talk about how great it has been to see each other and how urgent it is that they see more of one another. Therefore, they decide to get together. The ubiquitous appointment calendar appears and the ministers examine dates. After a great deal of sighing, they decide that the next date they are all free is six months away. Expressions of regret are forthcoming but there is a sense of pride over the success implied in each crowded calendar. One pastor's wife unintentionally exposed the pride inherent in the crowded calendar when she said, "We who are *leaders* have such busy schedules."

These models have some demonic qualities about them, because they contain elements of Christian success and are therefore seductive as well as virtuous in nature. The executive model appeals to the pastor's desire to minister effectively to specialized groups. Today, ministry to single adults is desperately needed. But to my knowledge the churches which have been most effective in this are those large enough to have a staff member or members who are specially trained and who have time to devote. In other words, I find that the ministry of one large congregation is often far superior in meeting the varied spiritual needs of our time to that of a half-dozen small struggling congregations. Therefore, a large staff—the executive model—becomes an important goal.

Sales are also important. The Great Commission has to do with sales—we are called to add people to the Christian ranks. Moreover, it does not always follow, as some argue, that the congregations with few sales are deepening the spiritual life of their members while congregations with large sales are always superficial in what they do. So the sales model has its valid claims as well as being seductive.

Christ called us to be peacemakers and prayed that we should be such. Therefore there is an element of Christian virtue in trying to keep the stockholders happy.

Similarly, virtue can be found in the crowded calendar

model. Although it traditionally has not been listed as one of the seven deadly sins, I contend that laziness is one for ministers. The minister, having no organized supervision, can easily become either a workaholic or a lazy individual. Unfortunately, I find many in the latter category, which is not virtuous. However, when one is busy—has a crowded calendar—there is a good possibility that the seduction of laziness has been resisted.

These models are demonic, also, because of the destructive powers which are unleashed as these models are followed. The demons unleashed by such models are legion. Several of the more prominent are easily identified.

Professional Gossip. Most ministers keep confidences but seem unable to resist sharing professional gossip. In an article for *Christian Ministry,* Larry La Velle affirms, "I'm not aware of any other professionals who so casually discuss and demean colleagues in their private and public conversations. We've all experienced it. It is one of those subtle, personal experiences that breeds distrust and increases isolation. I'm convinced that for some people it is as unconscious as a racist slur. Perhaps we should expose it on the spot for what it is: a petty and unprofessional way to enhance oneself by demeaning another."[9]

I have found that professional gossip is generally directed at the pastors of successful churches as measured by the executive model and the sales model. The rationale seems to be that pointing out the clay feet of the successful pastors enhances one's own standing as a pastor.

Gossiping is also often directed to former pastors. To be sure that the members are aware of how well he is doing, the new pastor will drop hints about the former pastor's weaknesses. His comments may include references to failure to keep proper records, inattention to shut-ins, lack of preparation of sermons, and non-cooperation with other ministers. Some may have a large measure of truth and others barely a few grains, but it really doesn't matter. The goal is to enhance oneself at the expense of the former pastor.

Gossiping which is based on jealousy often degenerates into the destructive force of bitterness, a bitterness which is then directed inwardly because one is not achieving and outwardly because the congregation is not permitting achievement. This bitterness can become a vicious attack which is unleashed against those who are not supporting the church in the particular way the pastor considers essential to his success. The pastor is then tempted to divide the congregation into the white hats, those who do what he says, and the black hats, those who either don't support his pet projects or who dare to oppose them. The jealousy-bitterness-anger poisons spread through the congregation from the pastor and destroy whatever effective ministry might have been possible.

Lack of Self-worth. It is axiomatic that self-worth is related to success. When a person feels that he or she is not successful, then that person has a low sense of self-worth. Lack of self-worth also undermines one's ability to serve.

There are many congregations which will never fit the executive or sales models. This is true not because of any fault of the pastor or congregation, but because of sociological factors. The church may be in a changing community; it may be in a static community; or it may be in a declining community. When the size of the organization and the number of sales are determinants of success, pastors in small, struggling churches are doomed to be considered failures. In turn, the feeling of failure keeps the pastor from being effective in areas of ministry which are possible. He loses his ability to function and his lack of self-worth is soon reflected in the congregation's view of itself. It becomes a vicious cycle in which all lose— clergy and laity alike.

Ministerial Isolation. The demon of ministerial isolation affects both the "unsuccessful" minister and the "successful" minister. The "unsuccessful" minister, as defined by the million-dollar-round-table model, is the minister of a small church or of a church with declining attendance. He feels threatened by ministers whose churches are showing remarkable growth in attendance. He believes that he will be looked upon as a failure and therefore isolates himself from ministers who might be eager to listen, encourage, and even suggest some possible steps in church development.

The "successful" minister also isolates himself. He is aware of the spirit of competition that is present among ministers and, therefore, of the envy and sour grapes which are directed towards those who are "successful." This awareness causes him to assume that because of his success he will be rejected by his peers. So he, too, isolates himself.

Unhealthy Competition. These models cause a great deal of unhealthy competition often leading to unethical practices in trying to secure members. A pastor may, with great reluctance (or so he says), indicate to a prospective church family that the church they had been considering isn't very spiritual (whatever that may mean), or that the pastor has a record of neglecting families once they join the church.

On another level, competition leads to wasted time and effort. New families in the community are visited by members and the pastors of several different churches. I've even had the experience of visiting with a family when another pastor has shown up. Time and effort are wasted in the duplication of ministries and in the neglect of ministries which require the cooperation of several churches.

Becoming Rather than Being. The executive and sales models lead the pastor to set his goal at *becoming* rather than *being.* He sees success not as Christian growth but as numerical and organizational growth. Ernest Mosley points out that the fruit of the Spirit presented in Galatians 5:22–23 is the basis of measuring spiritual growth and accomplishment. But he also adds that "the fruit of the Spirit is also the basic criteria for measuring success in all other areas of the minister's life and work. When love, joy, peace, patience, kindness, goodness, faithfulness, gentleness, and self-control are being expressed in any aspect of the minister's life, success is there. When any one of them is missing, success is limited."[10]

Mosley does not leave this concept in the abstract. In an excellent chart he relates these qualities to the following areas of ministry: myself, my spouse, my children, fellow church members, other ministers, others in the community, my work of teaching/preaching, my work of leading/managing, my work of counseling/caring, and my work of denominational responsibilities.[11] Such an approach keeps a proper priority of *being* over *becoming.*

The priority of *being* over *becoming* applies to the laity as well as to the clergy. Congregations should be conscious of their need for spiritual growth. Spurred on by the minister to become the largest in the community, many congregations develop the same characteristics as those of the church of Corinth. The members must still be fed milk rather than solid food. Growth in Christian maturity must be included in any standard of success for a congregation. This quality is difficult to measure, but it becomes evident when one measures a congregation against the goal of a servant community.

Neglect of the Difficult. The demon of the crowded calendar is the temptation to avoid those things one does not wish to do with the excuse that there is no time available. I have often noticed that I can excuse myself for not visiting a church family who needs my help but who irritates me. I can say that this week is too busy. However, the chance to visit someone who is a tither and might join the church can always find its place on the busy calendar.

This demon undermines the goal of Christian ministry, which is service. It is difficult to love the unlovely. It is time-consuming to counsel with the anxious, the troubled, and the perplexed. Therefore, those who need our love and ministry the most are the ones most likely to be the casualties of a crowded calendar.

Moving Syndrome. As mentioned, the average length of a pastorate is three years. One reason for short pastorates is the pressure to move to a larger church. If one wants to be cynical, one might say that the only time there is pressure to move to another church (other than when faced with termination) is when a larger church is involved. This moving syndrome promotes an unbelievable waste of money, to say nothing of ineffectiveness. Ed White, Executive Director of the National Presbytery, has ventured the suggestion that most pastors move too soon and leave too many tasks only half done.

Complete Outer Direction. Keeping the stockholder happy has its pitfalls as well. The pastor must determine the course of his ministry by the desires of the members of the congregation. As one wit has expressed it, the "prophet" motive is replaced by the "profit" motive. The pastor becomes completely outer-directed and must constantly check and recheck the pulse of the congregation to determine what he should be or do. The frenetic pace to which the pastor goes to please all church members leaves him exhausted and it causes him to be fearful of every innuendo that someone is unhappy.

Search for Praise and Adulation. In the president-of-the-corporation model, the congregations tend to see their own success or failure as coming from their professional leaders. This is how we gauge success in our free enterprise business system. Therefore, in this model, the minister is the one who receives all of the praise and all of the blame. Moreover, when everything is going well, the minister consciously or unconsciously encourages this model to receive as much praise and adulation as possible. The goal of the minister degenerates to a search for praise.

Brutalization. One facet of the demonic power of "numbers success" was expressed by a poet, Michael Harper. Harper has received recognition for his writing but, like most poets, he does not earn his livelihood by writing. He has taught at colleges in Oregon, California, and Illinois. When asked, "Does it bother you that you cannot write full-time or that more people don't buy poetry?" he replied, "I guess I have a few thousand readers. Some would say that's enough. I'd like to have more. Readership is important. But I'm more concerned with expressing poetic themes. Poets shouldn't be too concerned with the audience. *The worry brutalizes them.*" (Italics are mine.)[12]

My understanding of Harper's statement as applied to ministers is that when a minister becomes obsessed with audience response he loses his sensitivity—to God and to others. The minister is not able to hear the still small voice of God's will, nor is he able to hear the cries of those in need.

The brutalizing aspect of the numbers game was expressed by a pastor of a struggling congregation. In retrospect it was clear that this particular congregation was started in a moment of unreflective zeal. However, the congregation was a reality and a committee consisting of members from several churches was working with the pastor to determine courses of action. One member of the committee said, "You will have to visit more people so as to get more money." The pastor replied, "How can I visit a family with a goal of ministering to them when I see them as dollar signs?"

Sexual Indiscretions. Sexual indiscretions are often the by-product of inadequate success models. As described in chapter five, when the minister is being labeled as a failure, he becomes vulnerable to the sympathy and friendship of women parishioners. In most cases the problem begins as an expression of genuine concern and friendship on the part of the female friend. The sharing of frustrations and problems leads to greater and greater expressions of emotional support which can end in sexual involvement.

We can conclude from the observations listed above that our most common models of success in ministry are often destructive and demeaning to the church of Jesus Christ and to the clergy and laity who minister in his name.

GUIDELINES FOR MEASURING SUCCESS IN MINISTRY

Before seeking some specific guidelines for solving the problems related to success in ministry, it is important to dispel one misconception. Whenever ministers get together they tend to talk as if the problem lies with the inadequate views of success held by the laity. There is truth in the fact that a gulf separates the clergy and laity in their understanding of the purpose of the church and its ministry, and this difference will naturally cause conflict between them about the meaning of success. However, I want to make this point: There is enough blame to go around. Both clergy and laity have succumbed to our culturally influenced models of success.

Nathanael Guptill writes that the idol which the New Testament called "mammon" has the name today of "success."

> The worship of this idol symbolizes everything phony, shallow, empty, and inhuman about our culture. The cult of the beautiful people described in TV commercials who consume cosmetics, beer, cigarettes, soap, and crunchy breakfast food, who wear smart clothes, drive flashy cars, and "get ahead" in life is the great false religion of our day. A great many Christians and a great many pastors are secret adherents of this religion, but few will admit it; and many are torn apart inside because, although they profess a slushy form of Christianity, they know that down deep they really want more than anything else to be young, rich, beautiful, strong, and sexy.[13]

So the issue at hand is not for the clergy to offer to take the splinters out of the eyes of the laity while neglecting the logs in their own eyes, but for both clergy and laity to remove their own logs and, with unencumbered vision, to work together as they look for answers to the demons of inadequate models.

The key to success in ministry will be found in the statement of Jesus to James and John. The objection which Jesus raised was not an objection to the ambition but to the goal of the ambition. James and John wanted power and prominence. Jesus said that their ambition, instead of being for power and prominence, should be for service. Jesus urged them to seek greatness and even to be first. But greatness as defined by Jesus was service, and to be first was to be a slave. This standard of greatness was seen in Christ's life for he came to "minister and to give his life as a ransom for many."

This ultimate answer must be broken down to more proximate answers. I will seek to do this by providing some specific guidelines.

The first guideline is for both clergy and laity to define the meaning of the church and its ministry. A clear-cut definition on which both pastor and laity can agree is imperative (see chapter 7, "Role Conflict"). This means that with the divergence of views present in the church today not every pastor and every congregation will be able to work together in seeking success in ministry. When views are too disparate, the best answer is an amicable separation of ways. This is not a call to inflexibility in approach, but rather a realistic understanding of the differences that exist.

A second guideline is for the clergy to define success for themselves. Robert Kemper makes the excellent point that success in ministry is being defined today by the seminaries, the laity, the denominations, and the culture. In this process the clergy have had a negligible impact.[14] For example, the seminary is a school of higher education. Students write papers and meet the criteria academia has demanded. They are given grades as symbols of success. The clergy, therefore, see themselves, in part, as mini-professors. However, as Kemper asks, "What do you do when a congregation does not ask you to submit a paper at the end of a quarter?"

He then adds, "I am so bold as to advocate the creation of professional associations for clergy. I believe the fault lies not with the system but with the clergy themselves. They will get what they deserve, especially other people's answers to the questions about success in their profession. If they cannot answer those questions for themselves then they deserve to have to live with others' answers."[15]

Third, ministers and churches should set goals which can be measured in light of the specific program of ministry. Words such as faithfulness, concern, and fellowship are too general in nature. They can be used in ways that obscure mistakes and leave problems unresolved.

The planning committee for a city-wide revival asked an evangelist to change his customary procedure in giving the invitation. Instead of asking people to come to the front of the city auditorium, they were asked to come after the service to an inquiry room. The evangelist hesitated but finally agreed. His rationale was that as a Christian he was called to be faithful rather than successful; therefore, it really didn't matter what the outcome would be. The change in the pattern of the invitation was disastrous. The evangelist was uncomfortable; his uneasiness was conveyed to the audience; and the response was nil. After the conclusion of the services, the steering committee and the evangelist did not face up to their mistakes. Instead of saying "We blew it" or "We failed in our method of invitation," everyone said in unison, "We are called to be faithful, not successful." They may have assuaged their pain by that statement, but they left their failure unconfessed. They did not learn from their mistake.

Next, we should compare congregations sparingly. One of the biggest sources of difficulty lies in comparing one parish church with another. I suspect one major obstacle to solving the problem of success measurement is the practice of exchanging information about churches through newsletters, yearly statistical tables compiled by denominational executives, and brag sessions among pastors. These comparisons can be evaluated only in terms of the executive model or the sales model, and these models leave out the unique characteristics of each congregation and the gifts of the clergy and the laity. Ministry becomes not a response to the felt needs of the people in a given area, but an implementation of programs aimed at increasing the sales. As a result, the "weary and the heavy laden" that Jesus came to serve become objects to be manipulated for the ego-gratification of the minister and the congregation.

Each congregation must see its ministry in light of its ultimate goal of service, guided by the understanding of the gifts of the pastor and of the congregation and the location of the church. For example, some years ago a church contacted me in their search for a senior minister. At one time that congregation had been the largest in the community. However, a change in community—large homes made into apartments—brought about a steady decline in membership. The goal of the pastor search committee was to find a pastor that would be able to attract enough new members so the church would once more be the largest in the city. No thought was given to the needs of the surrounding neighborhood or how to minister to it. Members of the committee were thinking of success in terms of comparison with other churches, not in terms of service to a changing community.

We must also set spiritual goals. While it is very difficult to measure membership growth in light of the fruit of the Spirit, it is not impossible. Leaders within a congregation should work with the pastor to determine whether the membership has grown in love, joy, peace, patience, kindness, goodness, faithfulness, and self-control.

After a tragic accident which took the lives of two members of the church, I challenged the congregation to channel their grief and shock into a six-week effort of strengthening the bonds of Christian love within our fellowship. This effort was to include a conscious attempt to minister to all the members in love, even as the two families had been ministered to in their time of loss, and to make each worship service a time when we could demonstrate our oneness as followers of our Lord Jesus Christ. This six-week effort culminated in a moving celebration of communion.

The congregation reacted enthusiastically: We consciously set spiritual goals and as a family of faith, we grew spiritually.

Churches and pastors must set institutional goals as well as spiritual goals. The church is an institution. As a community of believers the church has a responsibility to teach, to make disciples, and to baptize. However, as an institution the church needs buildings, budgets, and members. There is, therefore, nothing wrong with setting goals of attendance, increases in membership, and increases in financial giving.

One can be so bold as to say that paving the parking lot may be a valid expression of success. Potholes, ruts, dust, and/ or mud are not an indication of spirituality in the congregation. If a parking lot is needed for people to park so they can come to worship, to study, to plan, to meet in Christian fellowship, then the paving of the parking lot may be seen as a valid expression of the ultimate goal of the salvation of mankind.

The warning I would give is that when institutional goals are used, they should be used by the congregation for an in-house study. Such a study can reveal both strong and weak points. When institutional goals are used primarily for comparison with other churches, one is back in the business of developing an unhealthy competition with its subsequent jealousy, bitterness, and peer isolation.

For example, at the first minister's meeting I attended, I received a sheet listing all the participating churches, the number of people in Sunday school, Training Union, new members, rededications, and even of decisions to enter church-related vocations. I was the pastor of a small congregation and the weekly statistical report from our church looked like a total failure when compared to the report of other congregations eight to ten times larger. My attendance at those meetings was usually a painful experience. And my feelings hindered my ability to relate to and learn from my peer group. I felt like such a failure that I didn't dare to ask for help in solving problems that I was facing, or to offer suggestions in areas where I was being successful.

Another guideline is to have services of celebration for achievements within the church—services that express thanksgiving to God and also a commitment to continued service. If the Holy Spirit delights in luring us to do our best, then it follows that we should give thanks to God when we see evidences of God's Spirit having lured the congregation to service and evidences that the congregation has responded.

Services of celebration can take place at the completion of specific tasks, on anniversary dates, at baptismal services, at the time of the visit of missionaries, at the dedication of a new building, after summer mission trips, and on any other occasion of authentic evidence of a ministry well done.

Unfortunately, for many years I approached such occasions as opportunities to challenge the congregation to greater service. I was afraid that to acknowledge any kind of victory was either an expression of self-righteousness or would lead to self-satisfaction. How wrong I was! I missed many beautiful occasions to help people celebrate the reality of the presence of God's Holy Spirit in our midst.

Fortunately, I have been able to find a more Christian understanding of ambition and success. As I stated above, Pelikan's statement on the theology of ambition has been a boon to me. Even as I write I am in the midst of preparation for the centennial celebration of the church where I am pastor. I am looking forward to that year-long celebration as an opportunity for spiritual growth and Christian success.

As a final guideline I would suggest keeping a daily log. A log can be of great help for an individual minister trying to determine his or her success. Because of the variety of demands which are placed on the minister's time, it is possible to come to the end of the week with many important tasks half done or totally undone. At this point it is helpful to refer to a log of the past week as a reminder of how time was spent. Such a process can be a boost when you see what has been accomplished despite the encroachment of less important tasks. When a log is kept for long periods of time, it can be studied by the minister either alone or with colleagues, and a valid picture of the failures and successes can be drawn.

*　　*　　*

Ambition, and its goal, success, can be compared to human sexuality. Both are beautiful gifts of God which have the potential to be abused and adulterated. The church has been unclear in its interpretation of both of these gifts. However, I believe that the church has been even less responsible in dealing with the meaning of ambition and success in ministry than it has been with questions relating to human sexuality.

In making such a statement I speak for myself and for most

ministers I know. I readily confess that ambition and success have been problems for me. I have been intimidated by the standards of the executive model, the sales model, the model of the president of the corporation, and the model of the crowded calendar. With one hand I've tried to hold on to these models and with the other I've tried to be a servant. As a result I have often seemed schizophrenic and have hurt myself and members of congregations where I've served. I do not offer excuses for my failures. I do express a plea that clearer guidelines be developed to evaluate success in ministry. Our neglect of such guidelines has caused clergy and laity alike to find fulfillment in ministry an impossible possibility.

Chapter 9

Until the Lord Leads or the Church Fires Me

He was calm now. The agitation so evident before was gone. I wondered what had caused the change. I thought back to the phone call four weeks before. It was a Monday morning when Jerry called. I had not seen him for about a year. Prior to that, we had seen each other often because our churches were in neighboring communities and we belonged to the same ministerial association. However, Jerry had accepted the pastorate of a church about a hundred miles away, and because our churches were in different ministerial associations, we had lost contact with each other.

I remember being surprised when I heard from him. Surprised, not because he had called, but because of the anxiety in his voice when he said, "Ed, I'm two blocks away at a coffee shop, and I wonder if you can come over and talk to me."

I replied, "Of course. I'll see you in about five minutes."

We talked for over two hours. He told me about the conflict in his church.

The names were different, but the scenario was well known. Both he and the members of the church had realized after six months that there was a mismatch. The church was in a small, conservative, county-seat type community. Jerry was in his early thirties, a mixture of a "new breed" minister and strong evangelical theology. This was his second church. He had been anxious to move because the first church had barely

157

provided subsistence-level income for himself, his wife, and his two small children. Neither he nor the church had any skills in clarifying their goals and expectations. Everyone involved had been as honest and above-board as they knew how. But the overriding consideration in the interviews had been that semi-magical belief that God would stop Jerry's being called if this was not the place where he was supposed to go. Some of the members of the congregation indicated that they had had reservations at the time his name was presented to the congregation for approval, but they had followed the age-old tradition of putting confidence in the pastor search committee. They believed that if God was leading the committee and the young man, they should stifle their reservations and vote in support of the recommendation.

Even though there were problems, there was hope that they could be worked out. Both the pastor and the congregation leaned heavily on the wisdom and maturity of the chairman of deacons. Jerry had been wise in seeking out the advice of the deacon chairman and had followed many of his suggestions. In turn, the congregation had been willing to accept the positive, hopeful stance of this long-time church leader. But his unexpected death left a vacuum within the leadership of the congregation and within the minister's support system. My friend didn't know where to turn.

Upon the chairman's death, the vice-chairman of the deacons assumed responsibility and in a few weeks called a special meeting of the deacons without the pastor's knowledge. He had indicated to the other deacons that they needed to look into some of the problems the church was facing. In the meeting it soon became evident that the problem which the new chairman had in mind was the pastor. The meeting broke up after some heated exchange. Many of the deacons realized the shortcomings of the pastor but did not believe that a secret meeting should have been called. It was obvious to several that the new deacon chairman was seeking to grasp by force the power which had been given to the former chairman as a result of his recognized leadership.

Because several deacons felt that the meeting was a mistake, they had no qualms about revealing the meeting to the pastor and disclosing what had happened. Their action put the pastor and the chairman at crossed swords.

My friend wanted to know what to do. We explored the various possibilities and reached some conclusions: First, he would meet with the deacons and try to clarify the points of difference; second, he would indicate to the deacons my willingness to participate in an advisory role; third, he would take the steps available in our congregational polity to try to relocate. We were both rather pessimistic about relocation because he had been at the church only one year.

After my first meeting with Jerry, two of the deacons asked if they could talk to me. We covered much of the same ground that my friend and I had. The deacons indicated that there were problems but were convinced that the congregation did not want to dismiss the pastor. Furthermore, they would try to work together with him, although they also agreed that it had been a mistake for him to have come to that particular church. The deacons assured me that they would continue to pray and seek God's help. I felt a certain sense of dismay because I took their statement to mean that they were not going to actively pursue a course of confrontation—speaking the truth in love. Rather, they appeared to be saying that they were going to do their best, be passive, and wait on God for action.

I initiated the second meeting with Jerry. I was going in the general direction of his home, so I called and asked if we could get together for a cup of coffee. There was a tremendous change in my friend. He was calm. We talked in generalities for a few minutes and then I asked, "What have you decided to do?"

He replied, "I've thought about this matter and prayed about it. I've come to these conclusions: God called me here; therefore, until the Lord leads me to another church or until the church fires me, I'm going to stay."

Two alternatives—until the Lord leads me or until the church fires me. I asked myself, "Isn't there a third alternative? What about negotiating an intentional ministry?"

The phrase "negotiating an intentional ministry" is a phrase that I had happened across just a few weeks before the meeting I have just described. It is a phrase that pulls together many things that I had felt at a gut-level for twenty-five years. It describes a style of ministry that can bring fulfillment to both clergy and laity.

This style of ministry is presented in *Creating an Intentional Ministry,* edited by John Biersdorf. Its rationale and its definition are found in the following statement: "We believe effectiveness and faithfulness in ministry result from negotiating an intentional ministry. Negotiation refers to the quality of relationships and transactions by which ministry is carried out. Intentionality refers to the style of faith and proactive behavior that is at the heart of effective ministry."[1]

I want to apply this style of ministry to two problems which I have observed—the lack of competence among ministers and the dilemma faced when it is evident that congregation and minister are moving toward destructive conflict.

AN UNNECESSARY REALITY—INCOMPETENCE

Many ministers are incompetent. Both Edward Golden and Laile Bartlett have described this incompetence and enumerated some of the complex causes.

Writing from the viewpoint of placement, Dr. Golden says that because our placement systems are so ineffective, "there are many persons in ministry who have not demonstrated effectiveness insofar as anyone knows. There are many who have not been successful." Some of the results of this condition are "poor morale, disillusioned churches, disharmony within the families of these clergymen, and the utter waste of a vast potential of human resources."[2]

The condition described by Dr. Golden exists because many church placement systems are little more than information centers supplying the names of individuals available or interested in a church position. Therefore, when a church receives the name of a minister from a church placement office, there is no guarantee that the individual recommended has the gifts necessary to minister in that particular church. Moreover, the placement office recommendations lull many congregations into believing that the suggested minister will meet their needs simply because his name came from a trusted service. Such was the case with the mismatch which I described in the opening paragraphs of this chapter. The members of the church had more confidence in Jerry's recommendation than it deserved because they were not aware that the placement office did not provide a thorough screening procedure for each person that they suggested.

Laile Bartlett describes a condition equally destructive. She contends that the nature of parish work has not been clearly recognized.

> As one church management consultant has suggested: "The parish *is* politics! Let's admit it and train for it."
>
> If this is shocking, it is also plain to see that clergy fall into two camps: those who enjoy "helping people relate and make their own decisions," and those who complain that "having a hundred bosses drives me crazy" and despair, as one of these latter put it, "of an institution with as imprecise a goal and commitment as an umbrella."
>
> The two camps have the same religious concern for the whole person, the same ethical fervor. Both views are valid. Each is appropriate for the person involved. But they have conflicting views of personal ministry. Those who enjoy *people* and *process* and *politics,* who are adept at keeping the show on the road and moving it along, are more "successful" in the specialty of presiding over a parish.
>
> Others, more task-, or product-oriented, or with single-track minds and the impatient urge to follow a particular channel— social action, theological scholarship, sensitivity training—are ministers, yes, but more suited to other kinds of ministerial specialty: teaching, counseling, campus ministries, for example.
>
> In the long run, the parish actually functions as a sort of screen, screening *in* those with political aptitude, screening *out* those who lack it. The woods are full of this second type who have, sooner or later, made their way out, or have been helped out, of the parish.[3]

Bartlett then asserts that incompetence in ministry could be solved if the difference between ministerial inclinations and talents were clearly recognized. She calls upon denominations to capitalize on the scriptural "diversity of gifts" in their recruitment, training, and placement of ministers.

I agree with Golden and Bartlett that incompetence in ministry is a major problem, and with their descriptions of some of its causes. However, I take the issue one step further and contend that incompetence is an unnecessary reality.

Why Ministers Are Incompetent. The quotations from Golden and Bartlett indicate that there are several reasons for ministerial incompetence. Some have to do with the denomination, but others relate to the action or lack of action of both clergy and laity.

First, *many ministers have determined their areas of ministry on the basis of their call experience and have neglected a long hard look at their gifts.* The call experience, as I have discussed it in this book, is an experience with strong emotional and mystical overtones (see chapter 4). When not interpreted along with gifts these emotional and mystical qualities can lock ministers into vocational pursuits for which they are not fitted. This is particularly true when it is assumed that the mystical and emotional qualities cannot be discussed or interpreted by the community of faith.

Specifically, many ministers believe that God has called them to be pastors. And they believe that to pursue another church-related vocation or a non-church-related vocation would be to turn their backs on God. Therefore, they pursue their task as pastor with great diligence. The result is tragic when these ministers do not have gifts to be pastors—tragic because they find themselves trapped by their theological interpretation of call. They cannot leave the pastorate, for this would be desertion. And when they cannot fulfill their tasks because they do not have the gifts for being a pastor, the end result is incompetence—incompetence made doubly sad because it is often coupled with sincerity and an earnest desire to be effective.

A second cause for incompetence is *lack of professional growth.* For many years it was assumed that basic seminary training provided skills to carry one through his whole ministry. This was the view when I graduated some thirty years ago. Today it is recognized by both educators and ministers that education for ministry must span the whole career. This approach is made imperative by the rapid and radical changes in the forms and context of ministry.

Although it has been implicit in the writings of many individuals, Mark Rouch has done a great service for the field of continuing education by explicitly relating continuing education to competence in ministry. He states, "Competence is the primary outcome of effective continuing education."[4] Moreover, Dr. Rouch's thesis is that effective continuing education breeds competence and, in turn, competence breeds a further desire to learn.

Unfortunately, a large percentage of ministers never avail themselves of continuing education experiences. A group of veteran continuing educators estimated that in the early 1970s, only 10 percent of all United States ministers participated in organized learning programs on an annual basis, while an additional 15 to 20 percent took part in one event every three years.[5] Therefore, attention must be given to involving a larger percentage of ministers in continuing education.

A third cause, closely related to the second, is the *lack of peer supervision*. This lack of supervision permits the growth of two problems which lead to incompetence. First is the lack of discipline in work habits. James Hatley tells how, in his experience as a minister, he came to the "realization that of all vocations in the world that of ministry is the greatest invitation to laziness of any vocation I know. I could get up when I pleased, drink my coffee, wander around the church, go downtown, shake hands, come home whenever I wanted to, and I reported to absolutely no one. It was difficult to come to the realization that I wasted valuable time. I would go home at night with a sense of guilt that I hadn't made all the hospital calls that I should have made. I had enough guilt to be uncomfortable but not enough guilt for self-discipline."[6]

Lack of peer supervision makes it difficult for a minister to grow in competence in the varied skills of his vocation. A minister has no peer group to evaluate his or her skills as a preacher/teacher, as a counselor, as an administrator, as a motivator. As a result a minister can develop serious flaws in the various facets of his professional responsibility.

Another reason for incompetence is the *lack of a relationship between competence and advancement and/or effective placement.* While the major incentive for competence should be service and not advancement, it is true that where there is no adequate recognition for competence there is a decline in the incentive to achieve it.

The authors of *Ex-Pastors* claim that the personnel practices in many churches are poor and that pastors sometimes receive shabby treatment in areas related to placement. Therefore, they affirm that clergymen "need some organization which functions the same as a labor union or a professional association, where concerted action is possible." In addition, they state, "Our study reveals a clear need for pastors to increase their power."[7] I interpret this need for power as a need to find more accurate placement and to provide opportunities to use areas of competence. I would confirm that where there are rewards for competence and that where pastors have a greater voice in decisions related to their vocations, incompetence will decline.

Ease in moving from one church to another has contributed to incompetence. When the "barrel" of sermons begins to run dry it is easier to move than to face the difficult task of studying for sermon preparation. It has been said that it is far more honest for a pastor who has been in the ministry for fifteen years to say that he has had three years' experience five times over rather than to say that he has had fifteen years' experience.

Short pastorates have not only kept ministers from developing skills which come from length of time in one location, but have also made it possible for ministers to continue to make the same mistakes over and over again. Bad habits developed in the first pastorate are often repeated in the second, third, and fourth.

The modern oversupply of ministers is making moving more and more difficult. But this condition may have some beneficial side effects such as causing ministers to face up to the task of increasing their competence rather than escaping it by moving.

Another factor that contributes to incompetence is what James Glasse has called *the "complain-conform syndrome."* When ministers get together they practically drown each other with tears of self-pity over the abuses which they are experiencing from their congregations. While there is a good measure of exaggeration in most displays of self-pity, it is a fact that ministers have too many demands placed on them. For example, it is unrealistic to ask that one person be equally competent in preaching, counseling, crisis ministry, administration, and fund-raising, or that a minister attend all committee meetings.

The problem is that ministers do very little about these demands. After complaining, they continue to conform to unrealistic expectations. This type of fatalistic mentality leads to incompetence because they continue to function in areas for which they are either not suited or not trained. Ministers must take greater initiative in correcting unrealistic expectations.

If a long list of reasons can be given why ministers aren't competent, just as long a list can be given as to why ministers do not need to be incompetent.

Why Incompetence Is Unnecessary. The style of ministry based on intentionality and negotiation points in the direction of overcoming incompetence. This style of ministry involves clergy and laity. Both must have a sense of direction for the church and its ministry. Both must be prepared to set goals, to seek to achieve them, and to be open to negotiation when differences arise. There are several very important steps which both clergy and laity can take to overcome incompetence.

First, *accept personal responsibility for the proper functioning of the office of the pastor.* Again, this applies to both clergy and laity. The minister needs to see his responsibility for intentionality in light of the teachings in the parable of the talents. The pastor has accepted an office, just as the men in the parable accepted sums of money. They accepted the money with the understanding that they would be responsible for its use. The servant who hid his money in the ground gave as reasons for his action that he was afraid and that the master was harsh. The master had no sympathy with these answers. But neither did he contradict the servant's evaluation of him as a harsh master. Instead, he said that this did not give the servant an excuse for inaction. At least the servant should have given the money to the bankers rather than have shown complete irresponsibility by hiding the money in the ground.

Speaking as a pastor, I say that too many of us excuse our inaction because the tasks are difficult. We abdicate our personal responsibilities because the tasks in the pastorate are so overwhelming. But personal responsibility and initiative are as much a part of ministry as prayer and dependence upon God are, and we must recognize this.

However, the entire responsibility does not lie with the pastor. The laity must also exercise personal responsibility for the competence of their pastors. There is a sense in which laymen consider themselves not skilled in matters related to the church and its ministry. This is not so. In its true sense the word *laity* means "the people of God." The difference between clergy and laity is one of office. While it is true that lay people may not be aware of the technical studies involved in preparation for the office of the pastor, they are able to judge the exercise of that office. Therefore, as fellow priests the laity have a responsibility for the competent functioning of those holding the office of pastor.

An example from my first pastorate can illustrate the point. One member told me that my Scripture reading was not effective because I read too rapidly. As a result of his observation, I started the practice of reading the passage of Scripture out loud and slower several times before the worship service. In the years which have followed, I have been complimented on several occasions for making the reading of the Scripture intelligible and meaningful.

When both clergy and laity assume responsibility for competence in ministry, a major blow will be dealt to incompetence.

Second, *develop and use appropriate feedback channels.* Every pastor knows that the members of the congregation are judging his or her competence in many different ways. "Roast preacher" for Sunday dinner may alleviate the frustrations of the parishioners, but it is an ineffective feedback system and does little to develop ministerial competence. By means of appropriate feedback channels, the congregation can help a minister understand how his competence or incompetence is perceived.

The minister should take the responsibility for setting up these channels. He has available to him questionnaires that can be used by the congregation or by peers to give feedback and evaluate competence. The Academy of Parish Clergy has identified twenty skills as basic to competence in the ministry. And Union Theological Seminary in Virginia has developed a list of seventy-seven competences that can be used as a standard for assessing knowledge and skills in ministry.[8]

Eugene Timmons of the Judicatory Career Support System of Kansas City has developed a practice whereby a group of ministers are evaluated both by the congregation and by each other. The ministers distribute evaluation forms to members of their respective congregations. They then take the responses, study them, and discuss them with the other members in their ministerial group.

The rationale for this practice is that ministers are less likely to be defensive in discussing the evaluations of performance with other ministers than with a representative group from their congregation. Therefore, there is potential for greater acceptance of the evaluation and, as a consequence, greater possibility for change. Moreover, it is felt that other ministers are able to determine with a greater degree of accuracy whether negative criticisms are justified.

Because of the many demands made on him, it is easy for a minister to fall into the trap of reacting rather than acting—of greasing the squeaking wheel. The pastor must *determine priorities*. In turn, the congregation must do the same thing. Then through negotiation, they can work together to *set common goals*.

An example of negotiation in setting priorities is the writing of this book. In July of 1979 I spent four weeks teaching at Midwestern Baptist Theological Seminary. During that time I did the first draft of four chapters. A second invitation to teach at Midwestern came in September of the same year. The deacons of my church agreed that four more weeks would be of help to me in my writing. They also agreed that this should be a priority for me and for the church. So a schedule was worked out where I preached each Sunday and did crisis visitation on Saturday. The deacons assisted the other members of the staff in hospital visitation, administration, and carrying out other duties that were normally my responsibility. By means of setting priorities and negotiation, I was able to do my writing and work toward the goals upon which the congregation and I had agreed.

Another part of the solution lies in *continuing education for ministers*. Reference has already been made to Mark Rouch's statement that "competence is the primary outcome of effective continuing education." But for competence to be achieved, it is necessary to understand and follow Dr. Rouch's definition of continuing education. It is "an individual's personally designed learning program which begins when basic formal education ends and continues throughout a career and beyond.

An unfolding process, it links together personal study and reflection and participation in organized group events."[9] It is important to note that continuing education is based on intentionality. It is a "personally designed learning process."

In emphasizing personal intentionality, Dr. Rouch does not neglect the other side of the coin—negotiation. He points out that ministers tend to select continuing education programs consistent with their own role expectations. "If these differ from those of our laity, continuing education only prepares us to do better what they do not expect of us."[10] Therefore it is important to negotiate with the congregation the kinds of continuing education to be pursued. Otherwise, continuing education can lead to a widening of the gap between what the clergy and laity consider to be important and vital in ministry and can serve as an irritant to the members who see the pastor as going off to study for his own enjoyment instead of tending to business.

If continuing education is to become a feasible reality for pastors, congregations need to provide time, monies, and incentives for it. As recently as 1968, 71 percent of Protestant ministers received no time for continuing education and 78 percent received no money for it. Fortunately, that picture is changing. Today, many denominations are providing funds as well as incentives. The United Church of Canada requires each pastor to enroll in three weeks of continuing education per year. Where the church polity is that of a congregational form of government, the official board can provide funds and require a certain number of weeks of continuing education in a given year.

Funds and expectations are not enough, however. Incentives are needed because many ministers do not use the opportunities available. Connolly Gamble, a leader in the field of continuing education for ministers, has pointed out six obstacles to continuing education. First, some persons do not understand the importance of continuing education. Second, the minister does not always have ready-made opportunities to share the results of study. Third, it is hard to maintain a disciplined life. Fourth, there is the problem of time and money. Fifth, the church as a system offers little incentive to continuing education. Sixth, for some ministers continuing education is the memory of a painful seminary career now seen as largely irrelevant.[11] These obstacles are real and ministers need help to overcome them.

The effectiveness of continuing education is increased when ministers involve their peers in their learning process. This is true both for study which is done in local groups and for that done in organized courses and seminars. For example, in the mid-fifties I was conscious of my lack of understanding of the writings of Albert Camus. I set for myself the goal of reading his major works. However, it was not until I joined two other pastors in making a commitment to a regular program of reading, studying, and discussing Camus's writings that I reached my goal.

My experience has also proven that I learn more from organized courses and seminars when I attend them with a colleague. In fact, this is so true that I make it a practice not to attend continuing education events by myself. I find that with a colleague we exchange feedback and suggestions for specific applications of the material studied as we discuss what we have learned.

The importance of sharing continuing education with peers is underscored by Gamble. He asserts that peer group participation is essential as one of the steps to overcoming obstacles to continuing education. Peer involvement makes it easier to keep a high priority on personal learning.

Finally, I would recommend *participation in the program of a Career Development Center.* Increased interest in career development has created a proliferation of career counseling services. In suggesting the importance of career evaluation and planning, I am speaking specifically of the services available at those centers affiliated with and accredited by the Church Career Development Council based at 475 Riverside Drive in New York City.

These centers focus on the needs of church professionals. The first center was opened by the United Presbyterian Church in November of 1965 at Princeton, New Jersey. One of the needs that this particular center sought to meet was that of providing guidance for development of a personal and systematic program of continuing education.

Gamble also relates the services of a career development center to continuing education. He writes, "A career counselor in a regional ecumenical agency can help you assess your needs where you are ministering, and at various stages of your life. The counselor can act as your advisor, support, coordinator, and colleague. I know a good number of ministers who regard their two and a half days at a career center as a turning point in their lives, a time when they began to perceive more accurately their strengths and limits."[12]

The Church Career Development Council identifies the purposes of the thirteen centers affiliated with them as follows:

- To provide an assessment of abilities and to guide professional church workers in the establishing of reasonable and meaningful career goals.
- To provide professional assistance in enabling professional church workers to use their capabilities more fully and effectively.
- To give guidance in developing a continuing education program to widen their range of capabilities.
- To provide vocational and occupational assistance to those considering leaving the pastoral ministry.
- To provide professional guidance for spouses of clients.
- To assess and give guidance to candidates for a church occupation.
- To give professional guidance to those facing a career crisis.[13]

When clergy and laity take the stance of negotiating an intentional ministry and avail themselves of the many opportunities already at hand, it can be said that incompetence in ministry is unnecessary.

An Avoidable Reality—Destructive Conflict

Destructive church conflicts are a reality. And the number of such conflicts is increasing. Indeed, the problem has become acute enough that in more than one of the judicatories affiliated with Southern Baptists funds are provided for ministers who resign under pressure (i.e., are fired).

I would be less than honest if I did not say that I write from an experiential point of view. I have been involved in conflicts which, in retrospect, could have been dealt with in a more constructive fashion. I have served as a consultant in church conflicts. And I have served a church which was traumatized by a major conflict.

There are two patterns which I have observed in church conflicts—both are destructive. The first is to avoid open and overt conflict. In these cases the minister relocates; the causes for the conflict are not acknowledged and, therefore, are never dealt with. The second involves choosing sides, with accusations and counter-accusations. Before the open conflict takes place, many church members withdraw their support of time, talents, and finances, while others move to neighboring congregations. The final result of open conflict can be twofold. Either a major split in the church occurs with the pastor remaining with one of the factions or the church remains intact and forces the pastor to resign under pressure.

In each of these patterns destructive forces are at work—self-righteousness, bitterness, intransigency, resentment, lack of self-understanding, failure to grow. Ministers move to other congregations unaware of their shortcomings, bitter at their critics, and prepared never to get themselves into the position where the laity has the upper hand. Congregations, in turn, become fragmented, lose enthusiasm, blame the pastor or other members for all of the problems, and do not develop an attitude of confession which can lead to self-understanding, change, and growth.

Is it possible that these patterns are an "avoidable reality"? I believe they are.

Causes of Destructive Church Conflict. One of the primary causes of destructive church conflict is incompetence on the part of the minister. The previous discussion within this chapter of that issue provides a basis for understanding the reasons for incompetence and also some of the solutions to the problem.

Incompetence can lead to conflict because ministers have a difficult time acknowledging their inadequacies. They are tempted to believe that they can walk on water. Similarly, congregations also have a difficult time accepting pastors' limitations. They expect them to be competent in all areas, and when one is not, there is a sense of disappointment that can lead to conflict.

The problem is compounded when pastors view their areas

of incompetence as having no consequence on their ministry. A case in point is administrative competence. Seminarians do not have the learning readiness to develop skills in administration, because they have not experienced firsthand the administrative responsibilities of a pastor. Moreover, their models of ministry place administrative duties at the bottom of the value scale. When they are finally confronted with the realities of administration, many ministers cannot overcome their prejudices enough to receive the necessary training. As it becomes apparent, church members criticize, and rightly so, the minister's administrative incompetence. At this point, if there is no negotiation between minister and congregation, the events which have been set in motion lead to conflict.

A second cause of church conflict is role conflict. The example just given involves not only incompetence but also role conflict. The minister does not see administrative skills as a part of his role as pastor. Therefore, he resists the requests of the congregation to develop skills in administration. As stated above, if there is no negotiation, then the inevitable result is conflict.

Another major cause of conflict is poor interpersonal relationships. Some would contend that this is the primary cause. I disagree. Incompetence and role conflict often lead to conflict between pastor and congregation, and it is easy to assume that the cause has been poor interpersonal relationships. It is true that in all destructive conflicts there are poor interpersonal relationships, but my contention is that poor interpersonal relationships are sometimes a symptom, not always the primary cause, of conflict.

However, situations do exist in which poor interpersonal relationships can lead to conflict. Such conflicts, which are often based on negative responses to authority figures, usually develop between the pastor and the congregation or between the pastor and other members of the staff. It is a well-known fact that many people have difficulties with authority figures. In a church the minister is an authority figure, and there are power structures which include other authority figures. As a result, a church is fertile ground for this type of conflict.

Sometimes the conflict results from a minister's inability to relate to congregation members who are authority figures, such as community leaders, wealthy businessmen, corporation presidents. The problem becomes more acute when the authority figures are individuals who have appropriated the authority for themselves rather than having received it by delegation. In other words, church bosses cause conflict.

Conflict arises also when the pastor is a church boss. Unfortunately, many congregations encourage the pastor to be a church boss because he is a professional. And the tendency of the lay person is to permit the professional to exercise great authority. When this is added to the common practice of "let the pastor do it," and he does, a perfect setting for the pastor to become a dictator is created. And dictators cause conflicts in voluntary associations.

The senior minister and other ministers on the staff are also likely to have conflicts. The same dynamics that relate to conflict between authority figures also work in this setting. Moreover, there is an added dimension if the other ministers and staff are looked upon as "hired help" rather than as colleagues of the senior minister. Many churches even encourage this attitude. Some expect staff members to look for other positions when the senior minister resigns or retires. This demeans the position of staff members and opens the door for conflict.

Conflict is also caused by abrasive personalities. One minister caused destructive conflict by habitually hanging up the telephone when he received complaints about his style of ministry. Such a display of arrogance will inevitably lead to conflict. Many church people—both lay and clergy—need to become aware of their own rudeness and take steps to alleviate it.

Sexual impropriety by the pastor is another conflict-producing problem. However, the conflict is often less destructive if the problems are openly confronted and admitted. It is then possible to take corrective action, which, in all the cases that I have known, has been resignation. Whether or not this should always be true may be a question of debate. In fact, it is at this point that the conflict usually develops. Some members believe that forgiveness should involve the opportunity to function in the same position. Others believe that forgiveness does not necessarily involve remaining in the same position in the same church.

The conflict is more destructive when there is evidence of sexual improprieties which is neither confronted nor admitted. In such cases, those who are aware of the sexual improprieties seek, on other grounds, to have the pastor resign or be dismissed. A smokescreen is erected to avoid the issue. Conflict then arises because church members either object to dismissal on the basis of the smokescreen reasons, or they object to dismissal because they don't believe the rumors of sexual improprieties.

A fifth cause for church conflict is inadequate models for the role of the pastor held by the congregation. Most church members look upon the pastor as the president of the corporation. Therefore, when the corporation drops in sales and in profits (i.e., church attendance and contributions decline), they believe the president of the corporation must resign or be fired. Conflict occurs because pastors and other church members do not view the pastor's role as that of president of a corporation. However, such a view is so dominant that I can't think of any pastors (except in situations in which there have been sexual improprieties) who have been fired when the church was growing in numbers and financial receipts!

The Pattern of Destructive Conflict. At this point I need to emphasize that I am speaking specifically about destructive conflict. There is no way to avoid all conflict, and conflict as creative tension can be valuable in the life of the church for both clergy and laity.

Before presenting some answers to destructive conflict, I want to describe what happens in the typical church conflict. The conflict generally begins when the minister and the official board have difficulty clarifying the priorities for the church. The difficulty stems from the fact that one, or more likely several in the group, including the minister, are vague about the purpose of the church and its ministry. The lack of clarity relates both to the meaning of the church as the body of Christ and to the meaning of the task of that particular congregation. Added to the lack of clarity is what appears to be a basic conflict between most clergy and laity—the conflict over whether the primary task of the church is to comfort or to challenge. Often the clergy places a greater emphasis on challenge and the laity, on comfort.

Because of the confusion and conflict a stalemate develops.

Discussions tend to go in circles and very little action is taken. The church is adrift without a rudder. The minister withdraws and as a result, the members of the official board complain that they can't get through to him. He listens politely but does not hear what is being said. He often becomes defensive and tends to lash out through sermons at those who oppose him. The opposition is labeled as immature Christians who do not know the true meaning of Christian discipleship.

As the tension mounts, members of the official board begin to withdraw in their participation. At first, withdrawal may manifest itself only as non-participation in the discussions. This is followed by non-attendance at meetings which leads either to waiting to rotate off the board or to resignation. Such action is taken in the name of harmony and out of a sense of frustration developed from an inability to solve the stalemate.

The withdrawal only aggravates the problem. Those who are most able to solve the problems through confrontation and negotiation are now on the sidelines. The "power vacuum" is filled by less capable and knowledgeable members. Generally, these are individuals who are on the "side of the pastor." They complain that the pastor is being persecuted by the power structure.

The former leadership, or power structure, continues either a silent disapproval or begins to withhold their financial contributions. The rift widens. The financial structure of the church is endangered.

At this point open hostilities are expressed at board meetings, congregational meetings, and in private discussions. The congregation is polarized between the pastor's supporters and his opponents.

In the next stage a few members begin leaving and going to other congregations. Others stop attending while keeping their membership in the church. The possibility for reconciliation has passed. Only two options remain. The pastor resigns, or the congregation fires him. In either case both the congregation and the pastor are traumatized.

When the pastor leaves he has the options of going to another church, hurt, bitter, and confused; going to a position as a denominational executive; or going to a non-church-related vocation.

Members of the congregation also have several options. Some

members give up attending church altogether. Others develop great anger and resentment over how unchristian Christians can be and become openly antagonistic toward the church. Yet others continue to do their best, but with less enthusiasm than before. In the end there have been no winners, only losers.

Answers for Destructive Church Conflict. The first answer is for the pastor and church to relate to each other in an attitude of negotiation based on intentionality. The key is negotiation. However, there can be no negotiation where there is no understanding of the purpose of the church and its ministry. It is this understanding that I call intentionality. When both clergy and laity have a clear understanding of what they are about they can avoid destructive conflict by relating to each other with an attitude open to negotiation. It needs to be recognized, however, that negotiation means a willingness to accept legitimate conflict as a creative force.

The attitude of negotiation can and should be based on several theological truths: the priesthood of the believer, the diversity of gifts, and the reality of sin.

The doctrine of the priesthood of the believer asserts that all Christians have spiritual insights which should be used for the building up of the body of Christ. Neither the pastor nor the members have a special pipeline to God. Therefore, it only confuses the issue when either clergy or laity resort to non-negotiable terms such as, "God spoke to me at this point," or "God has led me to take this position." In a church it should always be assumed that both clergy and laity are open to God's leadership. Moreover, it should be the practice of both to seek God's leadership. If the phrases "God spoke to me" or "God has led me" are to be used, they should be qualified to indicate how and in what way God spoke and led. Then communication can begin again.

Negotiation which is based on the understanding of gifts can solve most problems related to role conflict and inadequate role models of the pastor. In teaching seminarians I have found that many have a secret longing that God will endow a lay person with gifts of administrative abilities in each church where they will be pastors! Such an attitude is wishful thinking. A pastor can no more relinquish the role of administrator than he can the role of preacher.

When pastor and congregation assume that the pastor is gifted equally in all areas of his ministry, the stage is set for destructive conflict. There needs to be a continuous examination of the gifts of the pastor and congregation as they face ever-changing demands in ministry. Through cooperation and negotiation most new situations can be met successfully.

Pastors can be wrong! Deacons can be off base! All are human beings and therefore sinners. (We would hope, sinners saved by grace.) This reality can be coped with only through negotiation. Ministers need to admit their humanity and the laity needs to accept it. And the same holds true for the laity.

Although I have emphasized the theological foundations of negotiation, I would agree with John Biersdorf that negotiation "seems to be the most powerful word to sum up the professional life-style and work of the minister who serves the church as a voluntary organization."[14] Biersdorf presents a convincing case that negotiation takes its shape from one of the fundamental characteristics of American religious life, namely, voluntarism. He writes, "American churches and synagogues have been from the beginning, and continue to be, voluntary associations—democratic in nature even when official doctrine holds otherwise, forced to adapt to cultural, social, and economic influences, and to hold laity in high importance as they continually renegotiate their existence on the basis of the felt importance of the services they offer."[15] Therefore, for theological as well as cultural reasons, I see negotiation as one answer to destructive church conflict.

Another answer is the exercise of authority by the legitimate power structure in the church. I find too many lay persons wanting to be nice, pleasant, and "Christian" in the face of destructive forces. They define "Christian" as "let God do it." There are as many in the laity as in the clergy who take the attitude of passivity expressed in my minister friend's phrase "until the Lord leads or the church fires me." This passivity is not faith; it is placing the monkey on God's back.

All the power structures in the church must use their authority with intentionality and in a spirit of negotiation. Such an attitude is demanded where there is gross ministerial incompetence. After repeated attempts to increase the competence of the minister have failed, he should be asked and/or forced to resign. Such action should be taken in a spirit of patience and responsibility. Where authority needs to be exercised it should be done keeping in mind the goal of helping both the pastor and the congregation.

I find more cases of underused authority in churches than I do of overused or misused. Churches that take two to three years to fire a pastor do not help themselves or the pastors they dismiss.

Growth in interpersonal relationships is a third answer. This answer is self-explanatory. There is a constant emphasis today in both religious and secular circles to improve skills in interpersonal relationships. The small group movement has added impetus to the development of positive ways of relating to one another. I would add that within the church these skills should flow from a confessional approach—an approach where each person acknowledges the log in his own eye and seeks conscientiously to remove it before pointing out the splinter in the eye of his neighbor.

Clergy and laity need to agree on an everyone's-fault divorce. Such an agreement would provide an answer to destructive conflict when all other measures have failed. There are times when there is no answer other than for a church and its pastor to dissolve their relationship. When this happens, it should be with the attitude that it is everyone's fault. This is not to say that there should be an unwholesome mouthing of *mea culpa,* but that both clergy and laity should recognize themselves as individuals with shortcomings who have made mistakes.

When there is an agreement that divorce is everyone's fault, the climate is set for growth and change. The pastor is able to withdraw from the relationship and examine where he or she has failed, where he or she needs to grow. The same process can be followed by the congregation. This would avoid what I consider to be the most destructive force in a church conflict, namely, the development of an attitude of self-righteousness, placing all the blame on the other party.

An everyone's-fault divorce should include several practical steps for the pastor. He should seek greater self-understanding through counseling with peers or professionals. He should approach relocation with openness and carefully study the expectations of the new position. He should develop a program of continuing education based on needs identified in the conflict and in counseling. If possible he should delay relocation for three to six months.

The congregation also needs to take several steps. Financial provisions should be made for the pastor and his family during time of relocation. An interim pastor should be called to give the church time to overcome the trauma of divorce. Churches as well as individuals lose a sense of self-worth in a divorce, and time is needed to heal this wound. Churches should enter into an intensive time of self-study. Even if the conflict and divorce were the result of clear-cut differences about the meaning of the church, it is important to determine why and how the marriage took place. Caution should be exercised in the call of another pastor.

*　　*　　*

Negotiating an intentional ministry can be a means of dealing with two pressing problems in the life of the church—incompetent ministers and destructive conflicts. These two problems can and should be *unnecessary* and *avoidable* realities.

Chapter 10

Placement—
A Nine-Letter Word

There are some four-letter words which are frowned upon in polite society, but few four-letter words cause as much furor in some church circles as the nine-letter word "placement." This word conjures up thoughts of pastoral initiative, bureaucratic interference, computers, human decisions, absence of the Holy Spirit, denial of God's call, lack of faith in God and most everything else which is an anathema in our understanding of God's initiative and action in the lives of ministers.

Several unhealthy consequences follow our failure to discuss openly and publicly the question of placement. First, we neglect our responsibility to seek solutions for what is recognized privately as one of the most pressing problems facing ministers. Publicly we say little, and therefore, we do not harness our resources to solve this problem.

Another consequence of our avoidance of the question is that we permit and passively encourage a system which involves deceit, subterfuge, and feelings of self-loathing. For example, a pastor believes that he should move to another church. He becomes aware of a church that does not have a pastor. He contacts a friend and asks him to recommend him to that church. The minister asking for the recommendation knows that his friend cannot tell the church that he has been asked by the person he is recommending to write the commendation. The tacit understanding is that the initiative has come from the person making the recommendation.

The friend generally writes a letter something like this: "I want to recommend to you John Doe. He is the pastor of Peaceful St. James Baptist Church." At this point the writer of the letter, depending on how he feels the church may react, will take one of the following tacks: "John Doe would probably consider a change of pastorates at this time" (the more honest approach); "John Doe is very happy where he is but if the challenge is great enough, he would possibly consider a call to another church" (the more dishonest approach, but the one which will carry greater weight with a pastor search committee). In either case, no mention is made that the initiative came from John Doe.

The minister asking for the recommendation is aware that he is participating in deceit and is implicating a friend as well. His actions prompt strong feelings of guilt and self-loathing. I can attest to this statement, because I have been there.

I was pastor of a church where I found myself going under for the third time. As I look back on the situation, I see that I made many mistakes. But the decision to leave that church was, I still believe, the correct decision. Contacting friends seemed to be the best alternative. I spoke first to a denominational executive. I found it extremely difficult to go and say, "I need help. I want you to recommend me to another church." The executive listened attentively but in essence told me to have greater faith in God. I left that interview carrying a greater load of guilt and feeling that I was a mighty small person because I didn't have enough faith to wait for God's leading.

Several weeks passed and my suppressed feelings erupted and caused me to take further action. This time I wrote to two friends. Again, it was difficult to admit defeat and request that they contact a church and suggest my name, but not tell the church that I was the initiator. I maintain that any system which causes an individual to be demeaned for seeking relocation needs to be changed.

Another unhealthy consequence of our present system is that of a mismatch between congregation and pastor. This is usually followed by a period of agony in which neither the minister nor the church are able to take effective action. My interest in doing something about fulfillment in ministry received its first major impetus from my involvement in a situation in which a mismatch occurred. The incident happened at a church where I had been pastor. I knew the congregation well, and the new pastor was a personal friend. When it became obvious that a mistake had been made, I permitted both the pastor and some of the deacons to speak to me privately. Because all communications were confidential, I was not free to tell either party that I was talking to the other. This was my grave error.

The deacons' agony was genuine, and they were open to my suggestions. I recommended that they confront the pastor and also talk to a denominational executive. They did both, but with little response. The pastor had no suggestions. He knew that he and the church were mismatched, but he didn't know how to extricate himself from the situation. The denominational executive indicated that he had no power to act.

In turn, I tried to support the pastor. I pointed out that the problem was not with him as an individual. I offered to recommend him wherever possible. However, I knew what little value my recommendation would have considering the pastor had been at his present church for only six months. I did not have the courage or the faith to say to a pastor search committee, "There has been a mismatch. This pastor must move both for his sake and for the sake of the church." Inevitably the pastor learned that I had been talking to some of the deacons. He accused me of double-dealing. In the end, I lost a good friend.

The experiences related to placement which I have been describing are underscored and clarified by two statements. The first was written by Dr. Golden. After observing that one of the major problems facing some denominations today is the oversupply of persons in the ministry, he writes:

> Almost all the denominations have formal systems for mobility. However, most denominational executives would immediately concur that the informal systems are more operative. Most informal personnel systems are based upon four factors which are difficult to assess. Nevertheless, these factors function within the informal system of mobility. They are: (1) a person's effectiveness (whatever this means), (2) his successfulness (whatever this means), (3) his political contacts (who will speak favorably in his behalf), and (4) who will not relate unfavorable comments (refusal to speak

honestly). There are many persons in ministry who have not demonstrated effectiveness insofar as anyone knows. There are many who have not been successful. There are others who are politically isolated, naive, or conflicted. As a result it is my hunch that many thousands of Protestant clergymen are frozen in positions or churches, and their careers checked. The consequence of this condition results in poor morale, disillusioned churches, disharmony within the families of these clergymen, and the utter waste of a vast potential of human resources. In my opinion, those professional clergymen who are frozen should be identified, then assisted in making some assessment of their capabilities and potentialities. After such an evaluation, their respective denominations must develop strategies to assist these people in developing their careers. Undoubtedly, many persons will be identified who should not be encouraged to remain in the ministry. In this case, every effort should be made to assist them in making a transfer to some other occupation. It neither serves the individual nor the church to postpone such a confrontation.[1]

The second is from *Ex-Pastors:*

There are strong data to indicate that many of the men dropped out simply because they could not endure the long time it took to get placed. During the conflict situations, most of them wanted to move and could not. This created a serious morale problem which led both to withdrawal and, in some cases, to cynical disgust. . . .

The problem is a knotty one because the autonomy of the local church in many denominations militates against change; so also does the high competitiveness of the clergy and the church free-enterprise system which is operative. Yet we must face these questions:

1. How can we provide adequate support and evaluative structures for leadership during change periods?

2. How can we provide therapeutic support where needed during change periods?

3. How can we provide faster and more accurate placement for men and women who wish to move to a new position?

"More accurate placement" is an important phrase, for placement is not enough. Professional persons need placement in positions which maximize their strong points and minimize their weak ones.[2]

If these statements are accurate, and I believe that they are, then the surprising fact is not that so many ministers and congregations have been scarred but that they have survived. Without being flippant one must say that it is only by the grace of God.

The question which is posed is whether there are any solutions which can make fulfillment both for ministers and congregations a possibility in the face of an impossible situation. I believe there are.

WHAT IT MEANS TO THE CONGREGATION

First, *stop looking for a Messiah*. The chairman of a pastor search committee wrote in anger and despair, "This church is not looking for a pastor. It's looking for a Messiah, and we're overlooking the fact that the Messiah has already come."

Such an attitude is cause for alarm. It is demeaning to the role of the layman, destructive in its impact on pastors, and harmful to the witness of the church.

Looking for a Messiah accompanies the belief that somewhere there is a specific person who can solve all the problems of a specific church, and once that perfect pastor is found, there will be no more problems in the relationship—everyone will live happily ever after!

For example, a pastor search committee in Florida was evidently looking for a Messiah when it complained there was a shortage of pastors, for the committee admitted it had received close to one hundred recommendations. Another church in Texas took eighteen months to find the right man—its "Messiah." Unfortunately, it is not uncommon for churches to take between one and two years to locate a pastor.

Moreover, too many pastor search committees refuse to examine the problems of their church. They seldom ask, "What are our problems? Why did the last pastor leave?" The assumption is that a Messiah can take care of everything.

There may even be a predetermined image of this Messiah. He must be a young man with wide experience (usually this means a man between thirty-five and thirty-nine). He should have a doctor's degree (it matters little in what field it was received or what kind of school granted it). He should have good physical appearance. A perfect set of white teeth that gleam in the dark are not to be despised. He must work well with youth (this qualification is often listed as number one). In his previous pastorate, he must have had a yearly increase of members and budget of at least 10 percent for the past few years. He must have a charming wife and a model family. He must be a fearless preacher who pleases everyone (I have not figured this one out nor have I found a good biblical example).

As I said before, looking for a Messiah hurts the laymen, the pastors, and the witness of the churches.

It is assumed that laymen have little responsibility or impact in the ministry of the church. The laity's responsibility is reduced to supporting the program of the pastor. Laymen become priests in name only. However, by looking for a Messiah, pastor search committees are unwittingly destroying pastors. Telling a minister, "You are *the one* who can help our church reach its potential," can be like offering a forbidden fruit to tempt him into thinking he is "like God." The forbidden fruit is tasted and men are destroyed. They try to become Messiahs. But when they try to walk on water, they fail.

Similarly, the witness of the church is diminished. The concept of the pastor as a Messiah is not compatible with the biblical view of the church as a body. The Spirit's gifts to each Christian are overlooked. And whenever a successful pastor is found, there is a tendency of many church members to worship him, forgetting the true Messiah.

It is not enough to talk about the problems created by churches that are looking for a Messiah. We must do something to halt the practice. Here are some suggestions.

Both churches and ministers must recognize that to search for a Messiah is to court disaster.

Churches must believe in the power of prayer as a source of God's guidance. Instead of coming to God with mind made up and a description of the next pastor already non-negotiable, be ready to listen. God speaks.

We must develop more honest communication between pastors and laymen. Let us tell each other about our strong points and our weak points. God's spirit cannot work effectively with ignorance and masks. The best way to avoid a mismatch between minister and church is for pastor search committees and prospective pastors to consider whether they can complement each other's strengths and supplement each other's weaknesses.

Remember Paul's words: "Yet we who have this spiritual treasure are like common clay pots, in order to show that the supreme power belongs to God, not to us" (2 Cor. 4:7, TEV). It is time for churches to start looking for common clay pots with whom they can serve the Messiah who has already come.

Second, *the Holy Spirit does not observe the fifty-five limit.* Biblical and historical evidence point to the fact that the Holy Spirit has never observed age limits. But there is strong evidence that pastor search committees do. In fact, evidence suggests that for most pastor search committees age fifty-five is well over the limit. In *The Pastor and the People,* Lyle Schaller suggests, "At age forty-three a person is old enough to be elected president of the United States and young enough to be voted most valuable player in the American Football League but too old for a church."[3]

The worship of youth in a pastor has led to tragic consequences for both churches and ministers. It is important to see why such a practice has arisen and then to see the harm which has been done and the benefits which can come from lifting the age limit.

Congregations as a unit as well as individual Christian adults have been concerned with the church's ministry to the youth. This is a valid concern. But the cliché that the youth are the church of tomorrow is not so much the question (this statement sounds too much like institutional preservation), as the need of youth to have every opportunity to respond to the gospel.

Youth tend to stray from the institutional church much faster than adults. This has always been true and probably will always be true. Youth is the age of experimentation and of establishing one's own values. It is, therefore, a time of rebellion against the values of the adults.

It seems to me that these truths are often overlooked and there is great panic when young people do not automatically follow the religious traditions and practices of their elders. There is no denying that it is a painful experience to see one's child rebel against what one believes to be the most essential truths of life. However, it is harmful and dishonest to put such pressure on the youth that they are coerced or manipulated into following the pattern of their elders.

The search for a pastor who can "work with the youth" is a valid pursuit, but should not necessarily be limited to a youthful pastor. Although the assumption which is often made is that youth will be turned on by someone young and turned off by someone old, and it is probably true that any age group feels more comfortable with a person closer their own age, we must not ignore the value of experience.

Another reason why there is such a demand for young pastors is that a younger person does have greater energy than an older person. A church places many demands on its pastor. So it does help to hire someone who can work ninety hours a week instead of just sixty. However, there are unanswered questions related to whether quantity is always better than quality and whether the ability to put out so much quantity may hurt the church by permitting the laity to become lazy; the minister by giving him a Messiah complex; and the minister's family by never having him or her at home.

Enthusiasm is another mark of youth. When you are young, you are always ready to do battle. And most churches need a shot in the arm like that. But one wonders if sometimes the longing for enthusiasm may not border on desiring the sensationalism of the Messiah jumping down from the pinnacle of the Temple.

The point which I have been trying to make is twofold. There are some very definite strengths in youth. Therefore, a church seeking the best possible pastor will look to the strengths of youth. However, too often the strengths are desired for the wrong reason and the strengths can be liabilities. So let there be a question mark after youth, just as there should be after any age. What is important is not the age but the gifts of the minister in relationship to the needs of the church. The crucial issue is that of more accurate placement. The needs of a congregation may be such that the gifts of a sixty-five-year-old minister are needed rather than those of a thirty-five-year-old.

When examining the issue of placement, the advantages of

having a minister who is middle-aged (or older) should be considered. There is a greater possibility that an older minister will understand the meaning of the gospel more than a younger minister. Elton Trueblood once said that you have to be at least forty years of age before you can understand the gospel. He was making the point that you have to have lived long enough to have fallen flat on your face several times to recognize how desperately you need God's grace and how bountiful is his grace.

Closely related to this observation is the fact that a middle-aged person will be less likely to believe that he or she is the Messiah. As I mentioned before, the temptation to be the Messiah is very strong for ministers. Moreover, when they succumb to the temptation they destroy themselves and diminish the witness of the congregation. There is no guarantee that age will solve this problem, but there is the likelihood that it will help. You can only go down so many times when you try to walk on water before you learn that you either have to give up your Messiah complex or drown.

The experiences of churches that have had older interim ministers speak of the effectiveness of older men and women. I have known many cases where men in their late fifties and early sixties were called to be interim pastors. Because of their age, they had been ruled out for consideration as pastor by the pastor search committee. After a period of several months the relationship was so healthy that there was a desire to call the older minister as pastor. However, in most cases this was not done because the vocational decisions of the older ministers were such that they were not in a position to return to the parish ministry.

Another benefit of considering an older minister is the opportunity for new beginnings both for the minister and the congregation. If a minister is called to a church at age thirty-five and does not move before age forty-five, then it is likely the minister will remain at the same church until he retires (approximately thirty years). I recognize that there is disagreement over whether most pastorates are too short. But when a pastor remains at one church for thirty years, in many cases, he loses his effectiveness and the congregation's spiritual growth diminishes.

It has been shown that in middle age there is a natural desire to explore new possibilities. This I believe is a God-given desire. In middle age one faces the fact that all of one's dreams are not going to become realities. A desire to accomplish certain tasks before the curtain of retirement and/or death falls upon the play of our career grows within. Such a desire and the vitality which goes with it are often dampened by staying in the same setting. Conversely, there is a burst of new enthusiasm and the ability to dream new dreams in a different setting. Therefore, when a minister in middle age is forced to remain where he is even though he desires to move, he is denied the opportunity for growth and greater service.

There are times when a church benefits by a change in pastoral leadership. Churches go through certain stages just as ministers do. It is possible for one minister to serve through several stages. However, it is more likely that each clearly definable stage calls for different leadership. For example, it is a common assumption that a minister should move within two years after a major building campaign is completed. There is some wisdom in this assumption. The minister who is successful in leading a church to provide the facilities needed for ministry is often not the minister who is able to lead the church to develop new ministries. Therefore, it is a mistake for our placement system to force a congregation to retain a pastor for twenty-five to thirty years.

Although I am writing to the congregation, it seems appropriate to include a brief statement to pastors at this point. One important exception to the implied rules of ministers over fifty-five is offered when the minister is willing to go to a smaller congregation. This is a difficult thing to do. In other vocations many people at age sixty-five are at the zenith of their productivity. And it is unfair to say that the parish ministry is the one exception where age demands fewer duties and less responsibility. Moreover it is often true that the financial demands are great at age fifty-five. In many cases the college education of the children have either just been completed or the end is in sight. After these very demanding years there is a need to focus on adequate resources for retirement. This is not a good time to take a cut in salary.

Having said that, there may be greater benefits in going to

a smaller church at a smaller salary when compared with the tensions of staying at a church where both the minister and the congregation believe that there should be a change.

WHAT IT MEANS TO THE CHURCH

The Church needs to develop a sound, clear theology of placement. We have a theology of placement which is operative but which has not been clearly articulated or carefully thought through.

As Christians we believe in God's leadership. We also believe in God's initiative. Questions arise when we begin to apply these truths to the question of placement. To my knowledge we have not articulated how God expresses his leadership, what the channels are which God uses, and how much initiative a minister should take in finding God's leadership.

When the relationship between the minister and congregation is going well, we generally say that God led that minister to that congregation. When the relationship does not go well, we either say nothing or harbor doubts concerning God's leadership.

I know of one layman who has had his faith severely shaken because of a mismatch between a minister and the congregation. He was the chairman of the pastor search committee. As chairman he served diligently. He used the resources available to him from his denomination (which were not many), the wisdom of the members of the pastor search committee, and the insights of the congregation. Above all else he and the members of the committee spent much time in individual and corporate prayer. The end result was disaster, both for the church and the minister. The chairman of the pastor search committee could not understand how the mismatch took place. His theology had no room for the mistakes of man being able to override the leadership of God, even when it is conscientiously sought. As a result, he lost confidence in God's guidance and leadership. The last time I heard he had not returned to church.

One of the questions, then, which needs to be addressed in a theology of placement is: Are there any ways to guarantee not making a mistake when seeking God's leadership? If there are not, and I don't believe there are, what are the best ways to assure the possibility of finding God's will?

Another question which is going to have to be faced is that of human instrumentality. This question has not been thought through. On a thinking level, no one assumes that God works apart from human instrumentality. Specifically, I have not known of anyone who has reported that a pastor search committee learned about the minister who God would have them call either through a dream or through a heavenly messenger such as an angel. But on the feeling level, I suspect that many people believe that human instrumentality is not very important, at best only a necessary nuisance. Moreover, they believe that the less human instrumentality that we have, the better. That is, beware of denominational executives who might use too much power in the selection of a minister, distrust attempts to match a minister and church through computerized information, and beware of ministers who take too much initiative.

There is considerable resistance to the idea of the minister taking initiative on his behalf. For example, I remember talking to a member of a pastor search committee that had just endured an eighteen-month search for a pastor. I asked her if she or the other members of the committee would have considered a minister who approached them directly. She said absolutely not. When I retorted that I would assume at least 50 percent of the recommended names received by the committee had been sent by the individual through a friend, she was dumbfounded. Such naiveté as the result of not openly discussing placement leads to disillusionment when lay persons learn about it and to deceit on the part of ministers and those who recommend them.

My plea is for a sound and clear theology of placement.

WHAT IT MEANS TO DENOMINATIONAL EXECUTIVES

Use your influence—your power. This statement is made in light of the fact that there is a strong sense of congregational autonomy running throughout American Protestantism regardless of denominational labels. As Schaller points out, it

is not too strong to say that there is a definite anti-denomina-
tionalism bias in most Protestant congregations. This bias militates against the use of power by denominational executives.

Having said that, I believe it is also true that denominational
executives have great influence. Their influence and power
come from the people, and when the denominational executives
are held in high esteem by the people, they have considerable
power.

I suggest that denominational executives use their power
at three points: First, when there is a mismatch between a
minister and the church; second, where ministers have serious
problems and move from one church to another leaving havoc
and destruction in their wake; third, when a minister is fired.

In most situations in which I have known there was a serious
mismatch, the problem was recognized by both the minister
and the congregation within six months after the minister arrived. In such situations there is no need to prolong the agony
for both parties. But our present placement system militates
against a church considering someone who has been at a church
for only six months. Therefore, I suggest that when a mismatch
happens, the denominational executive should initiate a study
of the situation, both from the standpoint of the minister and
that of the congregation, to determine why it occurred. He
should be able to identify clearly the nature of the gifts of
the pastor as well as the nature of the gifts of the church.
Then he should use his influence to approach congregations
where he knows the gifts of that particular minister would
mesh and urge those congregations to consider him for their
pastor.

I believe that congregations would respond to such an approach. I am convinced that members of congregations are
aware that mismatches occur even when all precautions are
taken to avoid them. Therefore, if a congregation can be assured
of the nature of the gifts of the pastor and of the conditions
which caused the mismatch, I believe that it would consider
seriously the recommendation of a denominational executive.

The second area in which a denominational executive needs
to use his influence is with ministers who are troubled and
who are constantly causing trouble. Once again, the power
which the executive has is primarily the power of persuasion.

But persuasion based on sound facts and insights can carry great weight.

Obviously no minister (or anyone else) can be forced to face up to his problems or to get help. But a denominational executive can exercise power by pointing out to the minister the problems which have existed in his ministry. I have confidence in the average minister's ability to confront his problems when presented in a clear manner and in a spirit of concern. Moreover, many churches are willing to back their minister by providing time off and financial resources so he can seek guidance and counsel in resolving his problems. The key is to have someone—the denominational executive—take the initiative to urge the minister to seek help.

A third area in which denominational executives should use their influence and power is when ministers are fired or forced to resign. An increasing number of ministers are being dismissed, and very little is being done to help them and the churches that dismissed them.

There is a natural reluctance to get involved in a minister-church conflict. This reluctance stems from the realization that the issues are generally quite complex and that the fault lies both with the minister and with the church.

However, the denominational executive needs to step in and help both the church and the minister. If he doesn't, no one will. Admittedly, this will not be easy. At the time a minister is dismissed, both the minister and the church will be placing the blame on the other party and will be excusing themselves. Therefore, neither will be receptive to an offer of help. But the effort must be made for the sake of diminishing the trauma for both the church and the minister.

The task of the denominational executive is not to assess blame, but to provide love and concern for the minister. This can be done by being prepared to provide some financial help, plus encouraging the minister to seek counseling. In turn, he can help the church by encouraging them to discuss the conflict with respected denominational leaders, both lay and clergy.

The suggestions made in all three cases are only illustrative. Every capable denominational executive can come up with other and better ideas. But it is important that the denominational executive recognizes harmful situations created by vacuums of power, like the ones mentioned above, and that he uses his power and influence to correct the problems.

WHAT IT MEANS TO MINISTERS

First, take personal initiative. I mentioned above the problem of not having a clear and sound theology of call. One of the facets of this problem is the place of personal initiative. I believe that personal initiative is in keeping with the biblical teaching of God's leadership. Moreover, the failure to take personal initiative leads to unnecessary anxiety and misuse of God-given gifts.

John C. Harris, assistant to the bishop for clergy development of the Episcopal Church in Washington, describes the condition under which most ministers operate. He relates his experiences and those of a colleague and concludes by stating some of the unwitting assumptions which they made about the church as an occupational system.

> For one thing, we assumed we would be ministers for life, and that the church would "somehow" provide us with the right congregation, at least often enough to prevent us from getting stuck in one place. For another, we assumed the bishop was our ally: if worse came to worst, he would be willing and effective in recommending our name to any vacant church we suggested. Third, we unquestioningly accepted two seldom verbalized maxims: (1) never openly advertise your availability, and (2) never approach a vacant church directly on your own. In short, where work and vocation were concerned, we operated from a tradition of enforced passivity. In those years there was a part of me that relished that kind of dependence and never dreamed there might be a price to pay. As a result, in me the capacity to search for work remained largely undeveloped, as it has with many clergy. *I planned to work hard, shine brightly, and wait to be found.* (Italics are mine.)[4]

This approach contradicts the biblical teachings of personal responsibility, the exercise of proper control over one's life. The decision may be to remain where one is as a pastor. The decision may be to seek a position in another church or to search for a denominational position. No matter what the decision, it should be made with the help and guidance of friends, on the basis of Christian ethics, and seeking the guidance and direction which comes from prayer.

In talking over this question of personal initiative with a denominational executive, I found that he agreed a minister should take personal initiative, *short* of contacting a church directly. His one reservation was not theological but pragmatic. He stated that he felt that at the present time such action would do more harm than good. He is probably right. However, the system needs to change. We should not play games with church members. They need to know that ministers are taking initiative. When they are aware that this is the case and are convinced that there is nothing that is theologically wrong in such a position, I believe that laymen will not care whether the initiative comes through an intermediary or directly.

The objection can be raised that, if such a procedure were followed, churches would be flooded with too many recommendations. As it is, many churches receive well over a hundred recommendations when they are searching for a senior minister. I have a hunch that the opposite might be true. If ministers were in agreement that personal initiative is proper and acceptable, then there would be fewer ministers who would take it upon themselves to recommend a friend to a church. They would assume that their friend would take the initiative if he or she so desired. So, there might actually be fewer recommendations and requests for consideration.

Moreover, those recommendations which the pulpit committee received would be more likely to be those that would meet their needs. In making this statement I am assuming that a minister, if he took personal initiative, would be wise enough and ethical enough to study as best he could the church where he would recommend himself, and not to send a recommendation to situations where it would obviously be a mismatch.

The procedure I am recommending is based on the biblical teaching of gifts. It assumes that both ministers and congregations accept these teachings and are looking to find places where ministers' strengths can be maximized and their weaknesses can be minimized. This attitude would present a more honest setting in which pastor search committees could investigate ministers more openly and easily. Instead of spending weeks searching out information in a way which could do credit to the best CIA agent, the committee would approach the minister directly and say, "We want to search with you God's leadership relative to our church." It would be exactly that—a search.

This above-board approach would cause fewer difficulties for all concerned. Pastor search committees would not have to slip in and out of a church, trying to remain undetected, when they went to hear a minister preach. Congregations would not have to whisper and wonder if the carload of worshippers who arrived at the front door and then flew off in all directions like a covey of quail was, in reality, a pastor search committee. The pastor would not have to decide if the visitors present were newcomers or a pastor search committee.

Such procedure would avoid the trauma of knowing that a committee had come and then waiting for weeks wondering what had happened. As one pastor described the visit of a pastor search committee, "After the service, as I stood at the door, the pulpit committee members shook my hand and complimented me on the sermon. However, there was no indication they had been impressed to the point of a follow-up meeting. A week passed. Two weeks passed. I heard not a word from them. I began to think that perhaps they did not like my ministerial image. Perhaps I preached too fervently. Maybe they were looking for a much older man or someone more conservative in his theology. The anxiety began to mount. It would have been a relief to know that they were *not* interested in me. The suspense of not knowing anything increased from day to day. A check of the mailbox revealed no news. The telephone calls were only routine. With a wait-and-see attitude, I continued to perform my pastoral responsibilities. It was about six weeks later when the pulpit committee finally called me. They were still interested in me as a prospective pastor. They wanted to hear me preach a second time."[5]

Such agony is unnecessary. Personal initiative well-done and accepted by pastor search committees could save much time, effort, and anxiety, and the end result would be a better chance for God's leadership to be followed.

Second, *be honest with fellow pastors and denominational executives.* In searching for God's guidance, use the human resources which are available. Talk to fellow pastors and church executives openly about your felt needs, strengths, and shortcomings. Check out their understanding of who you are. Be willing to listen to both the positive and the negative which they see in you. This openness could avoid many future problems.

Under our present condition where we remain passive and/ or take initiative only through another person, we are unable to be open and honest about ourselves. We are afraid to tell fellow ministers and denominational executives about our faults and shortcomings. We realize that someday we may have to call on them for a recommendation. Therefore, we dare not let them see our faults.

What a waste of friendship! When we know that we are not completely dependent on others, we can be open. We will find that many times our fears and shortcomings are unfounded. It is possible to be under such pressure that we blame ourselves for conditions which are not our fault. It is a relief to get a true picture of our worth.

Conversely, we are often unaware of the mistakes which we are making. Our friends and associates will be able to point those out to us when we go and ask for help. Once again, since we are not dependent on them, we can take their suggestions without being threatened or becoming defensive.

Just recently I found myself troubled over the request for a recommendation. A church wrote me asking about a fellow pastor. I knew this minister and we were more than casual friends. However, our friendship had never gotten to the point where we could be completely honest with each other. We were both caught in the system and did not reveal ourselves to each other, nor were we ready to accept guidance from one another. Yet, he had given my name as a pastor who knew him. I could not in good conscience recommend him to the church that had contacted me. Neither could I go to him and tell him that I wasn't going to recommend him. Luck—I know no other word to describe the situation—was with me. While I procrastinated, he was contacted by another church. So I wrote to the pastor search committee that my friend was not available.

I am aware that I am speaking of the ideal and that what

I am saying is not as simple as it sounds. However, I contend that we have to have an ideal which will give us some direction to extricate ourselves from the quicksand which is pulling us down.

*   *   *

Placement is a nine-letter word. But it does not have to conjure up thoughts of absence of the Holy Spirit, lack of faith in God, or anything else which is an anathema in our understanding of God's initiative and action in the lives of ministers. Placement can stand for honesty, openness, responsibility, and proper use of those avenues given to us by God so that we can find his leadership and will. Placement can stand alongside another nine-letter word—happiness.

Chapter 11

It Is Painful to Kick
Against the Goads

The Greeks and the Romans saw the wills of the gods as unchangeable. To fight against the gods was, therefore, both painful and ineffective. From this belief arose the proverbial saying: "It is painful to kick against the goads."

Every major facet of life has its givens or unchangeable conditions. To reject this fact leads to unnecessary trauma, since trying to change the givens is both painful and ineffective. The way of wisdom is to pray, "God grant me the serenity to accept the things I cannot change, the courage to change the things I can, and the wisdom to know the difference."

Ministers need wisdom, serenity, and courage as they face the parish ministry in which there too are givens that cannot be changed. In my experience as a parish minister, I have identified nine givens which I have tried to find the serenity to accept in order to stop the painful kicking against the goads.

THE MINISTER AS A GENERALIST

The pastor is a generalist, not a specialist. The years of my college and seminary training taught me to strive for competence in my fields of study and as a result, I developed the mentality of a specialist.

The culture shock from classroom to parish ministry was devastating. I felt incompetent to deal with the variety of demands placed upon me. When I responded with the mentality of a specialist and sought to become a specialist in every area of my work, I soon found myself kicking against the goads.

The reality of the parish minister as a generalist is made clear in a study by the Episcopal Church Strategic Research Services. This study shows that a minister does not spend more than 16 percent of his time on any one facet of his work.[1] Therefore, the minister constantly lives with feelings that he must exhibit a variety of talents and that there will always be more tasks than can be accomplished.

In his book *Ferment in the Ministry,* Seward Hiltner focuses his attention on this problem. The thesis of his book is that "the ministry is a unity, a complex unity to be sure, but a unity nevertheless."[2]

Hiltner makes an excellent presentation of the unity from the standpoint of the functions of the ministry. His final advice is: "But unity contains ambiguity if it is the kind of unity that, in the mind of the minister, makes it hang together for him despite the variety of his activities seen in the usual categories. The ambiguity is deepened because the skills needed are very rarely present in high degree in any one person. But it seems to me it is just this ambiguity that adds to the zest of ministering, in any setting new or old. *Forget the perfectionism; do well what you can do well; shore up your weaknesses to some point—and then rejoice that you are not on the assembly line doing the same thing every ten minutes. For those who want assembly lines, the ministry is the wrong place to look.*" (Italics are mine.)[3]

THE MINISTER AS AN ADMINISTRATOR

Bruce Grubbs writes, "There's confusion today about who ministers are and what they do. A few years ago the Educational Testing Service conducted a study on ministerial identity. One thousand lay leaders in various denominations were asked to give adjectives and profile statements of what they considered to be an 'outstanding minister.' This information was then given to a group of psychological testers. The testers were not told who was being described. When asked to identify the person being described, they said, 'A junior vice-president of Sears-Roebuck.' "[4]

A minister friend upon reading this statement cried out, "I knew it! They finally found out what it means to be a parish minister." He was voicing the anguish and concern that most ministers feel as administrative responsibilities are thrust upon them.

Samuel Blizzard, in his classic study of ministers which provided the impetus for several subsequent studies, pointed out that ministers spend the largest portion of their time on those functions of the ministry which they least enjoy and which they are least prepared to fulfill. His study was amply supported by the research reported in *Ex-Pastors.* The most unanimous note struck by the pastors and ex-pastors was that their seminary did not train them in the practical skills necessary to lead in today's church, such as leadership training and business administration.[5]

A further irritant is that the minister is thrust into a leadership role from the very first day of his pastorate. Although he has had little opportunity to develop leadership skills, he is immediately expected to function effectively in that capacity. Even the boss's son does not take over the business the first day he comes to work!

Moreover, the pastor is unique in that few professionals "have organizations of laymen as both employers and clients, and professional associations so lacking in power to support and defend their members."[6] I would add that from an administrative standpoint there are few organizations where the employee (the minister) must serve as a supervisor. How does a minister deal with an incompetent committee chairman whom he is supervising when that chairman is one of his most influential employers?

There is no point in kicking against the goads. The parish church is an institution and, as such, demands administration and an administrator. The simplistic answer that there are administrators in the congregation who can take over some if not most of the leadership responsibilities is an answer which I have heard only from those who have not been pastors. There is no way to avoid the model of academic excellence when in school; and there is no way to avoid being an administrator the first day in the parish. The minister must learn to bite the bullet, and the laity must be patient with the anger and resentment of the young minister, as well as with his ineptness as an administrator.

INSTITUTIONAL RIGIDITY

Closely related to administration is institutional rigidity. Ministers see themselves as change agents. They are called to comfort and to challenge, even in the face of the institutional rigidity of the parish. But there is no easy or simple way to change an institution, whether it be governmental, educational, religious, or business.

John Biersdorf writes that one of the greatest stresses on ministers is their conviction that churches are unable to respond adequately to change and are not able to deal effectively with the needs of people in this time of rapid change. He states, "The minister feels the church is futile and ineffectual, and he is deeply angry, because he is caught in restrictive and oppressive structures that do not allow him to use his potential to move the church."[7]

This rigidity causes many ministers to leave the parish ministry—a tragedy. We cannot afford to lose those men and women who are most sensitive to the need for change. Certainly change can take place from the outside, but the most effective change comes from those working on the inside.

VOLUNTARISM

Few goads have been as painful for me as this one. Even though I refer to voluntarism in the American church in chapter nine, I believe that it needs to be mentioned again in the context of the ministry's "givens."

My first model of leadership was as a naval officer. When I became a pastor, I soon found that very few people in the parish respond to the shrill sound of the boatswain mate's whistle followed by the authoritative pronouncement, "Now hear this, now hear this."

The parish church is a voluntary organization and the pastor needs to cope with his role as a leader in a voluntary organization. A seminary professor writes pointedly but with a note of hope: "It is not putting it too strongly to argue that no one should attempt to minister within American congregations who is not prepared to take the characteristics of voluntary associations seriously."[8]

But to effectively carry out his role as a leader in a voluntary association the minister must accept certain limitations. One is the need to develop goals in conjunction with the laity. Hadden writes, "Leadership in a voluntary association involves a greater element of precariousness than in non-voluntary organizations. Voluntary associations are less likely to give their leaders a mandate to develop their own goals for the organization. The leader must operate within the boundaries of his prescribed role as leader. To deviate beyond the role prescriptions of his office is to invite conflict with the membership."[9]

Another helpful insight is that "it follows that one of the tasks of the leadership is to see that the organization continues to provide its membership with rewards that are satisfactory to assure their continued participation. If the leadership chooses to redefine the goals and rewards, they must either convince the membership of the efficacy of the new goals and rewards, or they must seek to recruit new members who share their definition of the organization. Failure to achieve one or the other of these tasks will result either in the demise of the organization or their loss of the leadership role."[10]

In emphasizing that voluntarism is a given in the American church, I am not suggesting that the minister must be prepared to compromise his beliefs to serve in the parish. Far from it. The minister is called first to do God's will and second to do the will of the parish. However, voluntarism calls for greater clarification of goals and understanding of the nature of ministry. With his goals clearly in mind, the minister can avoid conflicts of misunderstanding, although he cannot avoid conflicts of differing opinions. When there are conflicts over such differences, the minister must be prepared to find a solution without compromising his beliefs. If this is not possible, he must be prepared to resign as pastor.

There is no denying or getting around this very difficult given. It must be faced and dealt with honestly.

LIMITED CONTROL OF ONE'S TIME

Every minister can attest to the limited control he has over his time. It is easy to announce to the congregation that the pastor cannot be interrupted during the morning hours when he studies and for the secretary to screen all incoming calls. But the pastor, as a professional in the helping profession, is on call twenty-four hours a day. Genuine emergencies arise and need to be dealt with immediately.

Also, among the laity there is an unspoken belief that the minister should always be available. I am not sure this belief should be completely changed. Obviously there are limitations. A day off should be a day off. A vacation is a vacation. But the fact remains that the pastor is a symbol of Christian compassion and as such should be vulnerable to interruptions.

To cope with this given the minister must build *negotiable time* into his schedule. By this I mean time which has been specifically set aside for given tasks which could be postponed, such as random reading, going through the mail, filing, etc. There will of course be times when several days, or even a week, might go by without an interruption due to some crisis. However, that is seldom the case.

Limited control of one's time is a definite source of stress. In an excellent article titled "How to Survive Today's Stressful Jobs," the author quotes Dr. Robert Butler, director of the National Institute on Aging, "People who are healthy and live somewhat longer lives have a sense of predictability and control over their lives."[11] This statement says to me that a wise minister tries to find that thin line of demarcation between neglecting his duty to be available for real needs and permitting himself to be in a constant state of turmoil because of a lack of control.

POWER STRUGGLES

James Massey, Director of Church-Minister Relations for the Virginia Baptist General Board, states that power struggles are one of the most frequent causes of church-pastor conflicts. Conflicts do not have to be the only outcome of power struggles, but power struggles will always be present where two or more are gathered together.

The parish is a natural setting for power struggles. The primary reason for this is that power structures are seldom clearly defined or identified in a church. Moreover, there are formal and informal power structures. This is inevitable, since in a voluntary organization formal power has to be limited. Power resides in the members of the congregation and is delegated to both clergy and lay leaders on the basis of trust and confidence.

In addition, in a voluntary organization it is possible for informal groups to exercise power when a vacuum in the power structure is created or if some individuals desire to gain power.

Some pastors would say that a church is the one place where a powerless person, frustrated by his lack of power, is able to exercise power and to seek to gain self-esteem through that power. There is validity in this insight. If there are individuals, and there are some in every congregation, who need to exercise power to increase their self-esteem, they should be no more shunned or rejected than those who need attention and compassion because of the loss of a spouse. They must be accepted and given appropriate help. This is not easy. It is never easy to help a person who has a real need.

A far more dangerous and destructive power struggle comes when members, either because of their affluence or length of membership in the church, believe that they have the God-given right to exercise power. That is, power is seized on the basis of their understanding of themselves, not as the result of the delegation by the congregation.

The wise pastor will study both the formal and informal power structures in his parish. He will seek to work with the formal and legitimate power structures and be aware of the informal power structures.

When confronted with a power struggle which involves the usurpation of his delegated powers, the minister must be prepared to take a stand and avoid the takeover by those who seek to take power into their own hands.

Unfortunately, power struggles often end in church divisions. This usually happens when those who take undelegated power for themselves are denied power and as a result, either back away or, more likely, leave the church. These individuals should not be rejected. Every effort should be made to bring about reconciliation.

There are two safety measures which can be followed. First, when a pastor is being considered by a congregation, he can examine the track record of that church regarding its delegation and use of power. This can be done by contacting former pastors and those who have had close association with the church. If the prospective pastor finds that the church has a poor record in that area, he should either back away if he does not believe that he can handle the situation or, at best, proceed with caution. The second safety measure should be exercised if the minister decides to go to a church with a bad track record. He should speak candidly with a denominational executive and secure his promise to confront the congregation if it becomes obvious that there has been a flagrant misuse of power. If that fails, he should help the minister relocate if necessary.

SINGING THE LORD'S SONG IN A FOREIGN LAND

The psalmist was not the last to discover that structures and familiar settings affect one's joy in worship. Every pastor will be confronted with committed Christians who find it difficult to worship in the "new" church because it is not like the one "back home."

There is obviously a large measure of immaturity in such an attitude. But once again, a minister cannot simply write off an individual because he or she is immature. It is a given that has to be dealt with.

Moreover, there are many mature Christians who find it difficult to sing the Lord's song in a foreign land. A young couple had been actively involved in worship and ministry through the church where they were members. But a move to a completely different part of the country brought them face to face with congregations that were completely different in approach. In a community of some 40,000 people where Baptists were in the minority, there were thirteen different Baptist churches of various persuasions. Fragmentation was the order of the day. The young couple recognized what they were going through, but it was still very difficult for them to find a place of meaningful worship and ministry.

Furthermore, a pastor must recognize that in a mobile society there will be an unending stream of people longing for the "temple in Jerusalem." He must not permit this given to become a threat to him. It is not the minister's problem; it is the parishioner's problem. When the minister can accept this fact, he will be prepared to help those in captivity learn how to sing the Lord's song.

THE MINISTER AS A LINCHPIN

The dictionary defines a linchpin as "something that serves to hold together the elements of a situation." I do not believe that it is arrogance for a minister to say that he or she is the linchpin in denominational structures.

It is axiomatic for denominational executives to say that you have to get the support of the pastors. The result is a flood of mail which comes across the desk of every pastor. There are requests for him or her to participate and support dozens and even hundreds of causes. Moreover, there are all the demands of the local minister's association plus the requests of various civic, educational, and service-oriented groups.

In my private diary I once wrote a statement called "Depression and the U.S. Mail." My statement was in no way a criticism of the postal service. Instead, the statement came as a result of my trying to go through the second and third class mail that had accumulated during my vacation. One afternoon I decided to go through all of my mail. Now, I must admit there was also an accumulation of mail from several days before I had left. As I proceeded through the mail I found myself getting depressed. Before long I was at the point that I needed to get away from what I was doing. I tried to analyze my depression. It was obvious that it had to do with the mail that I was going through. But why should that depress me? As I thought further, I realized that I had spent more than two hours pouring over mail and each piece carried a suggestion on how to improve my ministry, or the announcement of an important meeting, or notices of continuing education programs which would better equip me for ministry, or reports of new programs that should be started in the church. You see, I heard the flood of mail saying to me, "You aren't a good pastor, you aren't a good scholar, you aren't supporting the denominational programs as you should."

Yes, the problem was mine. But the given was the overkill of mail because as pastor I am a linchpin. This, I say again, is not arrogance; it is reality. The denomination cannot exist without the support of pastors and churches anymore than a church can exist without the support of members. Therefore, the pastor must be sought out for support. Unfortunately, in a large denomination there are always more programs than can ever be supported or carried out. One can become callous and allocate all of the mail to "file thirteen." However, this is to deny the legitimate response which the pastor must make to his denomination and to other cooperating groups. Therefore, the answer is for wisdom on how to set priorities (i.e., wisdom on how to use "file thirteen," effectively).

THE UBIQUITOUS SERMON

A well-known story tells about a minister driving home from church on Sunday night, his hands tightly grasping the steering wheel as he mutters to himself, "Two more, two more." One Sunday was not yet over, and the minister was already apprehensive of the approach of another Sunday with the ubiquitous sermons.

While recognizing that he is a generalist, the pastor must also recognize that an important task in the ministry is to be a conscientious minister of the Word. There is no rationalizing away this central part of the minister's task.

Certainly, there is no task that is as demanding as the preparation of sermons. There are times when, as the result of random reading, ideas will flow together that will make the preparation and delivery of a sermon a very delightful and pleasant experience. However, there is no substitute for continuous and regular study. As with every other significant task, sermon preparation is 99 percent perspiration and 1 percent inspiration.

Every minister will develop his or her own style of study

and preaching. But the allocation of time, prayer, and effort to the preparation and delivery of sermons must be a common factor. They come every week.

*　　*　　*

The Greeks and Romans were right. It is painful to kick against the goads. It is also destructive. There is no way to eliminate these goads, but they can be identified and in part coped with. Beyond that, there is the way of wisdom to pray, "God grant me the serenity to accept the things I cannot change, the courage to change the things I can, and the wisdom to know the difference."

Chapter 12

We Have This Treasure

The apostle Paul was enthusiastic about the Christian message. He described it as a treasure. In words reminiscent of the parables of Jesus: Paul looked upon the gospel as a treasure to be desired above all other treasures; one so valuable that it awakened in him a deep desire to share it with both Jews and Gentiles. In fact, his desire to share the gospel led him to be all things to all people so that he might win some. Also, he subjected himself to strict discipline so that he might not be disqualified as a witness to the good news of God in Christ.

Moreover Paul was enthusiastic about his responsibility to proclaim the Christian message. He was enthusiastic about being an apostle—about being a Christian witness. He considered his call an expression of God's mercy—a call for which he didn't think he was worthy. In fact, he stood in amazement and thanksgiving at the thought that God had chosen him to be an apostle.

Paul's enthusiasm for his task stands in stark contrast to the apathy which grips a large segment of clergy and laity in their task as Christian witnesses. As noted in the preface, in a survey made in 1969 nearly two out of every three clergymen viewed their work as futile or ineffectual. While it is true that the '60s were years of great turmoil, there is no indication that the morale of the clergy has changed significantly in the '70s and '80s. If anything, there are signs suggesting that low morale among clergy is increasing. Tensions between clergy and laity are more prevalent today, and one knowledgeable church executive estimated that 80 percent of parish ministers would like to leave their present positions. In addition, there has been a continued increase in the number of clergy dismissed and/or forced to resign by the congregations they were serving.

I recognize that the clergy's lack of enthusiasm in response to their call to proclaim the treasure, which is the gospel, is strongly influenced by a loss of confidence in the institutional church as a means of proclaiming the gospel, and a loss of confidence in the church as an occupational system. However, the contrast with Paul still stands. Paul did not find the ministry as an occupational system very rewarding. As he wrote in 2 Corinthians 11:23–28, his experiences as an apostle included, among others, beatings, shipwrecks, imprisonments, often going without food, danger from robbers, and anxiety for all the churches.

Many of the laity are also discouraged with their call to be witnesses. They find it difficult to share their faith with friends and neighbors and are discouraged by the ineffectiveness of their witness through the parish church. In an old saw it is said that there are three classes of church members—the tired, the retired, and the tireless. I have found that over two-thirds of the church members fall into the first two categories. The tired and retired have found little joy in their ministry. The ministry which they perform is often minimal and done out of a sense of duty. There is seldom an indication that they are sharing a treasure.

Unfortunately, clergy and laity have not admitted to one another their feelings of discouragement. Therefore, they have not been able to help one another because they have not understood each other's feelings. I remember how on a deacons' retreat the obvious finally broke through to me. I had been going through a period of deep discouragement over the ineffectiveness of the parish ministry and was looking forward to the deacons' retreat as a time when I would receive encouragement from the deacons. I believed that my discouragement was due primarily to the thousand and one details which are involved in maintaining the institutional church. I reasoned, therefore, that the deacons, who were not involved in so many details, would have a more enthusiastic attitude about the importance of proclaiming the Christian gospel.

On the retreat, as a result of a very open and honest discussion, I learned that the deacons had as many questions as I did about the importance of what we were doing. If anything, they were more discouraged than I was. Moreover, they were looking to me for encouragement. We found that we had been looking to each other for help and were disappointed that we had not been getting it. When we discovered that we both had doubts and questions, we were able to begin looking together for a new sense of enthusiasm. And together we were able to make some progress.

One of the obstacles that must be overcome if there is to be fulfillment in ministry for both clergy and laity is the lack of enthusiasm in witnessing to the treasure which has been entrusted to us. Specifically, both clergy and laity need to help each other find the kind of enthusiasm which the apostle Paul had. Is this possible? My answer is "Yes." We can have a solid faith and conviction that the gospel is a treasure and that the parish ministry is a viable means of proclaiming and living the gospel.

However, in order to increase enthusiasm for ministering through the parish ministry, three questions need to be answered: Is the gospel a treasure? Is the institutional church a valid way to proclaim and live the Christian gospel? Is the church a viable occupational system? The first two questions apply both to clergy and laity, but the third applies only to the clergy.

Is the Christian Gospel a True Treasure?

Every Christian affirms that the gospel is a treasure. That is why they are Christians. But there are varying degrees of enthusiasm about the necessity of witnessing to the gospel. Some consider the Christian gospel an indispensable ingredient for understanding life and death. Others view it as important but not indispensable for a more abundant life or for bringing peace on earth.

My personal enthusiasm and commitment to the Christian gospel as a spiritual treasure and an indispensable factor in the life of every individual has grown in my thirty-four years as a pastor. And an insight by Harris Franklin Rall has had a great influence on that growth. He points out that the Christian gospel has three facets: It is a faith, a way of life, and a way of salvation.

Using Rall's insight as a base, I have molded my own *apologia* for my proclamation of the Christian message. This defense has been shaped further by my perception of my task as a minister in the local parish. Whether or not the reader accepts my *apologia* as a valid statement for himself, I contend that every Christian, clergy or lay, must have his own *apologia* if there is to be genuine enthusiasm for the Christian faith as a treasure. I am not speaking of a privatized religion, but of one's own personal understanding, forged by biblical and theological studies and tempered by experience.

I have elaborated on Rall's insights by noting the fact that every individual has a faith, a way of life, and a way of salvation. This has helped me recognize that the Christian gospel is not an addition to life; rather, it is a part of the very fiber of life. In reality, the gospel has to do with questions and concerns faced each day by every individual. The only questions that need to be answered are: Is the Christian gospel the best faith? The best way of life? The best way of salvation? My answer to each is "Yes."

Every individual believes something about life and the universe we live in—this is a faith. There is a wide gamut in the kinds of faith people live by. H. L. Mencken, the brilliant journalist whose influence was at its zenith in the 1930s, said, "Life fundamentally is not worth living. . . . What could be more logical than suicide? What could be more preposterous than keeping alive?"[1] In much the same vein, Albert Camus, who molded the faith of many individuals on both sides of the Atlantic following the Second World War, spoke of life as absurd.

At the other end of the spectrum is faith as proclaimed in the Christian gospel. Simply stated, the Christian belief is that there is a God, and that he is a God of love. God rules the world in love. He is present in the world, carrying out his purposes of love; and his ultimate will and purposes will be victorious.

My own belief is that most individuals have a faith that gives little hope or joy. Confronted by the absurd elements in life, they live with the suspicion that the future is basically meaningless—life is not moving toward a climax, but is simply winding down into oblivion. Because people cannot find much purpose or direction in life, the philosophy "Eat, drink, and be merry, for tomorrow you will die" prevails. The appeal of this hedonistic philosophy is its devotion to making every moment of every day pleasurable, regardless of the consequences.

Many times questions of existence don't arise until we face the realities of suffering and death. At those times we find that our belief systems surface. While the Christian faith does not offer a complete answer to the question of meaningless suffering, it does offer hope—a hope based on the victory of God in the resurrection of Jesus Christ.

As a parish minister I am forced to deal with the questions of suffering and death. It is easy to become professional and to parrot the proper "Christian answers." But such behavior provides little help. However, I am fully convinced that faith as understood in the life, death, and resurrection of Jesus Christ provides the best faith with which to meet life and death because it is a faith which offers hope. Our task as Christians is to learn how to interpret that faith in a way that relates specifically to everyday needs.

The Christian gospel is also a way of life. It is a statement on how we are to live.

Each of us lives life in a particular way. Yet, most of the time we give very little conscious thought to determining our lifestyle. It is caught more than it is taught. We generally reflect the lifestyles of our peers and of significant others. But this does not take away from the fact that we live by certain principles and goals.

The basic lifestyle of our time has been called that of the "me generation." While the term is new, the principle of self-centeredness is not. It was denounced by the prophets as they called for justice and mercy.

The Christian lifestyle is specific. As spelled out in the Sermon on the Mount, it includes forgiveness of others, going the second mile, turning the other cheek, striving for peace, hungering for righteousness, and praying for those who persecute you. In other words, it can be summarized in one word: *love*—the active concern for others. Reflecting those principles many years later, Will Durant, a historian-philosopher, distilled 2,000 years of history into three simple words of advice: "Love one another." He then added, "My final lesson in history is the same as that of Jesus. You may think that's a lot of lollipop. But just try it. Love is the most practical thing in the world."[2]

Our actions at home, at school, in the marketplace, and at social gatherings are determined by our lifestyle. The question which we must answer is this: Is the Christian lifestyle the best? If the answer is "Yes," then we have a treasure which needs to be shared in a world caught up in self-destruction.

The third facet of the Christian gospel is a message of salvation. We tend to think that salvation is a matter that no one is concerned about except those who attend church. Not so. In reality, this is the most pressing question before each individual. It is the question in life to which we give the most attention. We all recognize that there is something wrong in life, and we constantly seek to change life—to find a way of salvation.

In the truest sense, communism, materialism, science, and technology are all ways of salvation. They are all ways of coping with the realization of pain and evil and attempts to bring about change—to save us.

We are bombarded each day with thousands of messages of salvation, the basic theme broadcast in every advertisement. We are told that life can be changed and made beautiful by the right deodorant, diet, clothes, automobiles, drugs, etc.

The Christian message of salvation on both a personal and community basis is clear and simple. Its simplicity makes it appear childish in light of such tragedies as the Holocaust, the present reality of worldwide terrorism, and the possibility of nuclear destruction. The Christian gospel proclaims that the way of salvation is accepting the love and forgiveness of God's grace and living as a child of God—depending on God as our Father and loving all people as God's children and members of our family.

Admittedly, this way of salvation is difficult to relate to worldwide problems, but I believe that of all the ways of salvation it is the best, and the one to which all people must have the opportunity to respond.

I repeat that in my own experience this threefold understanding of the Christian faith has helped me to see that my task is a vital one. I am dealing with the basic questions of life, questions that are being dealt with each day by every individual. Moreover, I have found that the Christian faith, way of life, and way of salvation are the best. Again, I do not contend that my *apologia* is the only one, or even the best one, but it has given me a desire to proclaim the Christian gospel because I believe it is a treasure. However, I do contend that every Christian must have his or her own *apologia* in order to capture the conviction of the apostle Paul that we have been entrusted with a treasure. Only then can we find the enthusiasm which we must have to meet whatever obstacles may arise as we accept our call to be witnesses to God's action in Jesus Christ.

IS THE INSTITUTIONAL CHURCH A VALID WAY TO PROCLAIM AND LIVE THE CHRISTIAN GOSPEL?

The question of whether the institutional church is a valid way to proclaim and live the Christian gospel is more difficult to answer than the question of whether the gospel is a treasure. The difficulty in giving a positive response comes from many sources.

One source of disappointment with the institutional church is related to maintaining the institution. The "invitations to discipleship" at the close of most worship services are really appeals for people to give time and money to keep the doors of the institution open. The laity get tired of busy work and of being used. The clergy resign from their church positions every Monday morning because their expenditure of emotional energy did not seem to have any bearing on the vital issues of life. Sunday was just one more day of trying to keep the institution alive.

The need for greater and greater financial resources to keep the institution solvent presents another problem. The rise in the costs of building construction, utilities, and maintenance, plus increases in ministers' salaries, have placed heavy financial burdens on many churches. Therefore, greater effort must go into recruiting members. Churches compete with one another for the "tithers" who move into the community, wooing them more ardently than Romeo wooed Juliet. For each "Juliet" there are at least a dozen "Romeos," whispering promises of undying loyalty and devotion if only she will join his church. I might add that the Romeos even cut across denominational lines. All is fair in love, war, and recruiting tithers.

Recruitment also encourages "Christian gossiping." In the spirit of "trying to help," prospective members are told of the problems of other churches. The concerned pastor will say something like, "I have heard, and I must admit I am not positive about this, that the pastor at Northside Church is not as solid on the fundamentals as he should be. He seems to have some doubts about the interpretation of certain passages of the Bible. And we all know that if a church is weak on its stand on the Bible, then there is nothing to hold on to. I am only saying this because I want you to have all the information possible to help you find God's leadership."

This kind of competition brings about strained relationships between pastors. Those who have churches with declining memberships often look at those who are successful with an attitude of sour grapes.

Because increased attendance is equal to survival, recruiting tactics can become as devious as those of the most unscrupulous salesman. And the process damages everyone involved. The pastor feels uncomfortable about the tactics he has used. To survive, he stills his conscience to the point that he can no longer distinguish between right and wrong. The members wooed suffer "membership shock." After joining a church, they are frequently forgotten as the pastor runs after new prospects. Finally, the church suffers because the old members have to spend time keeping the new members happy and explaining the difference between what the pastor said the church is and what it is in reality.

These rather crass approaches to keeping the institution alive make sensitive souls wonder if there is validity in the institutional church. The competition seems sub-Christian if not outright pagan. For many, such practices raise questions about what fierce competition has to do with increasing the love of God and of man.

Another important factor to be considered is institutional rigidity. Although I described institutional rigidity as a given, the stress which this given causes ministers cannot be ignored. The Christian message is clear. Disciples are to be the salt of the earth, and the light of the world. They are to turn the world right side up. Therefore, if institutional rigidity blocks these goals, an alternative to the church as an institution must be found. However, there are reasons to believe that the institutional church is a valid base for change. Hadden puts it this way:

> Small cadres of clergy without an institutional base would be as powerless as any other cadre of individuals seeking to effect change. They would have power and influence only to the extent they could organize and coalesce others who share their views. In part, I am saying that to walk away from the institution of the church is to abandon one of the broadest bases of potential support for change that exists in American society.[3]

There are some who believe that a major problem for ministers as leaders in the institutional church is their decreasing influence. They are not the key figures they were a few years ago. This observation holds some validity. The problem I have experienced is not a loss of respect, but a feeling that my work is at the periphery of the important and vital issues of life. I have always been treated with great respect. But my goals, dreams, and longings to be involved in such a way that what I am doing through the church really matters have often been unfulfilled and shattered. Henri J. M. Nouwen expressed my deepest feelings when he wrote about "the wound of loneliness":

> The wound of loneliness in the life of the minister hurts all the more, since he not only shares in the human condition of isolation, but also finds that his professional impact on others is diminishing. The minister is called to speak to the ultimate concerns of life: birth and death, union and separation, love and hate. He has an urgent desire to give meaning to people's lives. But he finds himself standing on the edges of events and only reluctantly admitted to the spot where the decisions are being made.
>
> In hospitals, where many utter their first cry as well as their last words, ministers are often more tolerated than required. In prisons, where men's desire for liberation and freedom is most painfully felt, a chaplain feels like a guilty bystander whose words

hardly move the wardens. In the cities, where children play between concrete buildings and old people die isolated and forgotten, the protests of priests are hardly taken seriously and their demands hang in the air like rhetorical questions. Many churches decorated with words announcing salvation and new life are often little more than parlors for those who feel quite comfortable in the old life, and who are not likely to let the minister's words change their stone hearts into furnaces where swords can be cast into plowshares, and spears into pruning hooks.

The painful irony is that the minister, who wants to touch the center of men's lives, finds himself on the periphery, often pleading in vain for admission. He never seems to be where the action is, where the plans are made and the strategies discussed. He always seems to arrive at the wrong places at the wrong times with the wrong people, outside the walls of the city when the feast is over, with a few crying women.[4]

The laity have serious reservations about whether the institutional church is the best way to proclaim and live the Christian gospel. The picture of the "perfect" lay person drawn by the clergy is of one who tithes, attends all of the services, works hard for the institutional church, and keeps his or her mouth shut. After years of trying to live up to this ideal and also receiving little recognition for their ministry, outside the four walls of the church, the laity feel used. It is no wonder so many have joined the ranks of the tired and retired.

This situation creates an atmosphere in which both clergy and laity are tempted to take out their frustrations on one another, which further increases their doubts about the validity of the institutional church.

Having reviewed some of the problems within the institutional church, one is now faced with two questions, not just one: "Is the institutional church a valid way to proclaim and live the Christian Gospel?" and "Is there a better way to live and proclaim the Christian Gospel?"

My answer to the first question is, "Yes," and to the second is, "I do not know a better way." When I made these statements in a seminary class, a student asked me, "Have you looked for a better way?" I answered, "Yes. I have been looking, but so far I have found no better way. Moreover, I have found several very positive things about the institutional church."

First, the institutional church has many avenues whereby

to share the treasure which is the Christian Gospel. There are the worship services, Bible study groups, prayer groups, spiritual growth groups, prayer meetings, music activities for all age groups, retreats, one-on-one witnessing, youth mission trips, and many others. Moreover, the institutional church has a variety of specially trained leaders, both lay and clergy, to direct these programs.

The institutional church is aided in its mission of witnessing by excellent visual aid materials, twentieth-century English translations of the Bible, and an abundance of well-written books and tracts. The present day institutional church has greater total resources for proclaiming the treasure of the Christian gospel than it has had at any time in its 2,000-year history.

Second, people turn to the church for help. In the major crises of life, the church is still one of the most viable sources of help. In one area alone, that of counseling, it is estimated that more people turn first of all to their minister than to any other counselor. These people come in all shapes and sizes with a variety of problems, some that can be solved and some that cannot. Thus, a minister has opportunities unequaled by any other profession to serve people. The question is not whether people will turn to the church for help, but whether the pastor and the members of the church will have the expertise, time, and spiritual maturity to deal with all of the problems.

Third, both clergy and laity can take initiative in relating to people in need—both have chances to go to people who are facing crises in their lives. Wayne Oates has pointed out that the pastor is the only professional in our culture who *can* take initiative. He also calls ministers to task for adopting the medical model of remaining in the office and waiting for people to come to them rather than going to the people.

As I have indicated, there are more calls from people in need than can be met. But added to those calls are the opportunities to reach out to people. Visitation, although it is a more difficult art in today's fast-paced society than was true a few years ago, is still an important way to help people. However, I have found that by making appointments it is possible to visit in people's homes and to create an atmosphere in which significant discussions can take place. Many adult Christians have no one to talk to about some of their questions and doubts. If one is willing to give the time and to listen to what is being said, discussions can progress beyond subjects such as the weather, sports, and inflation. I have found great concern over biblical interpretation, but the range of subjects discussed during visits has strained my knowledge of theology, ethics, church history, and archaeology as well.

Initiative can also be taken in situations where there is family stress. I have yet to find an occasion when I have not been a welcomed visitor to a family in which a child had run away, a divorce was imminent, or some other crisis had arisen. Even when my calls have been unannounced and unsolicited, my concern has not been rejected.

Sometimes initiative is best taken by means of telephone calls and letters. Again, the response has seldom been negative. I am not saying that everything that I have ever done has met with great success; there are varying degrees of positive response. I am saying that as a pastor I am not looked upon as a meddler when I take initiative.

Fourth, the church provides leadership for other areas of community service. Sometimes the impression is given that church members only operate within the four walls of their buildings. Unfortunately, this is the case in too many churches. However, in community volunteer organizations many, if not most, of the positions are staffed by active church members. I have found that a majority of those people who work with advocacy programs for the handicapped, human rights commissions, legal aid associations, and rescue squad groups have been active members of local congregations.

The point is that the institutional church provides the incentive and the vision to serve in areas other than just church-related organizations. I must admit that for too many years I chafed under this condition. Having only institutional success as my standard of success for the church, I was often irritated at church members who were out doing good rather than attending another meeting at the church. Hopefully, I have come to see more clearly the importance of the contribution that church members are making, and also my need to commend them for the services which they perform in community activities.

Fifth, leaders in other vocations see the value of that which can be done through the institutional church. There are times when we need to take seriously what others say about us. Many times others can see us better than we can see ourselves. We may be too close to the trees to see the forest.

I have been impressed to find that those who know us best still have confidence and faith in us. Jeffrey Hadden concludes his sociological study of the church, *The Gathering Storm in the Churches,* with this statement: "Even in the midst of their faltering authority, I know of no other group in our society that has a greater potential and, indeed, a graver responsibility for generating a greater concern for human destiny than the clergy. In the name of MAN, I hope they succeed."[5]

Karl Menninger, the dean of psychiatrists in America, in a letter to Carlyle Marney in 1972, stated: "I think they are troubled in spirit. I think their morale is low. I do not think they realize what power they have at their command to do the very things they want to do, to be helpful and inspiring. But I think they must not fear to be reproachful. Jeremiah was not. Isaiah was not. Amos was not. Micah was not and John the Baptist was not. . . . This book I am writing is addressed to the clergy. Is that too presumptuous? I want to tell them that we psychiatrists do not know all the answers and it is no good trying to imitate us with or without fees."[6]

A journalist reviewing *Ex-Pastors* made this observation: "As men become increasingly skeptical of the effects of technology and reason, however, society is beginning to experience a religious revival marked by new popular interests in mysticism, the occult, and mind expansion through drugs, meditation and other means. Thus far this religious revival has gone on outside the established churches and it could become simply one more threat to an already frustrated clergy. On the other hand, it could provide clergymen with new opportunities for ministering in the most classic manner."[7]

James Glasse quotes this conversation with a physician. "A doctor once told me of his frustration in dealing with his patients. 'They won't come to me until they are so sick that it is an emergency; in these cases there is little I can do except try to get them well again; if only I had the opportunity you ministers have! What I want to do is prevent disease, not cure it. But my patients don't give me the chance. You ministers, through your preaching, pastoral visitation, and education programs have a golden opportunity to work with people along lines of prevention. I really envy you that *group* of people with whom you work.' "[8]

There are good reasons why one can be enthusiastic about the institutional church. With all of its shortcomings, the institutional church provides a viable and valid way of proclaiming and living the good news of the gospel. I know of no better way, and I am committed to it.

Is the Church a Viable Occupational System?

Both clergy and laity have a stake in the answer to this question. The degree of satisfaction which the clergy has with the church as an occupational system will determine the fulfillment which the clergy find in ministry and in turn will affect the fulfillment of the laity in ministry.

A negative answer to this question has been implied in much that has been written in this book. By dealing with the various facets of the ministry as an occupational system and by pointing out the shortcomings and the areas which need to be changed or strengthened, the implication is that the church is at best a poor occupational system.

Much of the research seems to substantiate the notion that the problem related to the "drop-out" from the ministry has nothing to do with a loss of faith. Rather, it has to do with a loss of confidence in the church as an occupational system. In support of this view, it should be noted that only 13.9 percent of the ex-pastors interviewed in one study accepted the statement that they had "left the ministry." Sixty-two percent saw themselves as performing a ministry within their current jobs.[9] The point is that many ex-pastors feel they have not left the ministry; they have left the church as an occupational system.

Edward S. Golden agreed with the conclusion reached at the First Annual Meeting of the Department of the Ministry of the National Council of Churches: "The Church has been morally irresponsible in the management of its manpower." He adds that unless the church dedicates itself more completely to helping ministers develop their potential so their professional and personal lives might have greater fulfillment, he for one would not want to encourage young people to enter the ministry.[10]

The conclusion reached in the chapter "The Church as an Occupational System" in the book *Ex-Pastors* puts the whole question in proper focus.

> We reiterate that the organization of the church has some structural elements which prevent it from adequately meeting the employment needs of its professionals. These elements are present regardless of whether the professional meets the need of the system, regardless of whether he has lost his faith, regardless of whether he is competent.
>
> We have shown the strains to be present in the training system, the hiring system, the work and reward system, the support systems, and the family and personality systems. We have shown that most of the strains are currently being experienced by many of the pastors as they have been by the ex-pastors. The strains are handled differently by different people.
>
> An individual clergyman comes to a decision either consciously or subconsciously that the system is not meeting enough of his needs to balance what he has to contribute to it. What does he do? Alvin Gouldner (1960, p. 269), says that he has three alternatives: 1. He can try to change the system so that more of his needs are being met. 2. He can remain in the system for his formal work but participate in other systems in order to meet some of his needs. 3. He can leave the system because the alternatives seem better able to meet his needs.[11]

My response as a pastor has been to try to change the system so that more of my needs are being met and hopefully more of the needs of the clergy and the laity will be met as well. This may sound presumptuous, but it is based on the conviction that the institutional church is a viable way to proclaim and live the good news.

In answering the question whether the church is a viable occupational system, it is proper to ask another question, "Would you want your child to be a pastor?" In answering that question, I would want first of all to answer the first two questions in this chapter. My response to whether I want my children to embrace the good news as a treasure is a thunderous "Yes." As to whether I want my children involved in giving their time and talents through the institutional church, my answer is an unconditional "Yes." But the question, "Do I want them to be pastors?" . . .

A few years ago my answer would have been "No." Today I would say, "If you know what is involved in the church as a vocational system and are prepared to develop a good support system, then I say 'Yes.' "

As a young pastor I used to wonder why so many dedicated church families objected to their children's decisions to enter the ministry as their vocational choice. I believe that I understand now. They had seen, as I have seen, too many scars and too many heartaches to want their children to be a part of the church as an occupational system.

Reinhold Niebuhr, writing in 1929, has a word for both clergy and laity about the church as an occupational system: "Having both entered and left the parish ministry against my inclinations, I pay my tribute to the calling, firm in the conviction that it offers greater opportunities for both moral adventure and social usefulness than any other calling if it is entered with open eyes and a consciousness of the hazards to virtue which lurk in it."[12]

*   *   *

God has entrusted us with a treasure. God, however, is not to be held accountable for the way we have developed the institutional church nor the church as an occupational system. We have done that ourselves. It is our task, then, to change the mistakes that we have made, so that both clergy and laity can rejoice not only in the treasure, but also in the institutional church and even in the church as an occupational system. At that point, both clergy and laity will find the goal which we all long for, which is fulfillment in ministry.

Notes

Preface

1. John E. Biersdorf, "A New Model of Ministry," in *Creating an Intentional Ministry,* ed. John E. Biersdorf (Nashville: Abingdon Press, 1976), 23.
2. Marianne Bernhard, "Clergy Burnout: When Stress, Overwork Overwhelm the Spirit," *The Washington Post,* 8 May 1981, B10.

Chapter 1

1. Gerald J. Jud, Edgar W. Mills, Jr., and Genevieve Burch, *Ex-Pastors: Why Men Leave the Parish Ministry* (Philadelphia: Pilgrim Press, 1970), 51. Copyright © 1970. Reprinted by permission.

Chapter 2

1. *Time,* 3 September 1973, 70.
2. William E. Hulme, *Your Pastor's Problems: A Guide for Ministers and Laymen* (Garden City, N.Y.: Doubleday & Company, Inc. 1966), 94. Copyright © 1966. Reprinted by permission of Doubleday & Company, Inc.
3. "Interview—Forty Years in the Ministry, A Conversation with Reuel Howe," *The Christian Ministry,* vol. 1, no. 1 (November 1969): 42.
4. Taken from a brochure describing the work of Interpreters' House, Lambuth Inn, Box 36, Lake Junaluska, N.C. 28745, 1972.
5. In quoting Dr. White, I am making reference to notes that I took at a conference entitled "Pressures of the Profession" held in Afton, Virginia, May 1969. This conference was sponsored by the Virginia Association for Mental Health in cooperation with the Virginia Council of Churches.
6. In quoting Dr. Glen, I am making reference to notes that I took at a Pastor's Renewal Retreat held in February 1970 at

the H.E.B. Foundation Camp in Leckey, Texas. Dr. Glen was a faculty member at the retreat.

7. Paul W. Turner, "The Minister's View of the Ministry," *Search,* vol. 2, no. 4 (Summer 1972): 35.

8. John C. Harris, *Stress, Power and Ministry* (Washington, D.C.: The Alban Institute, Inc., 1977), 3.

9. J. R. Dolby, "The Pastor—A Human Counselor," *Pulpit Digest,* vol. 1, no. 369 (November 1969), presented to the Waco Ministerial Alliance, January 1969, at Waco, Texas, Mimeographed. Reprinted by permission of *Pulpit Digest.*

10. John E. Biersdorf, "Crisis in the Ministry," *IDOC International,* North American ed. (New York: IDOC/North America, Inc., 1971), 18.

11. Turner, "The Minister's View," 38.

12. Robert G. Kemper, "Small Issues and Massive Revelation," in *Creating an Intentional Ministry,* ed. John E. Biersdorf (Nashville: Abingdon Press, 1976), 155.

13. Taylor Caldwell, *The Listener* (Garden City, N.Y.: Doubleday, 1960), 9f.

14. Larry Baker, "Pastors Should Not Be Lonely," *Arkansas Baptist Newsmagazine,* vol. 75, no. 20 (13 May 1976): 16. Reprinted by permission.

15. Loren B. Mead, *New Hope for Congregations* (New York: Seabury Press, 1972), 105.

16. Robert S. Glen, "The Psychiatrist's Role with Pastors Under Stress," *Pastoral Psychology,* June 1971, 34.

17. J. Lyn Elder, "You and Your Mental Health," *Church Administration,* July 1971, 47.

18. *Human Behavior,* May 1976, 38.

19. Janet Harbison Penfield, "Finding Out Who You Are," *Presbyterian Life,* 15 April 1972, 40–43.

Chapter 3

1. John R. Claypool, "Getting in Touch with Power," *The Quarterly Review,* vol. 39, no. 2 (January-February-March 1979): 12.

2. Henri J. M. Nouwen, *Creative Ministry* (Garden City, N.Y.: Image Books, 1978), xix.

3. Ibid.

4. Ernest E. Mosley, *Priorities in Ministry* (Nashville: Convention Press, 1978), 20f.

5. James D. Mallory, Jr., "The Enhancement of Ministerial Morale," a resource paper published in conjunction with a Consul-

tation on the Church's Use of Her Ordained Ministry, May 2–4, 1972, in Montreat, N.C., 50–57. Copyright © 1972 by Kenneth B. Orr, 3401 Brook Rd., Richmond, Va. 23227.

6. Claypool, "Getting in Touch," 13f.

7. E. Glenn Hinson, "The Spiritual Formation of the Minister as a Person," *Review and Expositor,* vol. LXX, no. 1 (Winter 1973): 84.

8. *Journal, Part I* (Minutes of the UPCUSA General Assembly, 1969), 100.

9. Hulme, *Your Pastor's Problems,* 120. Reprinted by permission of Doubleday & Company, Inc.

10. Ibid.

11. *The Best of John Henry Jowett,* ed. Gerald Kennedy (New York: Harper and Bros., 1948), 146f.

12. Hulme, *Your Pastor's Problems,* 105. Reprinted by permission of Doubleday & Company, Inc.

13. Ibid.

14. Ibid., 124.

15. Elizabeth O'Connor, *Call to Commitment* (New York: Harper and Row, 1963), 94.

16. Nouwen, *Creative Ministry,* xxiii.

17. Ibid., 108.

18. Walter D. Wagoner, *Bachelor of Divinity: Uncertain Servants in Seminary and Ministry* (New York: Association Press, 1963), 95.

19. John Killinger, *Bread for the Wilderness, Wine for the Journey* (Waco, Tex.: Word Books, 1976), 10f.

20. Paul Tournier, *Guilt and Grace* (New York: Harper and Row, 1962), 31.

21. Hulme, *Your Pastor's Problems,* 127. Reprinted by permission of Doubleday & Company, Inc.

Chapter 4

1. Henlee H. Barnette, *Christian Calling and Vocation* (Grand Rapids: Baker Book House, 1965), 17f.

2. K. L. Schmidt, "Kaleo," *Theological Dictionary of the New Testament,* ed. Gerhard Kittel, vol. 3 (Grand Rapids: William B. Eerdmans, 1977), 489.

3. Barnette, *Christian Calling,* 39.

4. As cited in Barnette, *Christian Calling,* 42.

5. Ibid.

6. F. L. Cross, ed., *The Oxford Dictionary of the Christian Church* (London: Oxford University Press, 1961), 988.

7. *The Washington Post,* 8 June 1979, C18.

8. As cited in Barnette, *Christian Calling,* 43.

9. Ibid.

10. As cited in John H. Leith, "The Theology of Call and Ordination," a resource paper published in conjunction with Consultation on the Church's Use of Her Ordained Ministry, May 2–4, 1972, in Montreat, N.C., 9. Copyright © 1972 by Kenneth B. Orr, 3402 Brook Rd., Richmond, Va. 23227.

11. Ibid.

12. Ibid., 3.

13. Elizabeth O'Connor, *Eighth Day of Creation* (Waco, Tex.: Word Books, 1971).

14. Carlyle Marney, *Priests to Each Other* (Valley Forge, Pa.: Judson Press, 1974), 9ff.

15. James Lowell Blevins, "Rethinking the Biblical Meaning of the Call," *Search,* vol. 2, no. 4 (Summer 1972): 10.

16. Everett B. Barnard, "God's Call and Its Relationship to Career Changes," *Search,* vol. 7, no. 1 (Fall 1976): 9.

17. Ibid.

18. Morris Ashcraft, "Christian Calling and One's Life Work," *The Commission,* vol. 41, no. 2 (February 1978): 33.

19. Leith, "The Theology of Call," 9.

20. Frank C. Williams, "Some Perspectives on the Needs of Clergy—Personal and Professional" (September 1970, Mimeographed), 15f. Copies available at the Midwest Career Development Center, 66 East 15th Ave., Columbus, Ohio 43201.

Chapter 5

1. Larry Jerden, "The First Year of Help," *Baptist Standard,* 1 August 1973, 8.

2. Edgar W. Mills and John P. Koval, *Stress in the Ministry* (Washington, D.C.: Ministry Studies Board, 1971), 55.

3. Laile E. Bartlett, *The Vanishing Parson* (Boston: Beacon Press, 1971), 126. Copyright © 1971. Reprinted by permission of Beacon Press.

4. Ibid., 127.

5. Wallace Denton, "Family Conflicts of the Modern Minister," *The Baptist Program,* March 1974, 15. Reprinted by permission.

6. Hulme, *Your Pastor's Problems,* 79f. Reprinted by permission of Doubleday & Company, Inc.

7. Marjorie Hyer, "A Family Matter," *The Washington Post,* 28 April 1978, C16.

8. Hulme, *Your Pastor's Problems,* 81. Reprinted by permission of Doubleday & Company, Inc.

9. Bartlett, *The Vanishing Parson,* 130.

10. Louis McBurney, *Every Pastor Needs a Pastor,* (Waco, Tex.: Word Books, 1977), 133.

11. Denton, "Family Conflicts," 7. Reprinted by permission.

12. Mosley, *Priorities in Ministry,* 20.

13. Denton, "Family Conflicts," 7. Reprinted by permission.

14. Mills and Koval, *Stress,* 56.

15. Kemper, "Small Issues and Massive Revelation," 157f.

16. Hyer, "A Family Matter," C16.

Chapter 6

1. Mills and Koval, *Stress,* 55.

2. Edward S. Golden, "Management and Support of Church Personnel," *Ministry Studies,* vol. 3, no. 1 (May 1969): 26.

3. Jud, Mills, and Burch, *Ex-Pastors,* 127f. Reprinted by permission.

4. Edgar W. Mills, Jr., "The Minister's Career Development," *Improving the Practice of Ministry,* 1 November 1971, Leader's ed., 13f. Available through the Office of Professional Leader Development, Board of Christian Education, Box 1176, Richmond, Virginia 23209.

5. J. Emmett Henderson, "The Ministers' Colleague Group," *The Baptist Program,* November 1973, 6.

6. *The Atlanta Constitution,* 8 June 1973, 18-C.

7. Mills and Koval, *Stress,* 54f.

8. Donald P. Smith, *Clergy in the Cross Fire* (Philadelphia: The Westminster Press, 1973).

9. Allen P. Wadsworth, Jr., "Drop-out from the Pastorate: Why?" *Journal of Pastoral Care,* June 1971, 124–7.

Chapter 7

1. Smith, *Clergy in the Cross Fire,* 13f.

2. Samuel Blizzard, "The Minister's Dilemma," *The Christian Century,* vol. LXXIII, 1956, 509–10.

3. Turner, "The Minister's View," 39.

4. Jeffrey K. Hadden, *The Gathering Storm in the Churches* (Garden City, N.Y.: Anchor Books, 1970), 239.

5. Smith, *Clergy in the Cross Fire*, 29f.

6. Jud, Mills, and Burch, *Ex-Pastors*, 119. Reprinted by permission.

7. H. Richard Niebuhr, Daniel Day Williams, and James M. Gustafson, *The Purpose of the Church and Its Ministry* (New York: Harper and Row, 1956), 50.

8. Bartlett, *The Vanishing Parson*, 37. Reprinted by permission of Beacon Press.

9. James D. Smart, *The Rebirth of Ministry* (Philadelphia: The Westminster Press, 1960), 17f.

10. Jeffrey K. Hadden, "Role Conflict and the Crisis in the Churches," *Ministry Studies*, vol. 2, nos. 3 and 4 (October 1968): 20f.

11. Biersdorf, "Crisis in the Ministry," 21.

12. Smith, *Clergy in the Cross Fire*, 81.

13. Ibid., 84.

14. Thomas J. Mullen, *The Renewal of the Ministry* (Nashville: Abingdon Press, 1963).

15. Ernest Mosley, *Called to Joy* (Nashville: Convention Press, 1973).

16. Hadden, *The Gathering Storm*, 247.

17. Thomas C. Campbell, "Arenas of Negotiation," in *Creating an Intentional Ministry*, ed. John E. Biersdorf (Nashville: Abingdon Press, 1976), 41–44.

18. Biersdorf, "Crisis in the Ministry," 48.

19. Reinhold Niebuhr, *Leaves From the Notebook of a Tamed Cynic* (New York: Da Capo Press, 1976), xi.

20. "Report of the Ad Interim Committee on the Church's Use of Her Ordained Ministry" (Minutes, Part I, submitted to the 114th General Assembly of the PCUS, 1974), 336.

21. Loren B. Mead, *New Hope for Congregations* (New York: Seabury Press, 1972).

22. Elisa L. DesPortes, *Congregations in Change* (New York: Seabury Press, 1973).

23. Paul S. Higgins and James E. Dittes, "Change in Laymen's Expectations of the Minister's Role," *Ministry Studies*, vol. 2, no. 1 (February 1968), 5–23.

24. Hadden, *The Gathering Storm*, 259.

Chapter 8

1. Nathanael M. Guptill, *How to Be a Pastor in a Mad, Mod World* (St. Louis: Bethany Press, 1970), 21f.

2. *Webster's Seventh New Collegiate Dictionary* (Springfield, Mass.: G. and C. Merriam Co., 1971).

3. Guptill, *How to Be a Pastor,* 20.

4. Jaroslav Pelikan, "Toward a Theology of Ambition" (Baccalaureate Address at Upsala College, East Orange, New Jersey, 1 June 1969, Mimeographed), 1. Reprinted by permission.

5. Ibid., 2.

6. Ibid.

7. Ibid., 3.

8. Ibid.

9. Larry La Velle, "The Question of 'Success' in the Ministry," *The Christian Ministry,* vol. 3, no. 2 (March 1972): 3f.

10. Mosley, *Priorities in Ministry,* 129.

11. Ibid., 131.

12. Michael Harper, "The Poet Who Saw Reality," *The Washington Post,* 9 March 1978, B4.

13. Guptill, *How to Be a Pastor,* 19f.

14. Kemper, "Small Issues and Massive Revelation," 167ff.

15. Ibid., 170f.

Chapter 9

1. John E. Biersdorf, "Negotiating an Intentional Ministry," in *Creating an Intentional Ministry,* ed. John E. Biersdorf (Nashville: Abingdon Press, 1976), 13.

2. Golden, "Management and Support," 26f.

3. Bartlett, *The Vanishing Parson,* 78. Reprinted by permission of Beacon Press.

4. Mark A. Rouch, *Competent Ministry* (Nashville: Abingdon Press, 1974), 10.

5. Connolly C. Gamble, Jr., "Continuing Education: An Essential or an Extra?" *The Christian Ministry,* vol. 5, no. 3 (May 1974): 6.

6. James W. Hatley, "My Personal and Vocational Needs as a Pastor," *Search,* vol. 7, no. 1 (Fall 1976): 40.

7. Jud, Mills, and Burch, *Ex-Pastors,* 127. Reprinted by permission.

8. Connolly C. Gamble, Jr., "A Lifelong Process of Learning," in *Creating an Intentional Ministry,* ed. John E. Biersdorf (Nashville: Abingdon Press, 1976), 116.

9. Rouch, *Competent Ministry,* 16f.

10. Ibid., 155.

11. Gamble, "A Lifelong Process," 109ff.

12. Ibid., 113f.

13. Undated pamphlet describing the history of the Church Career Development Council and the purposes, programs, and services of the centers that are affiliated and accredited by it. The Council is located in Room 770, 475 Riverside Drive, New York, New York 10027.

14. Biersdorf, "A New Model," 17.

15. Ibid., 16.

Chapter 10

1. Golden, "Management and Support," 26f.

2. Jud, Mills, and Burch, *Ex-Pastors,* 123f. Reprinted by permission.

3. Lyle E. Schaller, *The Pastor and the People* (Nashville: Abingdon Press, 1973), 30.

4. John C. Harris, "Getting a Job," in *Creating and Intentional Ministry,* ed. John E. Biersdorf (Nashville: Abingdon Press, 1976), 95.

5. Charles William Brown, "The Trauma of Changing Churches," *Home Life,* September 1973, 41.

Chapter 11

1. Biersdorf, "Crisis in the Ministry," 16.

2. Seward Hiltner, *Ferment in the Ministry* (Nashville: Abingdon Press, 1969), 8.

3. Ibid., 211.

4. Bruce Grubbs, *The First Two Years* (Nashville: Convention Press, 1979), 4.

5. Jud, Mills, and Burch, *Ex-Pastors,* 23. Reprinted by permission.

6. Edgar W. Mills, "Continuing Education as Role Socialization," in *Ministry in the Seventies,* ed. John E. Biersdorf (New York: IDOC/North America, Inc., 1971), 109.

7. Biersdorf, "Crisis in the Ministry," 42.

8. Campbell, "Arenas of Negotiation," 41.

9. Hadden, "Role Conflict and Crisis," 21f.

10. Ibid.

11. Pam Proctor, "How to Survive Today's Stressful Jobs," *Parade,* 17 June 1979, 4.

Chapter 12

1. Harry Emerson Fosdick, *Dear Mr. Brown* (New York: Harper and Bros., 1961), 28.

2. Pam Proctor, "From the Ages, With Love," *Parade,* 6 August 1978, 12.

3. Hadden, *The Gathering Storm,* 262.

4. Henri J. M. Nouwen, *The Wounded Healer* (Garden City, N.Y.: Doubleday, 1972), 87ff.

5. Hadden, *The Gathering Storm,* 266.

6. Taken from "I Think They Are Troubled in Spirit, So We Start There," a brochure describing the work of Interpreters' House, Lambuth Inn, Box 36, Lake Junaluska, N.C. 28747.

7. *The New York Times,* 22 February 1970.

8. James D. Glasse, *Profession: Minister* (Nashville: Abingdon Press, 1968), 55.

9. Jud, Mills, and Burch, *Ex-Pastors,* 39. Reprinted by permission.

10. Golden, "Management and Support," 26.

11. Jud, Mills, and Burch, *Ex-Pastors,* 88f. Reprinted by permission.

12. Niebuhr, *Notebook of a Tamed Cynic,* xii.